ANCIENT WARFARE
THE BASICS

Conor Whately

LONDON AND NEW YORK

Designed cover image: Alamy

First published 2026
by Routledge
4 Park Square, Milton Park, Abingdon, Oxon OX14 4RN

and by Routledge
605 Third Avenue, New York, NY 10158

Routledge is an imprint of the Taylor & Francis Group, an informa business

© 2026 Conor Whately

The right of Conor Whately to be identified as author of this work has been asserted in accordance with sections 77 and 78 of the Copyright, Designs and Patents Act 1988.

All rights reserved. No part of this book may be reprinted or reproduced or utilised in any form or by any electronic, mechanical, or other means, now known or hereafter invented, including photocopying and recording, or in any information storage or retrieval system, without permission in writing from the publishers.

For Product Safety Concerns and Information please contact our EU representative GPSR@taylorandfrancis.com. Taylor & Francis Verlag GmbH, Kaufingerstraße 24, 80331 München, Germany.

Trademark notice: Product or corporate names may be trademarks or registered trademarks, and are used only for identification and explanation without intent to infringe.

British Library Cataloguing-in-Publication Data
A catalogue record for this book is available from the British Library

ISBN: 978-0-367-55262-6 (hbk)
ISBN: 978-0-367-54918-3 (pbk)
ISBN: 978-1-003-09263-6 (ebk)

DOI: 10.4324/9781003092636

Typeset in Times New Roman
by SPi Technologies India Pvt Ltd (Straive)

ANCIENT WARFARE
THE BASICS

Ancient Warfare: The Basics offers an engaging introduction to warfare in the ancient Mediterranean World from the mythical Trojan War, through the rise of hoplites and conquests of Alexander the Great to Roman hegemony and the Arab conquests of western Asia.

This volume explores warfare in the ancient Mediterranean through art, literature, and archaeological evidence and covers a vast geographical area stretching from northern Europe to western Asia. After an introduction discussing the Trojan War, chapters explore warfare in ancient Greece from the Archaic to the Hellenistic period before shifting to the Persian army and the rise of Macedon. Whately then moves to Roman warfare, covering Rome's naval prowess, its wars against rebels and aggressors and its expansion in the east, exploring how Rome's way of war changed in the Late Antique period. The rise of the Huns, horse archery, and the last great war of antiquity – Rome versus Persia in the seventh century CE – close out the book.

This concise, accessible guide to ancient warfare is suitable for undergraduate and postgraduate students in Classics and ancient history as well as scholars and general readers interested in warfare in the pre-modern world.

Conor Whately is a professor of Classics at the University of Winnipeg. He has published a number of journal articles, book chapters, and books on topics ranging from the Roman frontiers and late antique historiography to Roman Arabia.

THE BASICS

The Basics is a highly successful series of accessible guidebooks which provide an overview of the fundamental principles of a subject area in a jargon-free and undaunting format.

Intended for students approaching a subject for the first time, the books both introduce the essentials of a subject and provide an ideal springboard for further study. With over 50 titles spanning subjects from artificial intelligence (AI) to women's studies, *The Basics* are an ideal starting point for students seeking to understand a subject area.

Each text comes with recommendations for further study and gradually introduces the complexities and nuances within a subject.

URBAN DESIGN
TIM HEATH AND FLORIAN WIEDMANN

PUBLIC RELATIONS (SECOND EDITION)
DEBORAH SILVERMAN

EDUCATION STUDIES
CATHERINE SIMON

DRAG
MARK EDWARD AND CHRIS GREENOUGH

BIOANTHROPOLOGY
MARC KISSEL

NEW YORK CITY
KATRIN B. ANACKER

HISTORICAL GEOGRAPHIES
PAUL GRIFFIN AND CHERYL MCGEACHAN

ANCIENT WARFARE
CONOR WHATELY

For more information about this series, please visit: www.routledge.com/The-Basics/book-series/B

CONTENTS

List of figures	vii
Acknowledgements	ix
Timeline	xv
Maps	xvii

Introduction: "The bronze gleamed around him like flashing fire": warfare in the Bronze Age Mediterranean, 1400–600 BCE ... 1

1 "The strong do what they can and the weak suffer what they must": warfare in archaic and classical Greece, 600–404 BCE ... 15

2 "Very well then, Alexander comes first": fourth-century Greece to the wars of the Diadochi, 404–275 BCE ... 37

3 Carthage and the "mutability of human affairs": the Hellenistic age and the Punic Wars, 300–200 BCE ... 59

4 "More fortunate than Augustus, and better than Trajan": from warlords to emperors, 200 BCE–117 CE ... 81

5 "They make a desert and call it peace": the Roman Empire, 117–284 CE   103

6 "If you want peace, prepare for war": the end of antiquity and the birth of the medieval world, 284–641 CE   123

Conclusion   143

Glossary   145
Further reading   157
Selected bibliography   163
Index   191

FIGURES

0.1	Lion Gate, Mycenae, Bronze Age, Wikimedia Commons	7
0.2	Hisarlik, Turkey (Troy), Wikimedia Commons	12
1.1	Bronze Helmet, Corinthian Type, 600–575 BCE, MET	19
1.2	Terracotta Oinochoe, three hoplites and shields, Amasis Painter, c. 560 BCE, MET	21
1.3	Tumulus at Marathon, Christopher Wordsworth, 1882, Wikimedia Commons	30
2.1	Soldiers of Xerxes I, tomb at Naqsh-e Rostam, Iran, 6th–4th century BCE, Wikimedia Commons	44
2.2	Battle of Cavalry and Foot Soldiers, Payava Tomb, Xanthus, Turkey, British Museum, Alamy	46
2.3	Alexander the Great commanding that the work of Homer be placed in the tomb of Achilles, anonymous, 1500–1550, MET	53
2.4	The So-Called Alexander Mosaic, Pompeii, Italy. Wikimedia Commons	54
3.1	Coin of Demetrius I, 222–180 BCE, Cleveland Museum of Art	61
3.2	Thureos Fresco, Istanbul, third century BCE, Wikimedia Commons	64
3.3	Carthaginian Naval Ram, Egadi Islands, third century BCE, Wikimedia Commons	67
4.1	Epitaph of Marcus Caelius, Wikimedia Commons	87

4.2	Masada Siege Ramp from the Hilltop, Carole Raddato, Wikimedia Commons	94
4.3	Boudica, Boadicea Haranguing the Britons (cropped), John Opie, 1793, Wikimedia Commons	96
5.1	Trajan's Column, Cichorius Plates, 1896–1900, Wikimedia Commons	106
5.2	Safaitic Graffiti, Jordan, Conor Whately	115
6.1	Persian Cataphract, Taq-e Bostan, Iran, 6th century CE, Wikimedia Commons	125
6.2	Plate with a Hunting Scene from the Tale of Bahram Gur and Azadeh, Iran, 5th century CE, MET	135
6.3	Walls of Halabiye, Syria, 3rd century CE (?), Wikimedia Commons	138

ACKNOWLEDGEMENTS

In October 2019, I drove down from Winnipeg to Brookings, South Dakota, to attend one of Graham Wrightson's "Many Faces of War" conferences to speak on the late antique military revolution, or lack thereof. When I arrived, I had received an email from Amy Davis-Poynter at Routledge asking whether I might be interested in writing this little book. I was on my second leave, had just completed my first major SSHRC (Social Sciences and Humanities Research Council of Canada) grant, and so answered with a yes. Like everyone else, I had no idea what was looming around the corner in the last quarter of 2019. Suffice to say, as I write these acknowledgements in the summer of 2025, this little book took a lot longer than I ever could have imagined.

The lack of speed wasn't only a detriment, however. For this gave me time to familiarize myself with all the material that was usually beyond my usual purview, like the scholarship on Greek warfare. I benefitted, in part, from inheriting Mark Golden's not inconsiderable pile of articles on Greek warfare. In the fall of 2022, when I first returned to teaching in person, I also got the chance to teach Greek warfare for the first time. In fact, as it happens, that term I taught one other course, an upper-year Greek language one on Herodotus, and in particular book 6 of his *Histories*. Somewhat surprisingly then, for one 'fleeting' term, I was a 'scholar' of the Greek world, no mean feat for someone who, classical forebearers of late antique historians aside, had generally shied away from this sort of material, at least in part. Of course, teaching at a smaller, primarily undergraduate university which, in my first few years, was Roman-heavy, meant that aspects of Greek culture and society featured in my teaching to some degree or another. And, as it turned out, I quite enjoyed teaching all this Greek stuff in that fateful fall of 2022. I even wondered why I had shunned it so much all those years earlier. On the subject of Greek classes, I also benefitted from teaching a different upper-year Greek class on Greek comedy in the winter of 2024. That class was about as far from my comfort zone as you could be, but, as before, I thoroughly enjoyed it – it turns out, Aristophanes' *Birds* is a fantastic play, and in preparing for and teaching the class, I also gleaned some additional insight into war in the Greek world. So, I'm grateful to have had those opportunities – and for the help and encouragement of my colleagues, particularly those who focus on Greek things, namely Peter Miller and Melissa Funke. I'll say too that I sent the very occasional (one or two?) email to Graham Wrightson and Jeff Rop on Greek warfare things, and I'm grateful for their advice.

There are other boons to finishing this book now, at the beginning of my seventeenth year in Winnipeg. In all those intervening years, I have taught a dizzying array of courses, and given the chronological, evidential, and geographical breadth of this book, all those courses have undoubtedly served me greatly. To give you, reader, but a sample of the subject matter, I have taught courses on Greek society and Roman society, both first-year introductory courses, as well as classical mythology and another on the ancient city. Besides Greek Warfare, I've taught on the Roman Military, the Punic Wars, and Romans and Barbarians. Other courses include one on Roman Arabia, another on the Fall of Rome, and another still on the age of Justinian. Finally, I've taught both Greek and Latin at all (undergraduate) levels, and in the process we've done texts like Aristophanes' *Birds* and Demosthenes' *On the Crown*, Pliny the Younger's *Letters*, and Vergil's *Aeneid*. It's been a wild, and not always smooth, ride, to say the least. But being able to do a wide range of courses has kept things interesting, and I owe my students a big debt of gratitude.

I've spent the entirety of my academic career here in Winnipeg, Manitoba, Canada. When I moved to Winnipeg from the University of Warwick and (Royal) Leamington Spa in the UK, I had no idea that living here would give me more of the island experience than the UK ever did. Living in Winnipeg is not for the faint of heart, even with all the modern amenities like central heating and reliable air conditioning. It's hard for those who live just about anywhere else to appreciate the travails of living in a place that sees a 60–70°C difference between winter and summer temperatures. In how many other cities can you go from wearing all the clothes to wearing almost none of them? And yet, for all the knocks that Winnipeg gets – it's too cold, there are too many bugs, the crime is too high, there's nothing to do – there is so much else about it to love. The food (and drink) is amazing and diverse, and the city has a vibrant arts scene, with everything from indie bands and a long-running folk festival to a symphony orchestra and a fantastic open-air theatre in one of the city's many big parks. The city is also close to some breathtaking natural landscapes, from the serenity of the island of Hecla and the sand dunes of Spruce Woods Provincial Park, to the beaches of Lake Manitoba and Lake Winnipeg. The big blue skies are also hard to beat.

But there's also the people. And so, here I want to thank some of those from my wider Winnipeg world who have made life here on this island that much better. For the past few years, I've been on a trivia team called Blue Thunder, which is composed of Brandon Christopher, current Associate Dean of Arts (and English professor); Alyson Brickey, acting chair of English; and Melissa Funke, my colleague in Classics. While I haven't made it to nearly as many trivia Monday nights as I'd like, largely due to family responsibilities (daughters' swimming and skating), they've been a blast, and even when we don't meet at trivia, the chat group often keeps me going. As always, I want to thank all my other colleagues here in Classics in Winnipeg for their invaluable support over the years. Melanie Racette-Campbell and Flavia Amaral are new colleagues who haven't made it into many of my previous book acknowledgements yet, so I want to single out Melanie for discussion of all things donut and related subject matter and Flavia for all things football/soccer. But I also want to give a shout-out to three of my colleagues down at the UofM (University of Manitoba). It's a remarkable thing to be in a city of close to 950,000 with two Classics departments. So, thanks to Lea Stirling for the various invitations to meet her students and to Mike Sampson and James Chlup for the now many years of friendship.

On the subject of soccer, two years ago I started playing again for the first time in nearly two decades for the Riverview Rowdies. It's amazing how much muscle memory exists after all this time even if the knees are long gone. As a longtime goalie, throwing my body around on an indoor pitch maybe isn't the best way to treat a 40-something body, but I've thoroughly enjoyed playing the beautiful game again, so doing something else far removed from the day-to-day. For decades now, I have swum regularly, and in Winnipeg that has been at the downtown YM-YWCA. Although endless metres of front crawl in the pool can be mind-numbingly monotonous, the regulars in the pool, the gym, and the front desk have made it a little less boring. I also want to thank another friend whom I've known here for more than 11 or 12 years, Richard Bailey. Rich, the friendly giant, was walking past my office when he noticed a replica of a Roman soldier's helmet and stopped in to chat. Since then, our families – now kids included – have become lifelong friends. Although the cycling around Birds Hill that used to occupy our time in the beginning is a thing of the distant past now, the chats poolside this past academic year while our kids were involved in competitive swimming training were fantastic. And, on the subject of activities far removed, at least a bit, from the day-to-day, I'd like to give a shout-out to "In Beer We Trust", a three-person chat group comprising Matt Gibbs (who used to be here), Peter Miller (here now), and me, which usually consists of pictures of beer we've known and loved.

I should also thank the Winnipeg Jets. In my 'youth', while thinking about prospective places I might end up, I was particularly keen to settle in a city with an NHL team. Moving to Winnipeg in the summer of 2009 meant I was 13 years too late, or so I thought. Imagine my surprise when Gary Bettman and True North Sports and Entertainment announced in the spring of 2011 that the Jets would return (i.e. the Atlanta Thrashers would move to Winnipeg). There was little doubt that this 'new' team would take the name of its predecessor. In 2026, the Jets will celebrate their sixteenth season. I have watched just about as many (too many even) games as a person could, mostly from the comfort of home (games are expensive). It has been a hell of a ride, even if they have not yet succeeded in claiming Lord Stanely's Cup. Two highlights were, first, their run to the semi-finals in 2018 and then the 'Manitoba Miracle' of game 7 in round 1 of the 2025 playoffs. If you don't know what that is, check out the highlights on YouTube – easily one of the most exciting and unexpected spectator sports experiences of my life. So, thanks Jets for all the highs (and really very many lows) these past 15 years.

Finally, to get back to where I started, I want to give my heartfelt thanks to all the people at Routledge for their efforts, from Amy Davis-Poynter for her initial invitation to Marcia Adams for all her subsequent help. The initial proposal was vetted by four reviewers, who each provided valuable suggestions that helped shape the ultimate form of this book. After the manuscript was completed (minus a few odds and ends), I submitted the book back to Routledge for review, and three of the initial reviewers came back with three lots of invaluable feedback. If there's anything wrong with what's in front of you, blame them! Just kidding. My experience with peer review has been fantastic. I was more than a little nervous when I submitted a book filled with Greek things, and I'm glad they didn't suggest I bin it all. But, as you might imagine, I'm grateful that they managed to catch all those infelicities that would have made this a far inferior volume. I also want to thank Stephen Poole for cleaning up my prose, and Thivya Vaudevan for bringing it all to fruition.

One final note: I always thank my family, and I'll save them for the end. Thanks to my wonderful wife Hannah and two fantastic daughters Ella and Penny for being themselves.

If, in the end, this book inspires you to read more about warfare in the ancient Mediterranean, I'll be pleased. In fact, I would encourage anyone who reads this to take it not as the last word but rather as the foundation for more detailed and wide-ranging reading on a subject that has more to offer than the traditional drum-and-trumpets history that the general public often associates with the subject matter. Indeed, as I hope you'll see, looking more closely at ancient warfare can reveal a great deal about the history, places, and lived experiences of these people who lived so long ago.

TIMELINE

	600 BCE–404 BCE	404 BCE–275 BCE	300 BCE–200 BCE	200 BCE–117 CE	117 CE–284 CE	284CE–641CE
Greece	Archaic to Classical Greece	Classical Greece to Hellenistic World	Hellenistic World	Hellenistic World to Roman Rule	Roman Rule	Roman Rule
Rome	Early Republic	Early to Mid-Republic	Mid Republic	Mid Republic to High Empire	High Empire	Late Antiquity
Western Europe	Celts and La Tène Culture	Celts and La Tène Culture	Celts and La Tène Culture			
North Africa	Carthaginians, Third Intermediate Period to Achaemenid Rule (Egypt)	Carthaginians, Ptolemies (Egypt)	Carthaginians, Numidians, Ptolemies (Egypt)	Numidians, Ptolemies (Egypt), to Roman Rule	Roman Rule	Independent Kingdoms Roman/Vandal Rule
					Roman Rule	
(West) Asia	Achaemenid Persians	Achaemenids Persians to Seleucids	Seleucids	Seleucids to Parthians	Parthians to Sasanians	Sasanians

MAPS

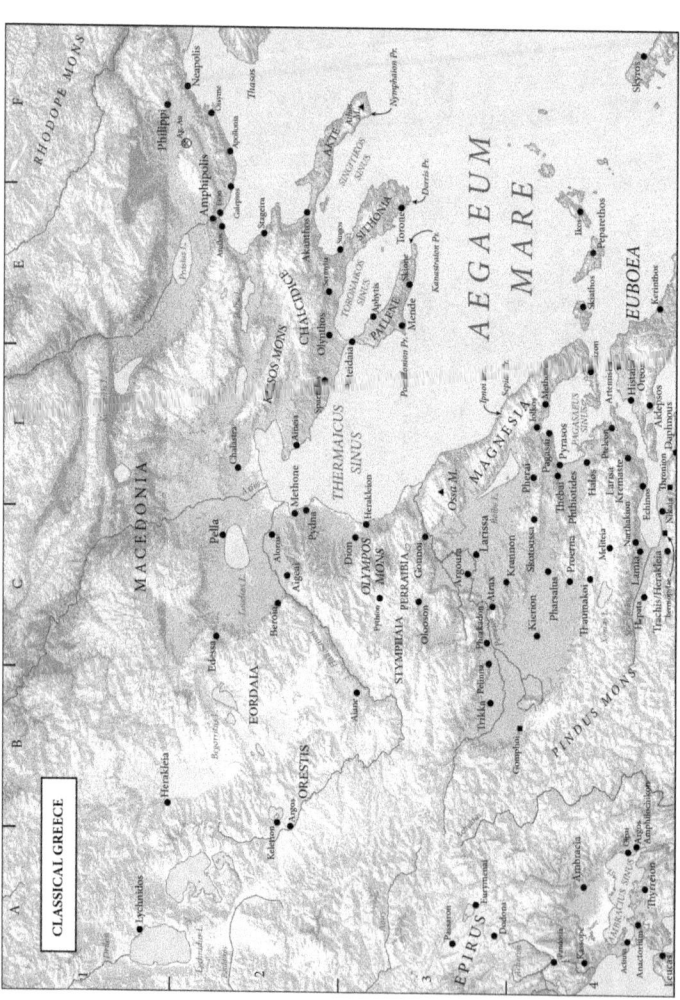

Map of Classical Greece, the North. *Atlas of Classical History: Revised Edition*, Edition by Richard Talbert, Benet Salway, and Lindsey Holman. Copyright © 2023 by Routledge. Reproduced by permission of Taylor & Francis Group.

MAPS xix

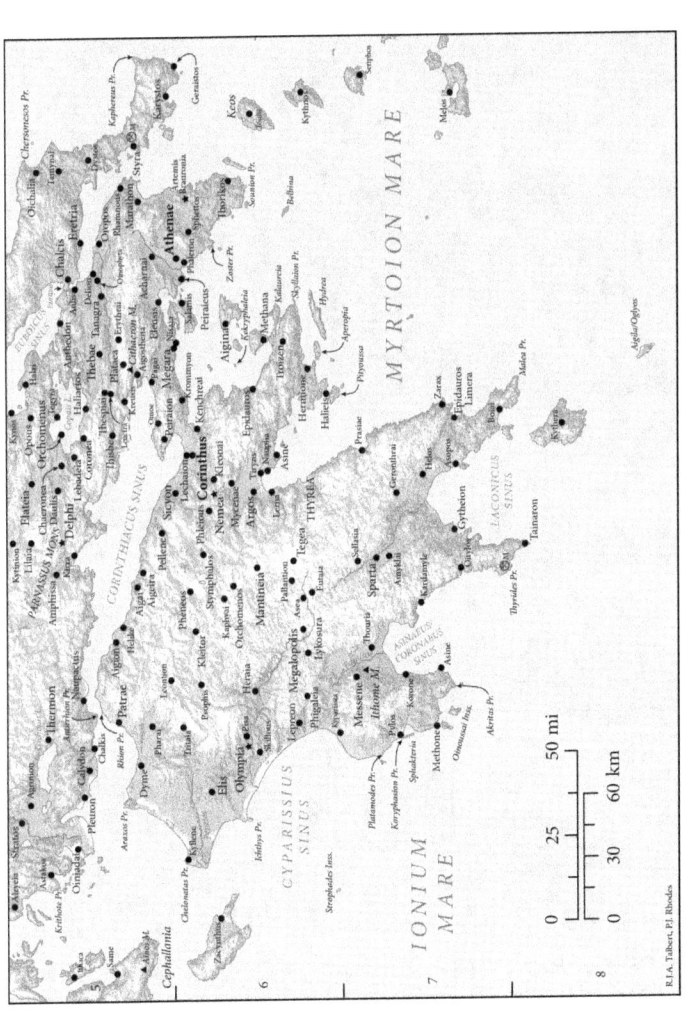

Map of Classical Greece, the South. *Atlas of Classical History: Revised Edition*, Edition by Richard Talbert, Benet Salway, and Lindsey Holman. Copyright © 2023 by Routledge. Reproduced by permission of Taylor & Francis Group.

xx MAPS

Map of the Western Half of the Roman Empire in 60 CE. *Atlas of Classical History: Revised Edition*, Edition by Richard Talbert, Benet Salway, and Lindsey Holman. Copyright © 2023 by Routledge. Reproduced by permission of Taylor & Francis Group.

MAPS xxi

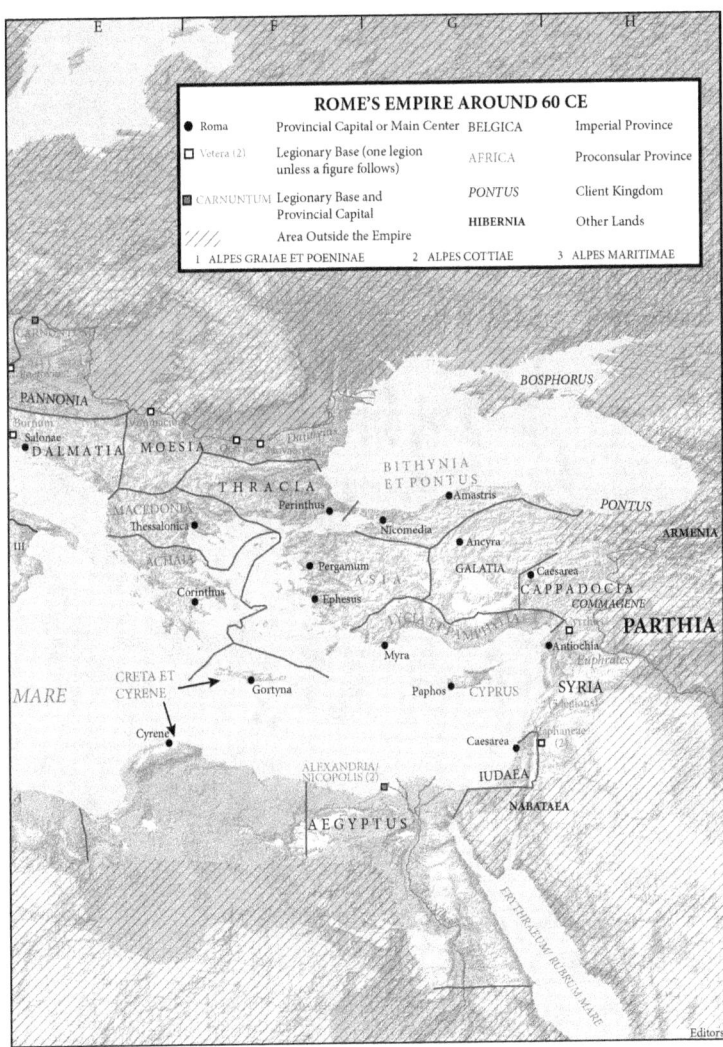

Map of the Eastern Half of the Roman Empire in 60 CE. *Atlas of Classical History: Revised Edition*, Edition by Richard Talbert, Benet Salway, and Lindsey Holman. Copyright © 2023 by Routledge. Reproduced by permission of Taylor & Francis Group.

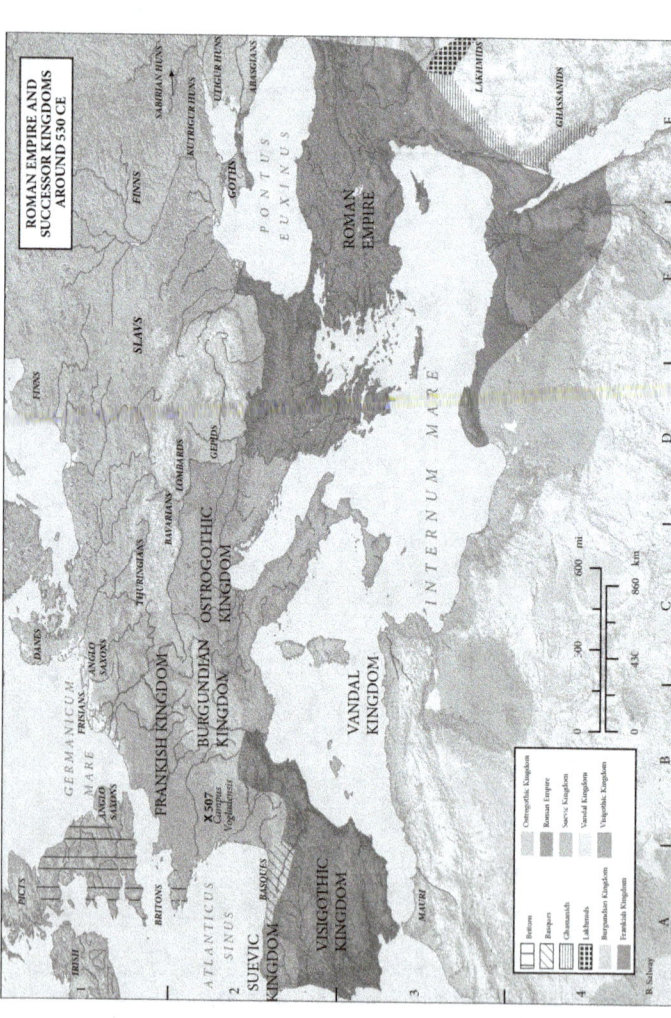

Map of the Roman Empire and the Successor Kingdoms in 530 CE. *Atlas of Classical History: Revised Edition*, Edition by Richard Talbert, Benet Salway, and Lindsey Holman. Copyright © 2023 by Routledge. Reproduced by permission of Taylor & Francis Group.

INTRODUCTION

"THE BRONZE GLEAMED AROUND HIM LIKE FLASHING FIRE": WARFARE IN THE BRONZE AGE MEDITERRANEAN, 1400–600 BCE

WAR THEN AND NOW

Early in 2024, when I was in the final year of writing this manuscript before submitting it for peer review, Apple TV+ released the miniseries, *Masters of the Air*, a follow-up of sorts to two earlier HBO television series: *The Pacific* and *Band of Brothers*. *Masters of the Air*, like the previous two, focused on the experiences and perspectives of a relatively small group of soldiers, here airmen (broadly speaking) of the USA's 100th Bomb Group from World War II, who operated Boeing B-17s. All three series provided visceral characterizations of American experiences of war drawn, in large part, from the personal accounts of veterans. One of the criticisms of the most recent series was the lack of firsthand monologues, a staple of past series, and a result of the timing of the series' release. That is, by the time it was released in 2024, there were few living veterans left able to talk about their experiences.

Writing this book as a forty-five-year-old Canadian male (who I hope will be forty-six by the time it sees the light of day), I've been fortunate to have had no direct personal experience with war. I watched *The Pacific* and *Masters of the Air* for entertainment purposes, and I was surprised by the much more pronounced emotional reaction that I experienced than I had expected. In the case of the former, it was the shocking and brutal violence depicted on screen and, presumably, on the field of battle that gave me pause, plus the rapidity, at least in the manner in which I viewed the episodes, with which key characters were killed, unfortunately one of the stark realities of combat in World War II. In the case of the former, the shock came from the horrors of the bomber flying experience, at least as depicted on screen, and the personal connection that came with it. My paternal grandfather, Desmond Whately, was in Canada throughout the war and was involved in the training of Royal Canadian Air Force personnel. On the other hand, my maternal grandfather, Alan Campbell, had flown in Lancaster Bombers for the Royal Canadian Air Force in World War II. While we had chatted occasionally about his experiences on long drives from Kingston, Ontario down the 401 through Toronto to Brantford, Ontario, these had been few and far between, and he had passed away decades earlier. In my mind (and based on what I remembered about Canada in World War II from high school), this had been a relatively "safe" means of participating in the war. While the Canadians, along with the British and other Commonwealth nations, fought at night, so limiting the danger at least a little, I never appreciated quite how close he might have been to death.

A different story brought to mind another aspect of the ancient experience of warfare and the ways in which fighting in ancient battles was far removed from the more recent combat experience. While walking to work in downtown Winnipeg one cool spring day, I was listening to the excellent CBC (Canadian Broadcasting Corporation) radio program, *The Current*, hosted by Matt Galloway. He was interviewing the acclaimed novelist Salman Rushdie, who had just released a memoir about the stabbing attack he suffered on August 12, 2022. One of the topics of conversation was the intimacy of the attack. Whereas with a gun, a would-be perpetrator could pull the trigger from some distance away (however small), with a knife, the perpetrator would have to be very close to the victim, as was the case in this instance. Rushdie commented on the intimacy of it all, including feeling the attacker's body on his as he fell down. Although Rushdie's experience came from a peacetime setting, the nature of the attack itself and the weapon employed suggested a reality of ancient warfare: the relative intimacy. Save for those who perished at the hands of artillery, a great many ancient soldiers would die not from missiles fired from afar, even though plenty would and did succumb to arrow and sling wounds. Rather, they would see, smell, hear, and even touch their killers before their lives were taken.

Collectively, these two anecdotes serve to highlight two realities of ancient warfare. One, as with *Masters of the Air*, in nearly every conflict from the ancient Mediterranean world, we don't have the firsthand accounts of soldiers who participated, with the odd exception, like Thucydides, Xenophon, Julius Caesar, Josephus, Ammianus Marcellinus, and Procopius. Second, the killing and the dying would have been a much more intimate affair than in the modern world, especially in an age when much modern conflict involves the use of unmanned drones and rocket-fired missiles coming from hundreds or thousands of kilometres away. There are other challenges in undertaking a project like this. Unlike those TV shows, this book is not about one division within an ancient army and how it performed in one conflict. So, how do we get from the warfare described by Homer in the *Iliad* in the eighth century BCE to the horse archery that dominates the *Strategikon* of Maurice, written near the end of the sixth century CE?

SIDEBOTTOM

This book will introduce you to the transformation of warfare over the course of those more than 1300 years, what brought it about, how we know about it, but also, especially, how it had an impact on those who lived through it. In other words, this is an introduction to warfare in the ancient Mediterranean which tries, where possible, to frame this history through the lived experiences of those who made, and lived through, it. Most of the warfare that we will see was fought on land, though occasionally we'll look at battles fought at sea. And while a lot of our attention will be on the bigger, more glamourous, open battles waged between two armies, we won't leave behind the sieges that made up such a big chunk of ancient warfare or the small-scale raids and more that often went unnoticed in our sources. The geographical locus is the Mediterranean Sea, though we'll travel far to the north to Scotland to investigate wars fought by Romans and Caledonians and down to the south and east to raids conducted by nomadic peoples in the deserts of Jordan and Syria.

This introduction is grounded in the ancient sources, whether they be Greek and Latin texts, black-figure vase paintings, colourful sculptural friezes, or Safaitic graffiti. But it's built on the work of generations of scholars – no scholar can hope to master the vast swath of ancient history encompassed in this book. And so I will, where relevant, draw readers' attention to their work.

On that topic, this is not the only little book on ancient warfare in English (to say nothing of other languages). Sidebottom's (2004) wonderful introduction to ancient warfare covers most of the subject matter that I would have hoped to cover in this book. And while his book is over twenty years old, it's full of prescient and relevant material. Indeed, in many ways, academia moves slowly, so what he has to say about topics like 'the Western Way of War' is just as important and relevant now as it was then. As a result, one of the big challenges, as I saw it, when sitting down to write this book, was to avoid duplicating him, where possible, and contribute something new. In some ways, I'm fortunate that Sidebottom's book came out when my graduate career was just beginning (I'm now 16 years into an academic position), and there has been no shortage of big developments in the study of ancient warfare. So, I see this book both as an introduction to ancient warfare and as a complement to Sidebottom's comparable volume. To illustrate some of this, and so set the stage for what will follow in subsequent chapters, I want to say a few things about the conflict that had the most significant impact on how the people of the Mediterranean thought about war.

THE TROJAN WAR

Despite so much evidence for war-making in the ancient Mediterranean world, observers, ancient and modern, have long recognized the challenges in trying to make sense of it. For ancient Athenians, one of the difficulties in determining the particularities of combat was the chaos of battle. A messenger in Euripides' *Suppliants* (680ff.) has this to say:

> The many horrors happening there I saw, not merely heard about, for I was at the spot [685] where the chariots and their riders met and fought, but which to tell of first I do not know: should it be the clouds of dust that mounted to the sky, or the men dragged this way

and that in the reins, [690] and the streams of crimson gore, when men fell dead, or when, from shattered chariot-seats, they tumbled headlong to the ground, and, amid the splinters of their chariots, gave up the ghost?

Theseus, the famous Athenian hero and king, and a key figure in the play, notes (*Suppliants* (Perseus), c. 850ff.):

These are idle tales alike for those who hear [850] or him who speaks, that any man amid the fray, when clouds of darts are hurtling before his eyes, should declare for certain who each champion is. I could not ask such questions, nor yet believe those who dare assert it; [855] for when a man is face to face with the foe, he could hardly see even that which it is his duty to observe.

Part of the explanation for the trouble was all those helmets, which offered fair protection from weapons but also hindered their wearers' senses. It was difficult to see and hear what was going on in the midst of battle while wearing a helmet. Another real problem, at least for some, is the undue influence of Homer's *Iliad* on Greek and Roman thinking about war for many centuries to come. This impacted how historians writing in both Greek and Latin composed works of history, especially works of history that focused on war, one of the principal categories of evidence for ancient warfare.

While legions of Greek and Roman authors clearly thought that much of the content of the *Iliad* was real stuff, for modern readers the story is different. But let's go back to the beginning. In 1184 BCE, or so many ancients would have us believe, the Greeks, led by Agamemnon, finally breached the walls of Troy and destroyed the city, bringing ten long years of war to a brutal conclusion. That war was immortalized in a variety of media, from Iron Age pottery to Archaic Greek poetry. No one did more to immortalize the war than the famed poet – whether real or not – Homer, whose 24-book *Iliad*, set in the waning months of a ten-year long siege, vividly captures the broad scale and impact of not only this war but the experience of war in general. Thanks in large part to Homer's vivid telling, this account of one siege of war had a significant impact on Greek and Roman culture for centuries to come. The quote that opens this chapter comes from the *Iliad*, and it reflects some of the complications around attempts to use the poem as a source for either the Bronze Age warfare that it purports to describe or the contemporary eighth-century BCE world in which the poet, Homer, was operating.

As noted, the *Iliad* covers only a small part of the wider conflict. Thanks to the survival of anecdotes in other works as well as coverage in other poems, we know not just the bare bones of the story but much else besides. Although there's no one, canon version for all things Trojan War, some details are well established and consistent. The gist of the story goes something like this. At the wedding of a mixed couple, the immortal Thetis and the mortal Peleus, the majority of Greek gods and goddesses were invited, save Strife. Outraged at the exclusion, she decided to sabotage the wedding celebrations by tossing in amongst the guests a golden apple (one of many) inscribed with something along the lines of "for the fairest". The competition over who was most deserving ultimately came down to three goddesses: Athena, Aphrodite, and Hera. Zeus, king of the gods, couldn't decide, and so the task was entrusted to a Trojan shepherd named Paris. Each goddess offered him something in return for the title, and he ended up siding with Aphrodite, who offered him the most beautiful woman in the world, then Helen of Sparta, married to Menelaus. As a result, Helen was taken to Troy to live with Paris. In revenge, Menelaus, along with his brother Agamemnon, king of Mycenae (Figure 0.1) and most powerful of the Greeks, called upon all those who had sworn the "oath of Tyndareus" to meet their obligations and join in a massive expedition to Troy to get her back. After delays for various reasons, which included Achilles' and Odysseus' initial unwillingness to participate and Agamemnon's dispute with Artemis, which led to (among others things) the death of his daughter, Iphigenia, the best of the Greeks finally landed at Troy. What they had hoped would be a short confrontation after some initial successes soon turned into a long, protracted war which stretched into ten years. The *Iliad* picks things up in year ten, with the two sides in a relative stalemate, the Greeks ensconced in an encampment made of their ships, many of them disillusioned and desirous of returning home. Over the course of a few weeks, Achilles, the best of all the warriors, Greek or Trojan, and his Myrmidons leave the field owing to a dispute with Agamemnon, which shifts the balance in the

FIGURE 0.1 Lion Gate, Mycenae, Bronze Age, Wikimedia Commons

Trojans' favour. Achilles finally returns to the fray after Hector, the best of the Trojan warriors, slays Achilles' companion Patroclus. He then hunts down and kills Hector at the walls of Troy but not before leaving a trail of destruction.

The war accelerates towards its inexorable conclusion following the death of Hector. Achilles himself is brought low by an arrow fired from Paris – possibly with the help of the god Apollo. In the ensuing dispute over Achilles' armour, the second-best Greek fighter, Ajax, takes his own life. Shortly thereafter, one of the Greeks, possibly Odysseus or Epeus, came up with the idea of the Trojan Horse, which is brought inside the city walls. While the Trojans slept (confident that they had won the war, with some exceptions, like Cassandra), some hidden Greeks, including Odysseus, emerged into the city and opened the gates, thus initiating the slaughter that would bring down the city and bring an end to its civilization.

Much of the scholarly discussion of the Trojan War and *Iliad* has focused less on the historicity of the conflict (at least to some degree) and more on its value as a source for Greek warfare. Because the

Iliad is an epic poem, it has a set of rules and patterns emblematic of the genre (dactylic hexameter and the reputation of formulaic phrases, among other things), a genre which was initially oral and so posed some practical restrictions on its tellers. The poem itself is full of all sorts of important themes, from human missteps and how we're seen by others to anger, courage, and injustice. Of fundamental importance, of course, are the honour, the glory, but also the horror of war. Much of the poem is replete with scenes of battle. We find heroes travelling to the battlefield on chariots, routs, and scores of single combats. Books 3 to 7, 8, 11 to 18, and 20 and 21 (in a 24-book poem) all detail combat in some form or other. There are lots of words for the toil of battle, the struggle, noise, the battle cry, and much more. And among all the scenes of fighting are plenty of episodes of single combat, like Menelaus' and Paris' duel in book 3, which was meant to end the war but didn't (3.340–382, 428–447). Although single combat, at first glance, seems a very Homeric thing, there are plenty of examples from other periods of Greek history. In a poem filled with combat, there are also all sorts of descriptions of wounds, usually graphic. Not only did the combatants suffer horrible wounds, but they usually died in one of three ways: the splitting of their head, a spear thrust to the body, or death by fire. There is, in short, no shortage of detailed descriptions of combat in the *Iliad*, and these scenes, and the characters who fill them, have been popular for centuries.

While the *Iliad* was meant, in part, to entertain, the abundance of warfare has meant that it has also attracted the attention of military historians, as I referred to above. Indeed, this isn't a new phenomenon; some ancient authors saw Homer as the first person to write about tactics in war, including the tactician Aelian (*Tactics* 1.1, ὅτι Ὅμηρος πρῶτος περὶ τῆς ἐν τοῖς πολέμοις τακτικῆς θεωρίας ἔγραψεν: "Homer first wrote the about the theory of tactics in warfare"). Ancient authors and modern military historians don't often agree on what was most important about warfare. Generally, those modern interpretations can be broken down into three viewpoints: first, Homeric warfare is pre-hoplite, filled with individual champions and melee fighting; second, it reflects the combat that was waged during Homer's own day; third, it is ahistorical. Beginning with the last of these, we have Finley (1971), who argued that the Homeric heroes served as models for later warriors but that the battles were inconsistent and unreliable. For Raaflaub (2008), there are a few issues: there are a mass of commoners, and the combat itself was extraordinary in length and is full of exaggerated and fantastic elements. There are no hoplites, but there is, indeed, mass combat. Latacz (1977, 2004) believes Homer provides consistent and plausible descriptions of pitched battle from his era, which mirrors what we find in the lyric poets of the seventh century BCE. So, there are dense phalanxes and no clear division between the pre-hoplite and hoplite periods. Van Wees (2004) brought in some compelling comparative evidence from Papua New Guinea because of the loose and fluid combat found therein. Sears (2010) tries to explain away all the nuances we see in Homer's account in terms of all the differing national units, each of which did their own thing, like the Myrmidons, both a national unit and elites at that. Regardless of whichever explanation you like best, it should be clear that the subject matter itself is murky. If we look more closely, albeit in summary form, the varied evidence for the Bronze Age world reveals a great deal of the diverse array of sources we have for ancient warfare, and this will set us up for subsequent chapters.

MAKING SENSE OF TROJAN WAR COMBAT

Although the *Iliad* as we know it was likely composed in the eighth century BCE or so, it depicts warfare set in the twelfth century. As it happens, thanks to many decades of research, we know much more than before about its states and how they waged war. We have images, osteological remains, and the remains of weapons and equipment. There are also a number of Linear B (the script used to write Mycenaean Greek) tablets. These tablets deal almost exclusively with administrative matters, but they do occasionally touch on the defence of the coast (PY An 657, 519, 654, 656, 661). All sorts of weapons, equipment, and types of soldiers are recorded. There are notices about guards too. While not specifically about war-making, these specific types of documents do give a good sense of the ability of some of the late Bronze Age Greek states to mobilize for war.

In Bronze Age society, as in the *Iliad*, being a man usually meant being a warrior, and elites tried to portray themselves as such. Archaeologists have found lots of spectacular graves of males with weapons. While, on the surface, they appear to be elite warriors, a closer consideration of the osteological (the scientific study of bones) remains of some of them has turned these assumptions on their head. For instance, some graves at Argos contained individuals of the wrong age (that is, boys and youths). Some had the wrong weapons – they were too elaborate to ever be used for actual combat. Some of the dead from graves at Mycenae show no signs of weapons trauma. On the other hand, there are graves of individuals who clearly had weapons-related trauma but no weapons. Those individuals were likely not members of the elite. Indeed, along those lines, the rank-and-file soldiers don't seem to have been buried with weapons at all.

As hinted at with the palace Linear B documents, we know a bit about the different types of soldiers the Mycenaean states could field in combat. There were both heavily armed and lightly armed soldiers, many local in origin, though some foreigners too were hired. The majority, however, would have been lightly armed infantry soldiers. Plenty of soldiers were adept as missile usage, whether slingers or archers. Chariots too were widely used. We find them in use not just by the Mycenaeans but also by the Egyptians, Hittites, and Mitanni, other Bronze Age peoples. Chariots were expensive, and their presence was usually confined to states that had the wherewithal to pay for them. When the palatial societies collapsed, the use of chariots dropped off.

The production of weapons was outsourced to villages, and in the collected documentary and archaeological evidence, scholars have identified evidence of involvement from all sorts of groups of labourers, whether craftsmen, farmers, shepherds, or some other group besides. The widespread involvement of many members of the local communities in war-making points to the importance of warfare to many facets of life in the Bronze Age and beyond. Many individuals are likely to have experienced warfare, whether as combatants or civilians caught up in an active conflict. But they also held warriors in high esteem, which is reflected in the presence of war gods and the burials filled with weapons and armour, among other things.

What about the war itself? Was there a Trojan War or wars, which could have inspired the poems and the epic cycle? Well, the Trojan War took place at the end of the Bronze Age, a period when many sites around the Aegean Sea were fortified, particularly towards its conclusion. This includes the famous cyclopean walls at Mycenae (and elsewhere), so called because of their size. Indeed, the Roman author Pliny (the Elder), following the Greek philosopher Aristotle, noted "towers were first erected by the cyclopes" (Pliny *HN* 7.57). The Bronze Age was filled with conflict, and two prominent parties, the Hittites and the Egyptians, were often at odds. This is perhaps best illustrated in the Battle of Qadesh (1274 BCE), which was led by the Hittite king Muwattali II and the Egyptian pharaoh Ramses II and which took place on the Orontes River near the modern border between Syria and Lebanon. Views differ on its outcome – or even its course – but it ultimately led to a treaty between the two, which was signed in 1259 BCE.

The Hittite Kingdom spread from its core in central Anatolia west towards the Aegean Sea, where they often interacted with contemporary Greeks, the Mycenaeans. Here in western Asia Minor, the Hittite vassal state Wilusa was the subject of several attacks, possibly involving those same Mycenaeans. Wilusa lay in the classical Troad, the region of western Turkey connected to Troy. In terms of language, Wilusa can be equated with the Greek word (W)ilios, or Ilion, terms often used in ancient literature for Troy. By most accounts, the Mycenaeans, the Achaeans of Homer's Troy, appear in select Hittite documents as the Ahhiyawa, who are occasionally at odds with the residents of Wilusa. Wilusa appears as one of several Hittite vassal states, including Miletus, which appears as Milawata, further south along that western Turkish coast. In fact, it even seems that Walmu, king of Wilusa, was overthrown in the thirteenth century BCE.

There's a surprising amount of evidence for war at Troy from the late Bronze Age. Cline (2014) notes the Greek epics, like the *Iliad* and others; Hittite records (diplomatic letters); Luwian poetry; and archaeological remains. Turkish Hisarlik (Figure 0.2), the ancient site of Troy, was destroyed two or three times between 1300 and 1000 BCE, within the purported period of the war. Two of the many archaeological layers, Troy VIh and VIIa, have the most notable signs of destruction while being closest in time to the ancient date for the conflict. On the other hand, the earlier instance (Troy VIh) is perhaps best understood as destruction wrought by an earthquake, while the latter might be better dated to the period after the

FIGURE 0.2 Hisarlik, Turkey (Troy), Wikimedia Commons

collapse of palatial states in Greece at the end of the Bronze Age (that is, just after the period in question). Nevertheless, collectively, there's enough material to tease out interactions between Greeks and Hittites and their vassals in this part of the world, some of which could well have led to conflict, at least on a small scale. In other words, there is plenty of incidental information about conflict around ancient Troy in the late Bronze Age, more than enough to have inspired the tales that came down to us as the Trojan War cycle.

WHAT'S TO COME

In the chapters to come, I aim to give readers as wide ranging an introduction to warfare in the ancient Mediterranean world as possible, both geographically and chronologically. So, while the Greeks and Romans will feature prominently, I'll devote plenty of space to the nomads of the Black Desert in western Asia, the Achaemenid and later Sasanian Persians, and the Huns in central Europe and the Britons in the northwest. But also, while I'll open each chapter with a quotation from some ancient author, I aim to introduce readers to the wide world of ancient evidence for war. Indeed, one of my principal aims for this little book is to show readers the diverse array of evidence at our disposal for ancient warfare, whether it be the remains of the Sacred Band at Chaeronea, the republican-era shipwrecks off the coast of Sicily, or Ammianus Marcellinus' Latin history of the fourth century CE. And, as with the story of the Trojan War, to make sense of warfare in these various eras of the ancient Mediterranean world, we often need to draw on as much varied evidence as possible, backed up by the immeasurable work of generations of scholars. Thus, I will close each chapter, this one included, with a little overview of some of the research that underpinned my discussions.

"THE STRONG DO WHAT THEY CAN AND THE WEAK SUFFER WHAT THEY MUST"

WARFARE IN ARCHAIC AND CLASSICAL GREECE, 600–404 BCE

The famous quote that opens this chapter comes from Thucydides' account of the Melian dialogue. In some ways, this captures well the often-stark differences in power between competing entities in the ancient world, where larger empires and federations, like Rome and the Athens of this quotation, went to war against smaller states like Athens' foe here, Melos. Thucydides' *History*, an account of the war between Athens and Sparta, the Peloponnesian War, is usually considered the first war monograph, a work of narrative prose specifically devoted to one conflict, in contrast to Herodotus' *Histories*, which is much more expansive. Herodotus too spends a lot of time on war, but the real emphasis is the antagonism between West and East, not just the wars between Greece and Rome alone. Works of narrative history, like those of Herodotus and Thucydides, often serve as our most important sources for warfare in the ancient Mediterranean, and the opening quote and topic make a fitting introduction to the subject of this chapter, war in Greece from the Archaic Age down to the arrival of the Macedonians under Philip II, father of Alexander, a period when big powers regularly went to war with smaller ones.

One of the most distinctive features of combat in this era was infantry in organized masses fighting against each other, especially

DOI: 10.4324/9781003092636-2

in Greece. In other words, this was the age of the hoplite, one of the most famed types of soldiers from the ancient Mediterranean world. As the intention of the book is to look at warfare from the perspective of more regular people, not only will I highlight hoplites and combat involving organized masses, I will also draw attention to a few points about the experience of battle and from the perspective of both men and women.

THE HOPLITE PANOPLY

For all that the warfare of this period often involved vast disparities in power (as epitomized by the quote), the type of combat often best associated with Greece is usually framed as a clash between equals. One of the most widely discussed soldiers from the ancient Greek world is the hoplite. Ironically enough, despite starting with ancient literature, we lack sustained, written, historical treatments of hoplites and their phalanxes, at least from the phalanx's purported heyday, Archaic and Classical Greece (c. 700 to 323 BCE). Rather, all the evidence comes from the material record and the visual arts, though some scholars have sought to supplement this with some experimental archaeology and what little bits we can glean from the literary evidence.

A hoplite was a heavily armed infantry soldier from ancient Greece named after its distinctive shield, the *aspis*, a Greek term (sometimes called *hoplon*). Although the soldier gets its name from a shield, there were, in fact, six key pieces to its panoply: the helmet with crest, the cuirass, greaves, a spear, a short sword or curved weapon, and the (usually) two-handed, rounded shield (*aspis*). All these elements appear in the archaeological record before 700 BCE. On the other hand, not all parts of the panoply were necessarily required or used by every infantry soldier.

Many would argue that our most important sources for Greek history and warfare are the historians like Herodotus, Thucydides, and Xenophon, and for good reason. The so-called father of history, Herodotus, made war and politics the focus of his *Histories*, and thanks to its success, his followers did the same, so making these subjects the principal focus of works of narrative history for hundreds of years thereafter. Some made contemporary or near-contemporary wars their focus, as was the case with Thucydides, who wrote about the Peloponnesian War, a war that seized all of Greece, and one in which he himself participated. In cases like this, that meant we sometimes had firsthand witnesses describing the action. Some authors, like Polybius, described both earlier and near-contemporary campaigns. Polybius described the rise of Rome, which meant going into detail about wars that predated him by decades, even centuries. This is the case for the Second Punic War, to which we will return two chapters from now.

Just because they described war, however, doesn't necessarily mean that they would describe all aspects of warmaking. For instance, why describe the Greek panoply when your audience already knew all about it? This is something we need to be aware of when we look more closely at these authors. Nevertheless, a few Greek writers describe aspects of the panoply, like Alcaeus of Mytilene, contemporary with the early phalanx, and Diodorus Siculus, who was writing later. Diodorus (15.44.3) gives the following memorable – if problematic (peltasts already existed, for example) – description of the changes in Greek armament:

> It will not be out of place to set forth what I have learned about the remarkable character of Iphicrates. For he is reported to have possessed shrewdness in command and to have enjoyed an exceptional natural genius for every kind of useful invention. Hence we are told, after he had acquired his long experience of military operations in the Persian War, he devised many improvements in the tools of war, devoting himself especially to the matter of arms. For instance, the Greeks were using shields which were large and consequently difficult to handle; these he discarded and made small oval ones of moderate size, thus successfully achieving both objects, to furnish the body with adequate cover and to enable the user of the small shield, on account of its lightness, to be completely free in his movements. After a trial of the new shield its easy manipulation secured its adoption, and the infantry who had formerly been called "hoplites" because of their heavy shield, then had their name changed to "peltasts" from the light pelta they carried. As regards spear and sword, he made changes in the contrary direction: namely, he increased the length of the spears by half, and made the swords almost twice as long. The actual use of these arms confirmed the initial test and from the success of the experiment won great fame for the inventive genius of the general. He made soldiers' boots

that were easy to untie and light and they continue to this day to be called "iphicratids" after him.

Writing much earlier was the Spartan poet Tyrtaeus. Often associated with the warrior culture of his native state, Tyrtaeus' poetry often touches on select aspects of warfare. In fragments of one of his elegiac poems (fr. 11.11–34), he says:

> So let each man bite his lip and abide firm-set astride upon the ground, covering with the belly of his broad buckler thighs and legs below and breast and shoulders above; let him brandish the massy spear in his right hand, let him wave the dire crest upon his head; let him learn how to fight by doing doughty deeds, and not stand shield in hand beyond the missiles. Nay, let each man close the foe, and with his own long spear, or else with his sword, wound and take an enemy, and setting foot beside foot, resting shield against shield, crest beside crest, helm beside helm, fight his man breast to breast with sword or long spear in hand. And ye also, ye light-armed, crouch ye on either hand beneath the shield and fling your great hurlstones and throw against them your smooth javelins, in your place beside the men of heavier armament.

The most significant item in the hoplite panoply was the shield. Over the course of the Archaic and Classical periods, the grip used in shields changed, enabling soldiers to carry heavier shields for longer periods of time. Shields were made of wood, commonly poplar and willow. One of the advantages of wood is that it would often bend but not break. On the other hand, as an organic material, wood rarely survived from the ancient world, which means not many shields survive either. Like much of the rest of the panoply, the shield came in many and varied types – not just one. Not only did shields vary in design, however, their manufacture varied too. Spears were an important part of the hoplite panoply too, but unlike in Homer, the Archaic and Classical era spears were thrust, not thrown.

Shifting from arms to equipment, as important as the shield was to the hoplite, the most distinctive feature for many is and was the helmet. Although the Corinthian helmet (Figure 1.1) is probably the best known, there were lots of different types, like the Attic type

FIGURE 1.1 Bronze Helmet, Corinthian Type, 600–575 BCE, MET

and the Boeotian leather cap. The helmets offered good protection but usually at the expense of situational awareness. Turning to the cuirass, they were often made of bronze, but many also had armour made of organic materials, like linen and leather. The linen armour, the linothorax, was light, flexible, and durable. Most importantly to the wearer, it did a fine job of offering protection.

As noted, we have some archaeological remains, like parts of shields. One complicating factor is not just the organic remains of much of the arms and armour but that, from the seventh century BCE onwards, we tend not to find men buried with weapons. Finding an entire hoplite panoply is a rare thing. Indeed, only at Metaponto in Italy have archaeologists recovered an entire panoply through excavation. In the absence of testable weapons finds, however, some have resorted to recreating ancient weapons to test their use, impact, and more. For instance, Rover (2020) carried out a series of tests to see if there was another way to determine if hoplites fought closely packed together, as is often assumed, or in some other way. He focused on swords, which could be used to perform three actions: stabbing, slashing, and hacking. He found that the slightly curved *kopis* was a hacking sword used only in close-order occasions, not in one-on-one duels or single combat. He also noted that the spear and shield were no good for single combat.

THE HOPLITE IN ART

Shifting from archaeology to the visual arts, while there's lots of evidence we do have, like Greek vase paintings, there's plenty that we don't. Pausanias (1.15), a Greek-language geographer writing under the Roman Empire, describes a lost painting from the Stoa Poikile at Athens which describes some heroic age (Bronze Age) combat, as well as some more contemporary action, in this case from the Graeco-Persian Wars. These wars pitted the Persians against a united force of Greek city-states in two invasions: one launched by Darius in 490 BCE, which included the famous Athenian defeat of the Persians at Marathon; the second, by the new Persian king Xerxes in 480 BCE, which included the famous Spartan defence of the pass at Thermopylae. These wars are the subject of Herodotus' *Histories*. Pausanias (1.15.3) describes the different parties coming to blows, the ships, and some of the more famous of Athenian commanders, like Miltiades. But he also notes (1.15.4) the "dedicated brazen shields, and some have an inscription that they are taken from the Scioneans and their allies, while others, smeared with pitch lest they should be worn by age and rust." The painting brings up an interesting point. While it's tempting to see any visual representation as an accurate reflection of reality, paintings, sculpture, and much more besides follow their own sets of rules. We need to bear this in mind whenever we use artistic evidence, just as we do with the literary material.

Though we might have lost some large-scale paintings, we have plenty of depictions of warriors from Greek pottery (Figure 1.2). One scholar investigated the reconstruction of Greek panoplies on pottery over time. Graells i Fabregat (2021) used 477 warrior representations on pottery (black-figure and red-figure) from the second quarter of the sixth century BCE to the third quarter of

FIGURE 1.2 Terracotta Oinochoe, three hoplites and shields, Amasis Painter, c. 560 BCE, MET

the fifth century BCE and looked at combat scenes only, not those scenes with just Greek arms or with soldiers arming for combat or soldiers on their way to combat. Graells i Fabregat found that the variety in representations was incredible, and well distributed across the period under consideration, though there were much more from the 25-year period between 550 and 525 than any of the others. In total, Graells i Fabregat looked at 60 images from 580 to 550, 168 from 550 to 525, 88 from 525 to 500, and 71 from 500 to 475. He found a decline in Corinthian helmets – the most distinctive of hoplite helmets – from 525 to 475. From 500 to 475, the kopis, a curved sword, became more common, while the number of swords in general went up. And though the one helmet decreased, another type, the Chalcidic, became more common. Closer to the end of the period under consideration, and especially the period from 475 to 450, early in the Classical Age, all the weaponry of the Persian Wars disappeared, with Corinthian helmets replaced by Attic and Chalcidic types in what depictions we have. Throughout these depictions, there were no standardized panoplies – that is, one version worn by all.

Arms and armament are interesting not just in and of themselves but because they can help fill in the gaps in other pieces of evidence. If we know what weapons Greeks used and what they wore while wielding them, we can get a better sense of how they might have acted in the heat of battle, which, in many cases, is just the sort of point that most ancient Greek historians, like Thucydides (at least for the most part), leave out – the ordinary individual in action. All those images of soldiers/warriors on pottery are useful for similar reasons. While they often don't give us the most accurate representation of a Greek man in combat, they often show plausible means of holding weapons. This too helps fill out the picture offered by the texts.

THE DEVELOPMENT OF THE HOPLITE AND THE WESTERN WAY OF WAR

All the discussions in this book build on the work of generations of scholars, and one topic which has attracted a lot of attention is the development of the hoplite. Nineteenth-century German scholarship imagined that hoplite battle involved opposing groups of hoplites with homogeneous equipment. One side might lure the other to battle by ravaging their fields and orchards. When the two sides drew up as a phalanx, a tightly packed formation comprising heavy infantry (usually), the clash would begin in quite a ritualized fashion, filled with rules, and, at some point, the push of the *othismos* (a real or imagined massed shove of combatants; more to come). This view gained wide currency, whether intentionally or otherwise, and later scholars sought to determine how, when, and why these changes took place.

Snodgrass argued for gradual changes to arms and armour which ultimately culminated in the advent of the hoplite. Lorimer, like others, pushed for technological determinism. The appearance of the double-grip Argive shield led to tactical changes. Some saw the development of the Greek *polis*, city-state, as key to the emergence of the hoplite, so arguing that it was essentially military in character and that it comprised a community of warriors.

One of the most influential scholars on Greek warfare has been Hanson, who saw the hoplite as an anti-aristocratic class. He tied the rise of the hoplite class to an economic revolution and connected the ideology of egalitarianism and ritualism to what he saw as the agrarian nature of the hoplite class. In turn, he saw the dawn of the hoplite system as the origin of the west. For Hanson's hoplites, the characteristic mode of combat involved the phalanx, and in particular one tightly packed mass of hoplites from one city-state lined up in a phalanx against another similarly armed and arrayed mass of hoplites. The two could crash together, and the one side that held out longest and best would be the victor.

Also of note, Ober had argued that battle was ritualized and that there were 12 rules of war. Picking up on this research, in Hanson's reckoning, these clashes would always be out in the open, the two sides would follow a set of rules (no surprise attacks, fight at a set time at a set place, and so on), and single battles would decide entire wars. In some ways, then, these phalanx-on-phalanx battles were decisive battles, which are battles that decide the outcome in a conflict. For Hanson, this mode of combat was distinctive of Greece, and after starting there it spread across the Mediterranean. This became the "western way of war", meeting an opponent head-on, out in the open, following, more or less, a set of established rules.

Today, no one accepts Hanson's thesis, both in terms of the development of the hoplite and regarding the ubiquity of the western way of war. Van Wees, for example, argued that phalanx-based combat, following on from Homer, was more dispersed than Hanson and others have let on. Even more seriously, Hanson focused mostly on the development and peak of phalanx combat (in his eyes) during Archaic Greece. Konijnendijk, however, has made a forceful case for the emergence of the phalanx only in the Classical Greek world and in the latter half of the fifth century BCE at that. Others too have noted the ubiquity of mass organized combat in other parts of western Asia like ancient Sumer, or Assyria, as well as the regular use of tricks and the presence of soldiers other than hoplites in battle. In other words, Hanson's 'Western Way of War' is misleading.

UBIQUITY OF WARFARE

How do you measure how much a society thought about war? Quantitative analysis is tricky in the absence of surveys from ancient populations. We can try to count how many different media discuss, portray, or engage with the practice of war. Though even here we might run the risk of privileging the viewpoints of elite members of a given society. In the case of classical Athens, there seems little doubt that powerful Athenians thought about war a great deal. *Strategos*, one of the chief military commanders in Athens (there were ten of them), was a year-long position elected annually and was held by some of Athens' most famous figures, like Alcibiades. But if we want to know what regular people thought about war, we'd have to look a bit harder.

One potential solution is offered by the world of theatre, especially comedy. Only a small number of the plays from classical Athens survive. These include select works of the tragedians Aeschylus, Euripides, and Sophocles as well as the comic playwright Aristophanes. It's the last of these that I want to mention here. The obvious example, for those in the know, is the *Lysistrata*, performed initially in 411. Comedies would be debuted in one of two Athenian festivals, the Lenaia and the Dionysia, in which new plays would compete for the top prize. Aristophanes won a few times, but we don't know how the *Lysistrata* fared. Regardless, the premise of the play, performed in the middle of the Peloponnesian War, is that the women of Greece would go on a sex strike until the men agreed to stop the fighting.

That's not the only play that points to the ubiquity of warfare. Aristophanes' *Birds*, about two Athenian men who leave their home and end up founding a new home in the air with the birds, Cloudcuckooland, also includes lots of direct and indirect references to warfare. Why Aristophanes provides such a clear example is because of both the audience itself and the language that he employs. Plays, even comedies, were presented in verse, but, for many scholars, they were written in the language that best approximated the language of the common person on the streets of Athens. So, if a play is filled with military language, there's reason to believe this would have been well received, or at least well understood, by members of the audience. The audience of Athenian comedies in the classical era would have been varied and diverse, if mostly male. You'd get men from high social classes as well as those from low social classes, the latter in part because some (many?) theatrical productions were subsidized. If you consider the war-themed jokes and offhand comments too, collectively this scattered evidence of warfare in the comedy of Aristophanes underlines just how much warfare featured in the public conscience.

BATTLE

We've seen a little bit about who fought and how they fought. But what happened when they did fight? We have little evidence for battle between the accounts of Homer and Herodotus. There are the aforementioned visual representations, which besides giving us a sense of the weapons and equipment soldiers might have used (or what contemporary artists thought they used), often attempt to illustrate combat in some way or other. Sometimes they show lines of soldiers, like on the famed Chigi Vase. Many more show one-on-one duels. These could be different kinds of encounters; they could also be two parts of the same battle, with the lines marching together and then dispersing when one-on-one combat breaks out.

So now that we've set the scene, so to speak, what do we think actually happened in the heat of battle? For one thing, there's no such thing as a typical battle. There are too many variables that could impact how a battle played out. That being said, there are a few things that we might expect to happen, to varying degrees, in combat. For one, battle was a feast for the senses, what with dust, shouting, crying, speeches, and music; for the participants the feel of weapons, their comrades, the enemy; gore – the sight, sound, smell, taste, and feel of it; and there was all that they ate and drank beforehand. We can imagine a wide variety of soldier types too. The soldiers themselves would be many and varied: some heavily armed, some lightly armed, many infantry, some cavalry, but also archers, slingers, and others who focused on missile fire. There could have been a rush as the two sides ran towards each other, followed by a crash. This is what is often called the *othismos*.

When it came time to fight, fear was a real problem, especially when the armies were composed primarily of untrained militia. Young Athenian men who were preparing for military service might swear an Ephebic oath: "I will not bring shame on my sacred arms nor will I abandon the man beside me, wherever I stand in line" (Christ 2006). To prevent this fear from taking hold, they might put the more timid in the front and the more experienced in the back, so to prevent them from leaving but also to calm the nerves. Being crowded together, relatively speaking, meant it might be difficult to see what's happening in the thick of battle, which could lead to problems of its own. Thucydides at Epipolae says (*Histories* 7.44.1): "each man hardly knows anything except what is happening to himself". We also get some insight in Greek tragedies. Euripides, for instance, was particularly skilled at conveying some of this fear. Orestes, in his *Electra*, says (*Electra* 377): "But shall I turn to warfare? Who, facing the enemy's spear, could be a witness as to who is brave? It is best to leave these matters alone, at random." Also, Theseus, in Euripides' *Suppliants* (*Suppliants* 850), proclaims:

> these are idle tales any man amid the fray, when clouds of darts are hurtling before his eyes, should declare for certain who each champion is. I could not ask such questions, nor yet believe those who dare assert it; for when a man is face to face with the foe, he could hardly see even that which it is his duty to observe.

Both sides would do their best to maintain order, and there may have been shoving (at least on occasion), often (even always?) involving their shields, which could be used offensively or defensively (again the *othismos*). There were likely several one-on-one displays, and inevitably one side would cave, turn, and flee. It was at this point, the flight, when most casualties would occur, a reality of combat across time and place in the ancient Mediterranean. The winning side would erect a trophy on the spot where the opposing side fled, so signifying their victory. One of the contentious parts of the hoplite battle was the aforementioned *othismos*, a nebulous concept and practice component that entailed shoving of some sort, possibly physical, possibly metaphorical, possibly both.

There is one important topic to discuss about the ancient Greek battle: the tactics of Greek armies. This has long been a popular subject, but some important recent research, by scholars like Echeverría and Konijnendijk, has allowed for a more nuanced understanding of the ins and outs of Greek tactics. They have concluded, among other things, that with the exception of Sparta, Greek armies were composed of untrained militias, and this amateurism had an impact on how they waged war. Terrain was a minor issue – much earlier work had implied that this was a central concern, but this doesn't seem to have been the case. Terrain was important, and armies would use whatever tricks they could to gain an advantage, but it wasn't the be-all and end-all. On that note, there were also no rules and rituals about where to fight and when. While we've focused mostly on hoplites (in large part due to their outsized reputation in the popular imagination), ancient sources include much more than hoplites in their accounts. We find light infantry, cavalry, and more. By some reckoning, there also doesn't seem to have been a post of honour in the classical phalanx (on the right or anywhere, though Butera and Sears disagree on this) and no set number of ranks required in a phalanx. For commanders, there were all sorts of limitations owing to the lack of training of their soldiers, the difficulty in transmitting orders in the heat of battle, and the tendency of those same commanders to fight in the front. With all these challenges, they unsurprisingly used whatever means they could to succeed. And once battle got going, there was little they could do to modify their tactics, with the exception of the trained armies of Sparta and Thebes.

Another contentious issue was the movement of the hoplites in battle, and it's largely thanks to some provocative comments from Thucydides. While describing one of the most famous infantry battles from Classical Greek antiquity, the first Battle of Mantinea, fought in 418 BCE between the Spartans and their allies and the Athenians and theirs, Thucydides notes the following (Thucydides 5.71.4):

> All armies are alike in this: on going into action they get forced out rather on their right wing, and one and the other overlap with this their adversary's left; because fear makes each man do his best to shelter his unarmed side with the shield of the man next him on the right, thinking that the closer the shields are locked together the better will he be protected. The man primarily responsible for this is the first upon the right wing, who is always striving to withdraw from the enemy his unarmed side; and the same apprehension makes the rest follow him.

Whether what Thucydides said was true of all battles or just this one is hard to know. Indeed, besides equipment and the frame of mind of Greek soldiers, the literary evidence has been used to document the movement of hoplite soldiers in battle, particularly in the phalanx. That said, relying on writers like Thucydides, whose understanding of combat differed from ours, presents all sorts of problems. At the beginning of this chapter, I noted that authors may not describe all things connected to war, even if it was the focus of their work. For one thing, many of their readers would have served as a hoplite themselves and so they would have felt no need to get into the nitty gritty. For another thing, they just understood battle in a different way from us. In his groundbreaking *Face of Battle*, a book on the experience of combat from the perspective of the lowest-ranking soldiers, John Keegan highlighted some of these differences. Ted Lendon took things further, so highlighting the peculiarities of Greek and Roman combat in a book and series of journal articles. So, it's not so much that Greek and Roman writers were inherently wrong in how they described combat; rather, they had a different understanding of what were the important characteristics in ancient warfare.

WOMEN AT WAR

A few pages earlier, I highlighted Aristophanes' *Lysistrata*, in which the women of Greece withheld sex until the men gave up making war. Comedic roles aside, women factored in manifold aspects of warfare in the Greek world, and the Roman world too, for that matter. In this section, however, I want to highlight some of the examples of the roles that women played in warfare in the Archaic and Classical Greece.

Although Aristophanes' women are dissatisfied with the war occupying the men, it's not the war itself that displeases them, but rather that their partners are ignoring their needs. In Sparta, according to Plutarch, Spartan women trained to protect family. Indeed, Spartan women were famous for their lack of tolerance for cowardly men:

> A Spartan, wounded in battle and unable to walk, was crawling on all fours. He was mortified at being so ridiculous; but his mother

said to him, "How much better to be joyful over your bravery than to be mortified at silly laughter." Another, as she handed her son his shield, exhorted him, saying, "Either this or upon this." Another, as her son was going forth to war, said, as she gave the shield into his hands, "This shield your father kept always safe for you; do you, therefore, keep it safe, or cease to live."

[Plut. Lacae. 6.15–16, trans. Babbitt]

We find women seeing men off to war and in a host of other support capacities, as Martinez Morales has set out so clearly. In sieges in particular, we find women throwing things, like bits of masonry or anything else they could get their hands on. Women bring weapons to the male combatants, distribute food, and, in the absence of medical professionals, care for the wounded. Sometimes, women were disguised as men on the city walls in a bid to trick the besieging side about the number of defenders (Aen. Tact. 40.4). We find women bringing water to victorious men (Xen. Hell. 7.2.9), cooking in garrisons (Thuc. 2.78.3), and carrying secret messages (Aen. Tact. 31.7). But we also find women building and repairing a city's walls, entertaining soldiers in army camps (Xen. An. 6.1.11–13), and even spying for others. And, in echoes of the later experiences in countries like Canada and the United Kingdom during World War II, Demosthenes even comments on women serving in paid employment while the men were away at war (57.30). Though we have only a small sample, we should bear all this sort of activity in mind in subsequent chapters. Even if our sources don't always spend a lot of time on the activities and experiences of women in war, their impact was unmistakable.

AFTER BATTLE

What happened when battle turned and one side gained the upper hand? Most casualties on the ancient battlefield took place when one side gained an advantage and the other turned and fled. In fact, the disparities could be quite dramatic. So, when we're talking about the dead from battle, we're often talking about those who fell in this stage. In this section, it's worth taking a look at what could happen to some of those who died after battle ended.

We know a great deal about the aftermath of battle in Athens, whether that is thanks to Thucydides' famous discussion of their funerals or the casualty lists that survive among the vast body of epigraphic material. There were three key elements to Athenian war dead: the funeral speech, the casualty lists, and the public cemetery. In his account of public funerals, just before the famous eulogy of Pericles, Thucydides said the following (2.34, Perseus):

> Three days before the ceremony, the bones of the dead are laid out in a tent which has been erected; and their friends bring to their relatives such offerings as they please. In the funeral procession cypress coffins are borne in cars, one for each tribe; the bones of the deceased being placed in the coffin of their tribe. Among these is carried one empty bier decked for the missing, that is, for those whose bodies could not be recovered. Any citizen or stranger who pleases, joins in the procession: and the female relatives are there to wail at the burial. The dead are laid in the public sepulchre in the most beautiful suburb of the city, in which those who fall in war are always buried; with the exception of those slain at Marathon [Figure 1.3], who for their singular and extraordinary valour were

FIGURE 1.3 Tumulus at Marathon, Christopher Wordsworth, 1882, Wikimedia Commons

interred on the spot where they fell. After the bodies have been laid in the earth, a man chosen by the state, of approved wisdom and eminent reputation, pronounces over them an appropriate panegyric; after which all retire. Such is the manner of the burying; and throughout the whole of the war, whenever the occasion arose, the established custom was observed.

At the end of a battle, the winner would erect a trophy, and the other side would admit defeat. The usual thinking is that the winner in a pitched battle would sustain far fewer casualties than the defeated, say a ratio of a loss of about 5% of the men for the victors and about 14% for the defeated. The losing side would usually come to claim its war dead. This would, on the surface, seem to be a significantly challenging task, but the Athenian conscription lists helped out a great deal. Bodies wouldn't be transported back to Athens, however. The fires made at the battle sites couldn't get hot enough to properly cremate the remains.

Once the public funerals had been performed, the remains might be interred at the public cemeteries, like at Kerameikos, where famous public individuals like Cleisthenes and Pericles were buried. As I noted above, we also have some casualty lists that identify not just the higher-ranking generals who might hope to have a prominent place in such a cemetery but also those from the lower ranks across various tribes or *phyle*. One such example, possibly from around 447 BCE, reads as follows (IG I3 1162, Attic inscriptions online):

> In the Chersonese of the Athenians these died. Epiteles, general. Of Erechtheis: Pythodoros, Aristodikos, Telephos, Pythodoros. Of Aigeis: Epichares, Mnesiphilos, Phaidimides, Laches, Nikophilos. Of Pandionis: Lysikles. Of Leontis: Chaires. Of Oeneis. Rhodokles, Eurybotos, Polites, Herokleides. Of Kekropis: Aristarchos, Karystonikos, Theomnestos, Aristarchos, Eukrates, Nikomacos. Of Hippothontis: Sotelides, Poseidippos. Of Aiantis: Diphilos. Of Antiochis: Kraton, Antikrates, Eudoxos.
>
> In Byzantium of the Athenians these died. Of Erechtheis: Nikostratos, Philokomos. Of Aigeis: Chionis. Of Pandionis: Philistides. Of Leontis: Lysimachos. Of Akamantis: Kallisthenes. Of Oeneis: Kallippos. Of Kekropis: Kniphon, Demoteles. Of Hippothontis: Haison. Of Aiantis: Nikodemos. Of Antiochis: Phanias.

> These died in the other wars: Of Erechtheis: Lysanias. Of Pandionis: Simonides, Aischylos, Archepolis, Smikrion, Charopides, Naxiades. Of Leontis: Philon, Eudemos. Of Akamantis: Protarchos. Of Kekropis: Chairias, Astyanax, Lysistratos. Of Hippothontis: Timonothos, Antiphanes. Of Aiantis: Kleinothos, Philios, Kallikles. From Eleutherai: Semichides.
>
> These by the Hellespont lost their gleaming youth doing battle, and brought glory to their fatherland, so that the enemy groaned, reaping the harvest of war, and they placed an immortal memorial of their excellence.

Beyond the public rituals experienced by all, there were the private emotions and more experienced by the individuals. One of the big debates among scholars is whether Greek soldiers, or any soldiers from the ancient Mediterranean world for that matter, experienced post-traumatic stress disorder, which is well established amongst the veterans of much more recent conflicts. On the one hand are the universalists, like Tritle, who hold that the innate humanity of soldiers then and now means that those soldiers from the ancient world suffered just like those from modern conflicts.

On the other hand, there are the presentists, who argue that the different nature of warfare then and now combined with the different life experiences and worldviews mean that those then did not suffer in the same way as those today. They argue that the lived experiences of ancient soldiers, both in the day-to-day but also in combat, meant they weren't exposed to the kinds of threats faced by modern soldiers. For instance, there was, perhaps, more death in their lives, whether that came from the threat of disease or the comparatively shorter lives, at least on average. Their combat was usually – but not always – restricted to daylight hours, which meant they were more likely to get more sleep and less likely to have to face an enemy with most of their senses all but useless. Some would argue too that there were far fewer head wounds, which often contribute significantly to the kind of injuries that are conducive to trauma. That Greek soldiers often stood close beside those they knew well probably also helped lessened at least some of their fears.

Of course, we lack detailed evidence from a soldier's perspective about what it was like and what they experienced in combat, at least at the sort of level that we find in today's militaries. They also didn't have the same understanding of the human body or necessarily characterize and treat wounds and injuries in the same way. All this makes it difficult to determine what, exactly, ancient soldiers experienced in battle. There are other problems, which I've hinted at already. The ancient battlefield was different from the modern one. You are, perhaps, more likely to be killed from a distance now than then and perhaps more likely to suffer wounds to the head.

But a human is still a human – there have been no profound biological changes in humanity between the ancient world and the modern one. With that in mind, some, more recently, have tried to combine what we find in ancient combats with what neuroscience tells us about what happens to the brain and body in traumatic (combat or combat-like) situations. Heidenreich, an evolutionary psychologist, and Roth, an ancient historian, teamed up to look at the neurophysiology of warfare in the ancient world, adopting an approach that takes ancient accounts of panic and then contextualizes this information in terms of what we know about how the body responds to these sorts of situations. In other words, they tested whether what we find in the ancient sources about panic matches what we know about how the body responds to these sorts of situations.

Using Onasander, though other ancient sources too, Roth noted that Onasander (and related textual evidence) was primarily concerned with what was happening to the soldier in the front, not the back or the side. As for the body, they noted the various ways that the body responded to stress (panic). This includes sweating, agitation, defecation, and urination, which are all neurophysiological responses to fear. Also associated with panicked soldiers are changes in heart rate, blood pressure, respiration, and incontinence. In other words, the body might respond in a host of ways to panic on the field of battle. A consideration of some of these responses was used to illuminate some of the more baffling episodes of soldierly behaviour in the context of battle. For instance, one of the most famous stories of trauma in battle is the blinding of the unwounded soldier Epizelus following the Battle of Marathon, an episode which has also been discussed by scholars like Tritle and which was initially recorded by Herodotus (*Histories* 6.117.2). They argue that his being struck blind might have been a neurological response to stress (the events of the battle). Livy (*Ab Urbe Condita* 2251.8) says that, at the Battle of Cannae, Carthaginians found Romans with their heads buried in the ground. They take this as an example of "the rational processes of thought being overwhelmed by an instinctual desire to dig oneself to safety" (Heidenreich and Roth 2020). These are only two of several examples that they adduce. Though only one small aspect of the ancient battlefield, research like this should allow us to probe a little deeper into the mind of the ancient soldier.

GREEKS IN SICILY VS. CARTHAGE

So far, owing in part to our often Athens-centric sources, I've been focusing on Athens. Athens is only one part of the Greek story, however. The Greek world was a big world, and before I shift to what came after, I want to move from mainland Greece west and south to Carthage, the powerful Mediterranean kingdom just across the sea from Sicily and the Italo-Greeks. I will come back to Sicily in Chapter 3 when we turn to the Hellenistic world and the Hellenistic Military Revolution. And in the next chapter, we'll take a closer look at the Greek soldier – the Athenian soldier in particular. Until that time, it's worth pausing to comment on the broad origins of the soldiers of some Greek states, in large part because it allows us to see how some researchers are using advances in genetic studies to broaden our understanding of aspects of the Greek world, war-making included.

Most think of the modern country of Greece when they consider ancient Greeks, but thanks to an ambitious period of colonization, Greeks could be found at various points across the Mediterranean, including – even especially – to the west in Italy and Sicily. These Greeks regularly came up against the Carthaginians, who lay just across the sea in much of modern Tunisia. Carthage's name came from the Phoenician *Qart Hadasht* (a reflection of their Levantine origins), which led to the Greek *Karkhedôn* and Latin *Carthago*, which meant "New Town". By the end of the sixth century BCE, Carthage was the premier power in the western Mediterranean.

Owing to their location across the sea from Sicily, the two western powers regularly found themselves at war. One of the most important of these conflicts culminated in the Battle of Himera, fought in 480 BCE between Gelon of Syracuse (in Sicily) and Carthage, one which the Sicilians won. There has been a lot of recent research on the aftermath of this conflict owing to an analysis of the deceased from the western necropolis at Himera, which dates from the seventh to fifth century BCE. Using DNA extracted from select remains from the thousands of deceased persons at Himera, researchers have been able to look more closely at the origins and backgrounds of those who fought in two battles at or near this location.

Himera offers one of the few mass burials from ancient Greece, and the deceased, many (most?) of whom were male, were likely fallen warriors who researchers believe had fought at Himera either in 480 BCE or many decades later in 409 BCE. Mass graves are often associated with conflict, because of the context. In the case of the aftermath of combat, we have a large number of individuals who have perished at one time who require immediate burial – immediate for both practical and cultural reasons: practical to avoid the spread of disease and related risks, cultural because of the widespread Greek belief in the importance of burial for the deceased – and the attendant difficulties in transporting their remains home in the aftermath.

What did they find? Well, some of their skeletons betrayed evidence of frailty, which would have put them at a greater risk of mortality. What's perhaps even more interesting, however, is just how many of these individuals weren't locals. In 480, some two thirds of all those bodies analysed (and it was the teeth of those individuals) were non-local; in 409, that total was about one quarter. The implication is that in Sicily, at least, they were hiring foreign mercenaries from distant places. In another recent study of the genome-wide data of 54 people from the necropolis, the results pointed to the careful placing of soldiers with similar backgrounds together. So, while we wouldn't want to generalize too much, this research does at least suggest we should assume that all Greek armies were reliant on a mixture of foreign and local soldiers in the Classical era, at least in the western Greek world.

CONCLUSION

In this first chapter, I've only scratched the surface of Greek warfare. I've tried to focus on the general at the expense of the particular. So, no long treatments of the two principal wars (or series of wars), the Peloponnesian War and the Persian invasions, which are well covered elsewhere. On the other hand, I've tried to stress the variety and quality of the evidence. Art can tell us a great deal about ancient warfare, and at times it can help fill in the pieces left by the gaps in our textual evidence – or even illuminate us on issues which the ancient authors don't even begin to appreciate. Another key aim of this chapter was to centre the discussion on the experiences of the participants, both soldiers and civilians, as early as possible, so we could get a sense of what ancient warfare was for them. What we found is that they fought in manifold ways – not just as hoplites in phalanxes. In addition, the soldiers came from all across the Greek world. In other words, war didn't just involve the soldiers of one Greek city-state against another. Whereas the focus in this chapter has been on the regular participants of warmaking, in the next chapter, we'll meet some towering figures of Greek military history, like Epaminondas and Alexander the Great.

"VERY WELL THEN, ALEXANDER COMES FIRST"

FOURTH-CENTURY GREECE TO THE WARS OF THE DIADOCHI, 404–275 BCE

One of the most entertaining satirists from the second century CE is Lucian, who wrote, among other things, a work called *Dialogues of the Dead*. Three of the dead who feature in one of the dialogues are three of Graeco-Roman antiquity's most famous generals: Alexander, Hannibal, and Scipio (Africanus). The three appear at the entrance to Elysium (something like paradise), and a discussion ensues about which general is the best. The ultimate arbiter of the decision is the famous Minoan king Minos. In the end, most of the debate, couched in occasionally humorous language, centres on who's better between Hannibal and Scipio, whom we will come back to in the next chapter. For many ancient and modern readers alike, it should come as little surprise that Alexander comes first. Alexander has regularly been held up as one of the greatest generals from any time and place in history. We'll say a little bit about Alexander closer to the end of the chapter and about leadership and how it was conceived of in the ancient world in general. Before we get to Alexander, however, we need to say a few things about the waging of war in the decades before he burst on the scene at Chaeronea. And I want to start by considering what motivated Greek soldiers to fight in the first place.

DOI: 10.4324/9781003092636-3

MOTIVATING GREEK SOLDIERS

Let's start with the Greeks. We already have some idea how they fought, thanks to the discussion of combat in the previous chapter, but we haven't gone over what drove them to fight in the first place. Love of country and self-defence might both seem like obvious and self-evident motivations, but there are others worth considering. The topic has been the subject of a lot of new and exciting research, much of it centred on Athens owing to the abundant source material, as we saw in Chapter 1.

The reason why a soldier might fight for their *polis* (city-state like Athens) in the first place emerges as a central concern right from enlistment. Recruitment in Athens involved a mixture of volunteerism and conscription, and various tools might be employed to motivate them, a necessary task when some who found themselves on conscription lists were not exactly enamoured with the prospect of going to war. In his play called *Peace*, Aristophanes (1180ff.) described this lamentable scene:

> Once back again in Athens, these brave fellows behave abominably; [1180] they write down these, they scratch through others, and this backwards and forwards two or three times at random. The departure is set for tomorrow, and some citizen has brought no provisions, because he didn't know he had to go; he stops in front of the statue of Pandion, reads his name, is dumbfounded and starts away at a run, weeping bitter tears.

It's fair to see why for the combat – and campaign – environment could be a challenging place for all sorts of reasons. Plato, the famed philosopher, noted this in his *Symposium* (219e220e):

> Now all this, you know, had already happened to me when we later went on a campaign together to Potidaea; and there we were messmates. Well, first of all, he surpassed not me only but every one else in bearing hardships; whenever we were cut off in some place and were compelled, as often in campaigns, to go without food, the rest of us were nowhere in point of endurance. Then again, when we had plenty of good cheer, he alone could enjoy it to the full, and though unwilling to drink, when once overruled he used to beat us all... But it was in his endurance of winter—in those parts the winters

> are awful—that I remember, among his many marvellous feats, how once there came a frost about as awful as can be: we all preferred not to stir abroad, or if any of us did, we wrapped ourselves up with prodigious care, and after putting on our shoes we muffled up our feet with felt and little fleeces. But he walked out in that weather, clad in just such a coat as he was always wont to wear, and he made his way more easily over the ice unshod than the rest of us did in our shoes..."Then, if you care to hear of him in battle—for there also he must have his due—on the day of the fight in which I gained my prize for valor from our commanders, it was he, out of the whole army, who saved my life: I was wounded, and he would not forsake me, but helped me to save both my armour and myself

The speaker here, Alcibiades, is describing the exploits of the philosopher Socrates, perhaps Athens' best-known citizen, though also a celebrated soldier. He makes it clear that Socrates was brave and saved Alcibiades' life. Some of his famed exploits in war came later in life: he was 37 when he fought at Potidaea, mentioned in the passage, and 45 when he fought at Delium, possibly a sign of Athenian desperation – having to resort to older men, though it might just as well have been less of an Athenian problem in general and more an issue with Socrates' own deme (Alopeke) or tribe (Antiochis). War was expensive for a hoplite like Socrates, and he could be expected to spend 75–100 drachmae for basic equipment, which was the equivalent to three months' wages for a skilled worker. So, fear of death aside, the financial challenges also posed a problem for would-be Athenian soldiers.

Nevertheless, Athenian soldiers were compelled to fight despite the circumstances, with two possible reasons being their patriotism and obligation. The *polis* was the birthplace of patriotism and patriotic warfare. But individualism was also important. How, then, to reconcile the needs of the many with the needs of the individual? Reeves has argued for a combination of coercion and compulsion, while Christ has argued that conventional motivations were not enough, and so soldiers had to be forced. But honour and its pursuit were important too, with Athenians obsessed with competing for it, and battle recognized as the ultimate place to achieve it. In other words, service provided a ready opportunity for individuals to achieve the honour they so desired.

During the peak of classical Athens, soldiers were recruited by means of the *katalogos* system, and by all accounts men weren't forced to serve. In a society obsessed with honour, rivalry, and competition, campaigning provided an opportunity for the would-be soldier to distinguish himself from his peers, and the best venue for achieving this was the field of battle. Success in battle might serve an individual in other aspects of life, like trials, where, if you ran afoul of the law, you might need to demonstrate the quality of your character.

In regard to combat itself, for one scholar (Crowley), it was the primary group that mattered most, the small group the soldier interacted with more often than not. For Athens, that small group was the deme, one of Athens' subdivisions. The *taxeis*, one of the larger Athenian units, didn't seem to have regimental identities of their own, at least not in the way that later regiments do or even the legions of Rome did. The *taxeis* were too short-lived, for they were only for specific campaigns. For Crowley, then, ultimately the Athenian hoplite endured the rigours of combat because of his fellow demesman and his desire to fight for his own socio-political system. Of course, the soldiers from other Greek city-states might be motivated by slightly different interests, owing to their varied outlooks and political systems. Nevertheless, this view for Athens does give us some idea of what impelled a Greek soldier to march out onto the field of battle.

THE FOURTH CENTURY

We shift now to the fourth century BCE, when some decisive changes led to some significant fluctuations in the balance of power of Greece. For one, the weakening of Athens and Sparta, the two dominant parties in Greece in the fifth century, coincided with the growing power of other Greek city-states. This increasing competition led to, among other things, an increase in fortifications across the Greek world as well as new developments in military technology. Diodorus of Sicily credits Dionysius of Sicily with inventing the catapult as well as other equipment too. This revolutionized siege warfare in Greece, which had been less developed than that practised by the Greeks' eastern Mediterranean neighbours – and predecessors. There were also changes in tactics, with peltasts, light-armed troops, used to great advantage, and the Athenian Iphicrates were particularly noteworthy for employing them. Mercenaries, though not new, became a bit more common too. None of this meant the end of the hoplite, but its role was gradually diminished.

A big development that came with the changes in siege warfare was an increase in the number of fortified settlements. One well-documented region is Arcadia, where the earliest walls were composed of a stone foundation topped by a mudbrick superstructure. In the late fifth and early fourth centuries, sites incorporated segments of high ground and rivers over manmade protection on at least two sides. All sites in Arcadia spaced their towers strategically, and a frontal or simple opening was the only attested type of gate. Posterns (secondary door or gate) were rare. Decades later, new fortified sites appeared throughout Arcadia, especially south, east, and north. Sites incorporated high ground and flat terrain, and they started to employ the regular spacing of towers with mostly the same gate types as before, but some new types, and posterns were also now more common.

From the fortification changes in one Greek region, we shift to the military record of a single city-state in another: Thebes. Thebes features prominently in a number of myths, especially the stories surrounding Oedipus. Its historical prominence grew early in the fourth century BCE when the Corinthian War against Sparta ended in 387. A treaty called the Peace of Antalcidas, which was intended to guarantee autonomy to Greek city-states across the world, was signed. As party to this agreement, Thebes would not act on behalf of its Boeotian neighbours, as would be the case for other city-states, whose independence would be safeguarded by Sparta, another formerly strong city-state. Sparta and its allies, the Peloponnesian League, were the ultimate victors in the Peloponnesian War. Their city-state was the most militaristic of Greek city-states, and their citizens, the Spartiates, were able to devote considerable time and energy to their own military. But this was due to their oppression of those on the lower rungs of their society: the Perioikoi and the Helots. While they were able to maintain this system for a while, declining population numbers among the Spartiates, among other things, eventually brought about their ruin. But let's get back to Thebes.

Around this time, an important relationship developed in Thebes between two prominent individuals: Epaminondas and Pelopidas. In the first quarter of the fourth century, Thebes went from strength to strength, which alarmed other Greek city-states. In 377, the Spartan king Agesilaus II and his allies marched against Thebes. The two sides met again in battle in 371, the Battle of Leuctra, which Thebes won, so establishing a period of Theban hegemony, which lasted until 362.

The Battle of Leuctra is, for many, one of the most decisive engagements from the ancient Greek world. Overall, the Spartan army was a bit bigger than its Spartan adversaries. The Spartan king, Cleombrotus, put cavalry in the centre and his best troops on the right (their usual practice, as most say). The Thebans put their best troops opposite. In their case, Epaminondas included Pelopidas' Sacred Band – which we'll return to shortly – and deployed them 50 ranks deep, quite a bit deeper than usual, even though the Thebans were known for using deeper ranks. Epaminondas and the Thebans (Pelopidas led the Sacred Band) launched a quick and successful surprise attack on the Spartan right, which happened before the Theban right wing had even engaged the Spartan left. That Theban attack on Sparta's right wing brought Thebes victory, and in the melee, King Cleombrotus died, and the Spartan army crumbled thereafter, so bringing an end to the superiority of the Spartan phalanx for good.

Despite the victory, however, the Thebans suffered too. Three of the seven Boeotarchs (Boeotian commanders), nearly 50% of its high command, died at Leuctra. Still, Theban success was commemorated in the following, relatively well-known, inscription (Rhodes and Osborne 2007:151 no. 30):

> Xenocrates, Theopompus, Mnasilaus.
> When the Spartan spear was dominant, then Xenocrates took by lot the task of offering a trophy to Zeus, not fearing the host from the Eurotas or the Spartan shield. "Thebans are superior in war," proclaims the trophy won through victory (*or* bringing victory) by the spear at Leuctra; nor did we run second to Epaminondas.

Indeed, as much as Thebes suffered, this was nothing compared to what transpired in Sparta. Their power crumbled, a new Arcadian federation was established, and they lost the Helots and Messenia, on which they depended for the running of their state, especially when Spartiates (chief Spartan citizens) were preoccupied with war. The Thebans attempted to seize the advantage and Epaminondas led four expeditions into the Peloponnesus between 370 and 362, including one with a particularly large army, comprising 60–70,000 men, which included Pelopidas, the leader of Thebes' famed Sacred Band.

So, what was the Sacred Band? By some reckoning, a band of boyfriends. Indeed, the language sometimes used for this group is similar to the language we sometimes find connected to marriage. The biographer (among other things) Plutarch credits the Theban Pammenes with arguing that it was better to draw up an *erastēs*, a lover or active lover, next to an *erōmenos*, a beloved or passive lover. Most claim that Pelopidas was the man responsible for carrying out the reforms that led to the establishment of the band. But looking back in time and myth, we can find traces of this notion of Theban love, including this epigram dedicated to the god Apollo outside a sanctuary (A.P. 13.22 IL.4–8, trans. Davidson):

> Direct the arrow of Eros at these here bachelors, that, bold in the love of youths, they may defend their fatherland; for it [the dart] fires boldness and of all the gods he [Eros] is supreme at exalting the front-line champions.

Regarding myth, it's worth noting that Thespiae, another Boeotian city, was the homeland of Narcissus and Eros, both with strong connections to love.

Relationship status questions aside, there is widespread agreement that this was an elite group of soldiers, for some even a professional force. They do seem to have been kept ready for deployment year-round for special missions. They were also a short-lived phenomenon, some 40 years, like Thebes' success more broadly – at least in the time frame of this book. And, as famous as they were, they were only ever a small part of the Boeotian war effort whose fame perhaps outstretched its impact on their success. On that topic, they featured in only four major battles: Tegyra in 375, Leuctra in 371, Mantinea in 362, and Chaeronea in 338, all fought in Boeotia. That last battle marked their demise, but we'll come back to that point later.

THE PERSIAN ARMY

So far, I've all but excluded one of the ancient Mediterranean world's most important entities, Persia. Early in the fifth century BCE, the Achaemenid Persians twice invaded Greece, and famous battles were fought at Thermopylae, Marathon, and Salamis, among other places. The Greek historian Herodotus claimed that, during the second of two invasions, they marched from their territory with an army that numbered 1,700,000, by all modern reckonings a clear exaggeration (Hdt 7.60). But there's no doubt their army was of significant size and varied in its capabilities. That invasion army consisted of a dizzying array of different people (Figure 2.1), including Persians, Medes, Cissians, Hyrcanians, Assyrians, Bactrians, Sacae (Scythian people), Indians, those from the Persian Gulf Islands, and many more besides. We find them depicted on sculptural reliefs in the heart of Persia and elsewhere in modern-day Iran. Though the languages of its soldiers were varied, the principal language of the state and so its military was Aramaic. We don't have detailed Aramaic historical narratives laying out their war-making and so we rely on a mixture of Greek and Latin sources and assorted documentary texts. Nevertheless, we know a few things about their war-making.

The Persian state was led by a king, who would convene a council to decide on war and battle. The army was called *spāda* in Aramaic, and it was composed of infantry, *pasti*, cavalry, sometimes called *asabāri*, or "horse-borne," sometimes *ušabāri*, "camelborne", charioteers, and camp followers. It was organized on a decimal system,

FIGURE 2.1 Soldiers of Xerxes I, tomb at Naqsh-e Rostam, Iran, 6th–4th century BCE, Wikimedia Commons

and the elites – the Persian nobility at least – received lots of training on a regular basis. But there would also be soldiers levied for specific campaigns, and at various points the Persians hired Greek mercenaries, like the famous Greek author Xenophon. Xenophon was a prolific author and general, who is usually considered one of the great historians of the classical Greek world. He wrote about horses, philosophy, and much more besides. Arguably the most celebrated text he produced was the *Anabasis*, the story of Xenophon and some Greek mercenaries' great escape from the Persian Empire. Besides providing some valuable details about the mechanics of Greek combat, it tells us a lot about the personal relationships within Greek armies, the composition of Greek expeditions, and something of the dietary challenges of an army on the march. It is an extraordinary piece of work, which also provides some important information about the Persians.

The most famous of their soldiers are probably the ones called the Immortals by Herodotus. Herodotus' term might be a reference to Anushiya, the name of a unit in Old Persian, which could mean "behind death" or "deathless". These were elite Persian soldiers, the crème-de-la-crème of their military, and there are places where they seem to be depicted, like some palace tiles from Susa, the Persian capital. There's one last group of soldiers to note, the frontier soldiers, who are comparatively well documented, thanks to the survival of numerous papyri from Egypt, long part of the Persian Empire. One particularly well-documented garrison was based at Syene, along the Nile, in Egypt. Its garrison was diverse and included Judaeans, Aramaeans, Egyptians, Babylonians, Persians, Medes, Caspians, Chorasmians, and Bactrians. A wide variety of names are found in the surviving documents, and we find, among the soldiers, fathers and sons. Some soldiers are anonymous, some are named things like Mithraxa and Cithraxa. They were based in a few spots in Egypt, and while their backgrounds seem to have been diverse, the highest-ranking officers might well have been Persian. Their units ranged in size between 120 and 1000. Although the papyri don't show the soldiers in combat, they do provide invaluable evidence of the lives of soldiers beyond the field of battle, that is where soldiers spent most of their lives.

This, then, is the Persian military in a nutshell. While it had its share of problems, whether in its invasions of Greece a century

FIGURE 2.2 Battle of Cavalry and Foot Soldiers, Payava Tomb, Xanthus, Turkey, British Museum, Alamy

earlier or against the Scythians to its north and west, the Persian military was a formidable force. They could field a huge number of soldiers, with a diverse range of capabilities, and they inhabited a massive empire. This was not a force to be taken lightly. The great mass of infantry soldiers were not trained professionals and so, by some measures, less capable than other infantry, but when they were used in conjunction with the Persian military's fast and mobile cavalry (Figure 2.2), and in combination with their artillery, the whole could cause big problems for any army. And yet, for all its might, one of two Macedonian generals, in the second half of the fourth century BCE, decided to do just that, invade Persia.

THE RISE OF MACEDON

One of the most significant events of the second half of the fourth century BCE was the rise of Macedon. Formerly (from the perspective, say, of a citizen of classical Athens) the home of backwards Greeks (perhaps not even real ones – Greeks debated the issue fiercely), Macedon soon produced two of the most famous generals and leaders from any part of the pre-modern world: Philip II and his son Alexander III. The former is reasonably well documented and is in turn credited with transforming the Macedonian military. By some reckoning, he professionalized the military and broadened its capabilities, carefully integrating the disparate parts into an excellent whole, so making Macedonians masters of combined arms and, for some (Sears), the ancient world's best army.

Before we turn to all the things that Philip accomplished and I give you a précis of the Macedonian military and combined arms, I want to highlight the high regard in which he is held. I'm usually loath to talk about revolutions and the ancient world, but there are, on occasion, instances which bear closer consideration. One of the clearest considerations of revolutions in the context of military studies comes from Brice, who settled on five criteria for an RMA, a "revolution in military affairs", a term adapted from research on more recent periods of history. Those five criteria are, first, it should take no more than two generations (60 years) to be implemented; second, it should be new in conception or employment; third, it should include dramatic changes in doctrine and operational and organizational concepts; fourth, it should force every opponent to adapt or be defeated; and, fifth, it should have socio-political implications or repercussions.

The Macedonians had long had an effective, though unexceptional, cavalry. But they started using it as a shock force in conjunction with their infantry, with troops often formed into a wedge. That infantry on its own underwent significant reform, even a revolution. Most Macedonian phalangites wore a leather thorax, not bronze. This was much cheaper, which made service in the military more affordable while not sacrificing the safety of the soldiers. Another big change came in the form of the introduction of the sarissa. This was an extremely long spear, which was two-handed and which in turn made the Macedonian phalanx hard to penetrate. To enable the soldiers to hold the sarissa with two hands, they used small shields linked around their arms. Of course, lighter armour and new weapons can only do so much. So, Philip implemented a full-time training regimen, which meant they could, if desired or needed, fight any time of year. Even the cavalry wasn't immune to change, for it was now composed not only of Macedonian elites but also Thessalians.

Other key components of this military were the bodyguards. The royal bodyguard units comprised infantry and cavalry, and both protected the king and served as elite soldiers. On a whole, these varied components worked together seamlessly, so that when the Macedonians attacked their foes it wasn't just one part, like heavy infantry, against their enemy. Rather, it was more than one, like heavy infantry, archery, and cavalry working in unison, over the course of battle. This apparent mastery of combined arms warfare made the Macedonians a very difficult opponent indeed.

Thus, based on what we know about the Macedonian past, Philip's reforms led to a military considerably different from what came before in a comparatively short period of time. The kingdoms that succeeded Macedon all adopted his fighting techniques. Plus, Macedon's victories brought about a new world across the Mediterranean. So a revolution in military affairs it was. The impetus for many of these changes seems to have been some time that he spent in Thebes, where he was exposed to the efforts of Epaminondas and Pelopidas. The Athenians might also have left their mark, for some argue it was Iphicrates (of Athens) who introduced the idea of a long spear to Philip.

THE BATTLE OF CHAERONEA AND THE DECISIVE BATTLE

In the previous chapter, in the context of the development of the hoplite, I discussed the idea of a decisive battle and in particular whether all those supposed hoplite-on-hoplite battles were decisive. Whether they were or they weren't, here, at the end of the classical (Greek) era, we find one battle that almost certainly was. The Battle of Chaeronea, waged in 338 BCE between a Greek alliance and the Macedonians, marks the end of Greek independence until the modern era. It also marks the debut of Macedon's most famous leader and general, Alexander III, or Alexander the Great. Unfortunately for us, this battle is not well documented.

Macedon wasn't a new entity to the Greeks to the south, for they'd long featured, in some capacity, in Greek history. They'd never been an especially powerful group, however, at least not before the rise of Philip II. At this point in time, Athens and Thebes were often enemies, but unlike Macedon, they were both democracies and their people saw the Macedonians as a legitimate threat. One of Athens' most famous orators from any era, Demosthenes, was alive during the rise of Macedon, and he used his rhetorical skill to help persuade Thebes to change sides and fight with Athens against the Macedonians. In several speeches, which we are fortunate to have today, Demosthenes rails against the danger posed by this northern Greek kingdom and its people. Here's one small sample (Demosthenes, Philippic 3):

> But if some slave or superstitious bastard had wasted and squandered what he had no right to, heavens! how much more monstrous and exasperating all would have called it! Yet they have no such qualms about Philip and his present conduct, though he is not only no Greek, nor related to the Greeks, but not even a barbarian from any place that can be named with honour, but a pestilent knave from Macedonia, whence it was never yet possible to buy a decent slave. Yet what is wanting to crown his insolence? Not content with the destruction of cities, is he not organizing the Pythian games, the common festival of the Greeks, and if he cannot be present in person, sending his menials to act as stewards? [Is he not master of Thermopylae and the passes into Greece, holding those places with his garrisons and his mercenaries? Has he not the right of precedence at the Oracle, ousting us and the Thessalians and the Dorians and the rest of the Amphictyons from a privilege which not even all Greek states can claim?] Does he not dictate to the Thessalians their form of government? Does he not send mercenaries, some to Porthmus to expel the Eretrian democracy, others to Oreus to set up the tyranny of Philistides? Yet the Greeks see all this and suffer it. They seem to watch him just as they would watch a hailstorm, each praying that it may not come their way, but none making any effort to stay its course.

As we've seen, Demosthenes, the Athenians, and the Thebans had good reason to be afraid, for Philip had honed his military into a well-tuned fighting force. Although Demosthenes' diplomatic efforts certainly helped the Greek case, it couldn't prevent outright war, and eventually the two sides met at Chaeronea in 338 BCE. At first glance, the two sides were probably fairly well matched, but the southern Greeks didn't have generals of the calibre of Philip and Alexander on their side. By the battle's conclusion, the Sacred Band would be no more, and Alexander would raze Thebes to the ground a few years later, though Athens, owing in part to its rich cultural heritage (and the Macedonian crown's relationship with certain Athenians), fared much better.

Thebes had already been in trouble some decades earlier. The second Battle of Mantinea, waged in 362 BCE, pitted Agesilaus' Sparta alongside Athens and assorted other allies, who had maybe 20,000 infantry and 2,000 cavalry, against Thebes and its allies' 30,000 infantry and 3,000 cavalry. The Thebans' famous general, Epaminondas, was mortally wounded in the battle, which led to chaos and confusion among Thebans, who managed to win the battle in spite of this. So, while this is an important battle, it's not decisive – Thebes continued, even if significantly weaker thereafter. But let's get back to Chaeronea.

This important battle is not well documented, as I noted above, though we find a bit in the literary sources. Diodorus Siculus, Plutarch's *Life of Alexander*, and Polyaenus all provide a few details on the events. But we also have a great deal of supplementary evidence provided by studies of battlefield topography and even some excavations. For instance, archaeologists found the grave of the Theban Sacred Band under the lion monument, which stands on the site of the battle.

That Sacred Band had played a big role in Theban war-making for some time, and they feature prominently in the research on this battle. Both Philip and Alexander were present, with Alexander leading the cavalry against the Sacred Band, and probably on the left of the Macedonian battle line, rather than the right wing, which seems to have been his preferred side. In the course of the battle, Philip used feigned flight to lure the Athenians into a pursuit. They were then caught and defeated uphill while in formation. Overall, however, the battle seems to have been a close-run affair with the Macedonians finally pulling off the victory only after a closely fought contest. Plutarch says that, by the end, the Sacred Band were wiped out and that Philip was moved to tears by their deaths.

One of the most contentious parts of the battle was Alexander's struggle against the Sacred Band. There is some doubt over whether he used cavalry against them in the first place. Scholars used to think that the young (18-year-old) Alexander had charged them on the left. But more recently, questions have been raised, mostly because of questions over whether horses would charge at disciplined, heavily armoured, infantry (i.e. the Sacred Band). Two scholars, Sears and Willekes, have pushed against this, however, drawing in part on the work of a third (Liston). To address this contentious issue (would horses charge at armed infantry), they looked at horse behaviour and the skeletal evidence provided by the excavations.

Starting with horse behaviour, initially, as some scholars have argued, it seemed that horses would not have charged. After all, horses are hard-wired to flee danger. On the other hand, horses are also herd animals, and this aspect of their behaviour is a big part of their training. We have an ancient, near contemporary (by ancient standards) account of horse training, Xenophon's *On Horsemanship*. He discusses the role it plays in his understanding of horses. It turns out that, yes, horses don't want to be prey, but they're also scared of being left behind by the herd. So, horses could be trained to charge against heavily armed soldiers.

Of course, just because they could, that didn't mean that they did, and to address this, Sears and Willekes had to bring in the work of Liston on the skeletal evidence from Chaeronea. Liston showed that blade and blunt weapon injuries were evident from the battle, but so too were other injuries. All but one of the skeletons had experienced blunt force trauma to their face. Some had experienced gruesome head injuries, some had lost teeth, one had had their face amputated, and another had a cut above the knee. The evidence of some wounds points towards the use of swords in phalanx combat, a point which helps underscore some of the realities of phalanx combat. While much of it was organized – the integrity of the line was key – there were clearly moments of individual combat, where swords were more valuable than spears. The armour they used also illustrates how a Greek soldier's panoply changed over time. Few hoplites were wearing bronze armour by Chaeronea, and while there was still some headgear (helmets), not everyone was wearing them.

This is all evocative, but also gruesome, stuff that really drives home the violence of ancient combat. But what does it have to do with whether Alexander charged the Sacred Band on cavalry? Well, as it happens, despite all those varied wounds and evidence of varied weapons and armour, the bodies also have wounds which imply that they were struck from above. And the only way that they could have sustained these was by attackers on horseback, namely Alexander's cavalry. We don't have many battlefields from the ancient world, but when we do, they often not only provide remarkable insight into the nature of ancient combat (especially how it was experienced) but in select cases can help address tactical questions like these ones. It seems certain that Alexander did lead cavalry at a charge against the infantry of the Sacred Band.

ALEXANDER THE GREAT

Chaeronea brought about the end of Greek independence, and for that reason alone, we should consider it a decisive battle. It also served as Alexander's great coming-out party. By the time he died, he was one of the best generals who had ever lived. Later writers, from the ancient world through modern times, have been enthralled by his military prowess, with later Roman generals, from Marc Antony in the late republic to Julian in late antiquity, striving to match his success, especially in the eastern Mediterranean. At the beginning of this chapter, we discussed the dialogue concerning who was the best general, with Alexander the victor. We also saw, if briefly, Alexander's emergence in the Battle of Chaeronea in 338 BCE. What, if anything, was special about Alexander's leadership and how did he become the general we know him as?

Greek military leadership went through many permutations. Throughout much of the period under consideration, leaders were expected to fight in the front with their men rather than to hang back and manage the armies from the rear. The historical value of Homer's *Iliad* is mixed, but throughout the poem, we find the leaders of the various Greek peoples fighting amongst their men against the Trojans – and vice versa, for that matter. Two excellent cases in point are the actions of Achilles on the Greek side and Hector on the Trojan. That said, the practice adopted by Priam was something else, with the aged king never participating in the fighting in the *Iliad* and instead managing affairs from afar. The fighting from the front eventually shifted to fighting from the back, where generals could manage the movement of their units. To some degree, this also went along with the rise of military science and those sophists who pushed their knowledge of military affairs. Alexander and his Macedonian brethren, however, preferred this fighting from the front, and, in many respects, Alexander represented the peak of

FIGURE 2.3 Alexander the Great commanding that the work of Homer be placed in the tomb of Achilles, anonymous, 1500–1550, MET

the heroic general, for he regularly led the charge himself, so often bringing himself and his cause into danger. In fact, Alexander, who was believed to have been descended from Heracles, was inspired by Achilles and made a point of visiting Achilles' grave after he crossed the Hellespont early in his conquest of Persia (Figure 2.3). In more ways than one, perhaps, Achilles marked a fitting model for the famous Macedonian general.

For one thing, Alexander had the distinct advantage of inheriting the army put together by his father Philip, who had already by this point created a well-oiled military machine, at least in some respects. Alexander's great achievement, from the perspective of a small book on ancient warfare, was his remarkable conquest of Achaemenid Persia. At the start of a campaign around 334 BCE, he had a 50,000-strong army, composed largely of Greek, especially Macedonian, soldiers. The majority of the infantry were foot companions, called *pezhetairoi*. The cavalry equivalent were (just) the companions, *hetairoi*. They had advance scouts, *podromoi*, light infantry, composed of their neighbours, including Agrianian mountaineers. They also had Macedonian, Thracian, and Cretan archers and even some Thracian cavalry. Much of the initial core of this army was Greek (or Greek-adjacent), but owing to deaths, attrition, and more, the composition of his army changed over time, with the next major shift coming in 330 BCE following his big victories over Persia. From 328 or 327, he started making extensive use of eastern troops.

Alexander's first major victory over the Persians came in 334 at the River Granicus in what is now Turkey. A year later, he defeated them again at Issus, again in Turkey, only this time down in the southeast in the Levant. This was followed by the siege of Tyre, the conquest of Egypt, and the 'establishment' (quotes because there was a pre-existing indigenous settlement) of the most famous of his Alexandrias, the one in Egypt, all in 332.

The decisive victory, however, came at Gaugamela, in what is now Iraq, in 331. This battle, or perhaps Issus, was depicted in a famous mosaic from Pompeii, Italy: the Alexander mosaic (see Figure 2.4). Darius was murdered shortly thereafter, and Alexander was declared king of Asia. During the last, fateful, battle, the Persians outnumbered the Macedonians (as they often did) by a significant margin. Darius III's army had anywhere from 100,000 to 1,000,000 troops, the latter surely an exaggeration, while Alexander's army had something like 31,000 heavy infantry, 9,000 light infantry, and 7,500 or

FIGURE 2.4 The So-Called Alexander Mosaic, Pompeii, Italy. Wikimedia Commons

so cavalry. As was invariably the case, Alexander lined up on the right with the cavalry, while his army as a whole was arranged in an oblique formation. He attempted to draw the Persians to the sides, so leaving the centre weak. Darius, meanwhile, was in the centre with his best infantry, with cavalry, chariots included, on both flanks. Darius attempted to encircle the Macedonians, but Alexander's companions, in a wedge formation, broke through his line and won the day.

While this might have made a fine place to halt his advance, Alexander decided to go further east and capture the Persians' eastern lands and some more territory besides. At the Battle of the Hydaspes River, near the borderlands between Pakistan and India in 326, Alexander won again, this time against King Porus. Eventually, his soldiers had had enough, however, and from 326 to 324, Alexander and his army marched back west to Babylon, the capital, and Mesopotamia. A year later, he was dead, and his empire soon shattered into several smaller pieces, though after some often brutal fighting.

With a record like this, end aside, it's hard not to look back on Alexander and judge that he deserved his title "the Great". He never lost a battle. While using his father's tactics, he managed to incorporate just about every unit type available in combat. But he made two tweaks which made the Macedonians' use of combined arms tactics even better. One was the adoption of an oblique formation, which had been used previously at Chaeronea and Leuctra, and the other was Alexander's tendency to charge on the right flank. Thus, in Wrightson's estimation, he perfected the use of combined arms warfare. This system was so successful that his successors adopted the same system, though they relied more on the phalanx than the heavy cavalry.

Of course, Alexander wasn't perfect. Plenty of scholars have pointed out some of the problems that he faced in command of the military and his fledgling empire. There were one or two mutinies, one at the River Hyphasis in 326 (the contentious one among scholars), the other at Opis in 324. At times, he was overly rash and nearly succumbed to enemy attacks, as at Guagamela. Alexander took quite a lot of men with him from Macedon, which left a comparatively small number behind – this, in turn, contributed to minor issues of instability. Some too have questioned the quality of his opposition. At Granicus, he didn't face the king in battle (so making for an easier battle). At Issus, the king he did face, Darius, was by some reckoning mediocre at best. Alexander also launched a number of costly sieges, like the siege of Tyre in 332.

Many of his problems occurred in the latter stages of his campaigns. Given how long they were and their geographical scope, it's not surprising that he would run into problems at some stage or other. Indeed, despite being outnumbered at the Hydaspes River, King Porus and his army, comprised, in part, elephant cavalry, and fought well even if Alexander still managed to win. In fact, his entire campaign into the eastern stretches of Persia and beyond, into Afghanistan, Pakistan, and India, has been questioned. And then, his march back west through Gedrosia, after his men had reached their limits, was itself questionable, particularly in the stretch of land in the desert. Although it provides us with one of the most famous examples of Alexander's generally positive relationship with his men, exemplified by his regular desire to share their trials and tribulations (his dumping out water from a helmet when his men couldn't drink also), it's safe to say they shouldn't have been put into this position in the first place.

There are other complaints. Grainger argues he had no grand strategic vision – though many would argue no pre-modern leader had this – and, along similar lines, he was not a brilliant strategist or politician. The impact of Homer might have driven him to take unnecessary risks. And he did, as I noted above, possess what could be called the ancient world's best army. This gave him a leg up over other generals – the odds were in his favour right from the beginning. It could be, then, that what made Alexander great was not so much his conquests but his public relations, which left behind a record that has dazzled people for centuries.

CONCLUSION

A healthy dose of scepticism isn't a bad thing when looking at the exploits of a famous historical figure like Alexander. Some moderns may question Alexander's prowess as a general, but ancient writers and commentators (such as Lucian, as we saw above) had no doubt. Alexander, building on the efforts of his father before him, managed to motivate a huge number of Greek soldiers, build on some of the advances we saw already in places like Thebes in the fourth century BCE, and with other changes overcame that long powerful Persian army. In the next chapter, we'll meet that other great empire from the ancient Mediterranean world, Rome.

CARTHAGE AND THE "MUTABILITY OF HUMAN AFFAIRS"

THE HELLENISTIC AGE AND THE PUNIC WARS, 300–200 BCE

As we have seen already, sometimes our best sources for ancient history weren't contemporary, even if they themselves were from the ancient world. The passage above is taken from a second-century CE Roman historian, who wrote in Greek, named Appian, who discussed the Punic Wars, and the second in particular. The line itself comes from the lips of a Carthaginian envoy named Hasdrubal Eriphus, who appeared before Scipio Africanus after he defeated the famed general Hannibal at Zama in North Africa. That battle effectively ended the war between the two western Mediterranean powers, Rome and Carthage, and Carthage, which had been the most powerful state in the west, was about to be brought low. So, the envoy cautions the Romans to treat the Carthaginians fairly as what has happened to them could later affect Rome (App. *Pun*. 8.51–52). In this chapter, we'll look at select aspects of the clashes between Rome and Carthage. To do so, we have to go back to the end of Alexander's great, but short-lived, empire, for the clashes in the aftermath brought about the dominance of Rome and the end of Carthage. Before we get there, I'll start with the rise of "military science," which, for some, revolutionized how war was fought in the Mediterranean world.

DOI: 10.4324/9781003092636-4

HELLENISTIC MILITARY REVOLUTION

Two chapters ago, I looked at hoplites and phalanxes, a subject connected not just with a supposed western way of war but also with a purported revolution in war-making. Few would call the advent of the hoplite a revolution, even if the political changes that accompanied it were significant, but that doesn't mean there weren't other, potential, military revolutions, or revolutions in military affairs, as scholars of more recent military history and strategic studies call it. They're easy to find in other eras, with Michael Roberts proposing and Geoffrey Parker advancing, for example, a military revolution from 1550 to 1650 in early modern Europe. This revolution took many forms, from tactics and strategy to the larger-scale and greater impact of the era's warfare.

In the previous chapter, I touched on Brice's arguments for a revolution in military affairs under Philip II of Macedon. Many of the changes in warfare were adopted by the armies of the successor kingdoms in the Hellenistic age. This was the period of big powers in the eastern Mediterranean, often at loggerheads with each other, that rose out of the ashes of his empire, especially the Ptolemies in Egypt, the Seleucids in Syria, and Antigonids in Macedon. Even smaller powers, like Pergamum in Asia Minor (northwestern Turkey) or Demeterius I of Bactria (northwest India, Pakistan, Afghanistan), were regularly embroiled in these conflicts. So, Hellenistic armies, like Philip's and Alexander's armies, had infantry with smaller shields and giant sarissas. But the Hellenistic world produced some change of its own. We tend to associate significant developments in arts and science with the Greek world, and the classical world of Athens especially. After all, this was the age of the dramatist Aristophanes, the philosopher Plato, the sculptor Praxiteles, the historian Thucydides, and many more besides. On the other hand, a number of important developments, like standardization of many texts and some important changes in the Greek language, took place in the Hellenistic world. Hellenistic thinkers were concerned with, among other things, accumulating vast amounts of knowledge. The Hellenistic age also saw major developments in the world of science, and more scientific documents survive from the Hellenistic period than any other type of text.

CARTHAGE AND THE "MUTABILITY OF HUMAN AFFAIRS" 61

FIGURE 3.1 Coin of Demetrius I, 222–180 BCE, Cleveland Museum of Art

In fact, some speak of the rise of "military science" at this time, owing, in part, to the rise of specialized military engineers, *technai*. Indeed, an unknown engineer might well have invented the torsion catapult. Sometimes, leaders brought in engineers from afar, for Demetrius the Besieger, an early third-century (BCE) Macedonian king, brought in engineers from Greece, Carthage, and Italy. Arguably, one of the most famous inventors (and engineers, mathematicians, and polymaths), Archimedes, dates to this period and allegedly employed a range of inventions during the Roman siege of Syracuse in 213 BCE. He even features in the most recent Indiana Jones movie, *Indiana Jones and the Dial of Destiny*.

But let's get back to the texts. Some of these abundant Hellenistic scientific texts were texts of military science, which go by a lot of names and which first appeared around this time, if not slightly earlier, in the fourth century BCE. Arguably the earliest of these texts,

Aeneas Tacticus' *How to Defend a City*, comes from the middle of the fourth century BCE. It covers some social, economic, and cultural aspects of a siege and was possibly written at Stymphalus in Arcadia (Greece). The next lot of texts appears a century later, with another one on sieges, Philo Mechanicus' *On Sieges*. It includes lots of technical discussion of fortification work. So, while it goes over how to survive a siege, it also covers catapults and much more. Jumping ahead a century (or more), we come to Biton, who wrote the *Construction of War Machines and Catapults*. This, then, covers some of the same material as Philo, only Biton concentrates much more on the machinery of war, like the helepolis, sambuca, and the non-torsion catapult. There are two more writers who were writing in the Hellenistic era: Athenaeus Mechanicus, who like Biton wrote a work, *On Machines*, focused on military machines, and Asclepiodotus, whose *Tactica* takes a different approach – order, the phalanx, and pitched battle. Those authors are just the surviving ones, for Polybius, for instance, the famed historian of the rise of Rome, wrote a now-lost *Tactica*. The Greek king Pyrrhus might also have written a manual.

One side of this period of military intellectual fervour is all those texts. Another side is all the inventions. Thucydides referred to all sorts of siege machines, from rams and incendiary devices to shields and tortoises (Thuc. 7.43.1). So, while some siege implements are well attested, others are a little less so, like the catapult. There's some debate over whether the catapult was discovered or rediscovered during the Hellenistic age. One issue is evidence. The most common type of archaeological evidence we have for them is the washer, which, on its own, makes it tough to determine how widespread they might have been and how early. Fortunately, we have some of that textual evidence (and more) referred to above. What we can say is that the earliest mentions of them in the Greek world come from Diodorus Siculus, who notes their use in Sicily in 399 BCE. Most evidence does come from the third quarter of the fourth century BCE. In Athens, both bow and torsion catapults were in use. Despite the introduction of some newer types, this was a slow process with outdated models in use often alongside the older ones. The biggest changes, however, came in the last third of the fourth century BCE.

From sieges, we shift to another theatre that witnessed some big changes, the sea, and here the 'big' refers not just to the significance of the changes but also to the size of the things changing. Naval warfare wasn't a new thing. The battles of Salamis and Artemisium stand out as two of the most famous of ancient naval battles, and both took place during the second Persian invasion of Greece. But the size of the participating ships had stayed relatively consistent, with triremes dominating. Triremes had three rows of oars and had served the Greek world well. We can thank another Macedonian king, this time the first king of the Antigonid Empire – the Macedonian successor state to Alexander's larger empire – for instigating a naval arms race in 315 BCE. Antigonos the One-Eyed launched the Hellenistic age's race for ever-bigger ships, the gigantism that was a staple of the ships. Attempts were made to replace ships with three rows of oars with ships with four rows, five rows, and even ten rows. Antigonos' successor, the aforementioned Demetrios the Besieger, had a flagship seven-rowed ship equipped with bolt and stone-throwing artillery. Nearly a century later, Ptolemy IV Philopator, yet another Macedonian king, took things to even more ridiculous lengths, for he had ships with an astounding 40 rows of rowers. Athenaeus, a third-century CE Greek writer, had this to say about these giant ships in his *Deipnosophistae* at 5.203e (trans. from lacus curtius):

> Philopator constructed his forty-bank ship with a length of four hundred and twenty feet; its beam from gangway to gangway was fifty-seven feet; Fits height to the gunwale was seventy-two feet. From the top of the stern-post to the water-line it measured seventy-nine and a half feet. It had four steering-oars, forty-five feet long, and the oars of the topmost rowers, which are the longest, measured fifty-seven feet; these, since they carried lead on the handles and were very heavy inboard, were yet easy to handle in actual use because of their nice balance. It had a double bow and a double stern, and carried seven rams; one of these was the leader, others were of gradually diminishing size, some being mounted at the catheads. It carried twelve under-girders, each of them measuring nine hundred feet. It was extraordinarily well proportioned. Wonderful also was the adornment of the vessel besides; for it had figures at stern and bow not less than eighteen feet high, and every available space was elaborately covered with encaustic painting; the entire surface where the oars projected, down to the keel, had a pattern of ivy-leaves and Bacchic wands. Rich also was the equipment in armament, and its satisfied all the requirements of the various parts of the ship.

On a trial voyage it took more than four thousand men to man the
oars, and four hundred reserves; to man the deck there were two
thousand eight hundred and fifty marines; and besides, below decks
was another complement of men and provisions in no small quantity.

This naval arms race didn't last, however, for ships started to get smaller again in the second century BCE. It's also the case that the notion that "bigger is better" didn't apply only to ships, for Hellenistic armies tended to be bigger too, Achaemennid Persia's massive armies aside. To give one example, at the Battle of Raphia in 217 BCE, which pitted the Seleucids (roughly Syria) against the Ptolemies (roughly Egypt), the former's army numbered close to 62,000 infantry and 6,000 cavalry, while the latter's army 70,000 infantry and 5,000 cavalry (Polyb. 5.79–85).

There were other changes to Hellenistic armies. New, hybrid soldiers, such as the *thureophoros*, appeared (Figure 3.2). A *thureos*

FIGURE 3.2 Thureos Fresco, Istanbul, third century BCE, Wikimedia Commons

used a single-grip, large, flat shield and was a medium-armed infantry soldier. They could fight at a distance with a javelin or close up with a sword. Cavalry also underwent changes, which were initiated by the reforms of Philip and Alexander, discussed in the previous chapter. There are plenty of archives which provide valuable insight into warfare in the Hellenistic age, like those found at the cavalry headquarters at Athens, the Hipparcheion.

ROMAN NAVAL WARFARE

But let's now ship west to Rome. By the third century BCE, after Alexander had died and his empire had been divvied up into a number of smaller kingdoms, Rome had managed to take over most of the Italian peninsula. Along the way, they overcame a long-remembered siege and sack of the city around 390 BCE by the Gauls. In the first quarter of the third century, a Greek general named Pyrrhus invaded Italy on the invitation of some Roman rivals in southern Italy. Although he had some success, his victories were usually accompanied by significant losses. In fact, his losses were so great that he was eventually forced to withdraw from Italy, so giving rise to the phrase "pyrrhic victory".

By the middle of the third century, Rome found itself at odds with its Carthaginian neighbours over parts of Sicily. At the start of the First Punic War, the first of three wars fought between Rome and Carthage from 264 to 241 BCE, there was little doubt, in the western Mediterranean at least, that Carthage had the superior navy. The Romans of the early third century BCE were much better known for their prowess with infantry on land than with ships at sea. In the course of the war, however, this would change dramatically. Owing to some spectacular finds off the coast of Sicily, we are fairly well informed about at least one battle in this conflict: the Battle of the Egadi/Aegates Islands. Before we get to that battle, a quick look at Roman naval tactics.

At the start of the war, Rome was much better known for its prowess at land-based warfare than its naval prowess. The tactics of much of this warfare on the surface were not sophisticated: one side often won because they had more boats, or, if the numbers of ships were comparable, they had more marines. One side's ship might also try ramming another's. As simplistic as ramming might seem, it was no mean feat to try to puncture a hole in an opposing ship which didn't want to sink. To ram a ship effectively, the attackers would need skilled rowers and helmsmen. Men from the lower classes usually provided the bulk of Rome's sailors, with enslaved peoples used only in the most desperate of situations.

The tactics weren't always so straightforward. Some of the more complicated manoeuvres that ships could deploy include the *diekplous*, crashing through an enemy's line of ships and then back out again, and the *periplous*, which meant encircling the enemy to hit them from the rear or on a vulnerable side. But it wasn't just a matter of trying to crash through an enemy's ship or ships. Larger ships might have artillery with a range of up to 200 m, which could be useful not only in naval combat but also when besieging coastal cities. Sometimes the main approach was to try to get one's marines to board an enemy vessel. This is the context of Rome's famed *corvus*, or crow, which was an invention from the beginning of the First Punic War that allowed a Roman vessel to latch onto an enemy vessel so their troops could board with relative ease. It doesn't seem to have been in use after about 256 BCE, however, which implies that the Carthaginians might have found a way to counter it.

Naval combat played a big part of the First Punic War. At the start of the war, the Romans had a small navy. Over the course of the war, Roman navies got bigger owing to a mixture of good fortune, Roman determination, and economic might. By war's end, the Roman navy was a significant force. The Battle of the Egadi Islands took place near the end of the war, on March 10, 241 BCE, and was the final Roman naval victory. Besides the spectacular archaeological remains, we have Polybius' description. As noted in Chapter 1, Polybius was a Greek historian who wrote about the rise of Rome. He himself was also a general, who wrote a tactical manual and was, effectively, a prisoner of war of Rome and later a friend of the Scipiones. His surviving history isn't fully extant, but what we do have provides an invaluable account of aspects of Rome's rise and its wars with Carthage.

In the build-up, the Carthaginians had been making a supply run to Sicily led by a commander named Hanno. En route, he and the Carthaginian fleet were intercepted by the Romans under Lutatius. According to Polybius, he had found out about Hanno's arrival and intentions and decided to act quickly to cut them off, even though the weather conditions weren't ideal. The alternative was that, in delay, Hanno would be able to meet up with the general Hamilcar and his land-based forces. So, Lutatius' well-trained forces raced to the Carthaginian ships, which were laden with cargo and had a crew that was a little less experienced and so a fleet that was a bit sluggish. They succeeded in engaging the Carthaginian forces, sinking 50 ships and capturing 70 more.

When the items on the seabed were found in our day, the nature of those items, their spatial orientation, and their dating confirmed that they formed part of the battle landscape of this engagement. Most of the finds lay where they were first deposited, though some had been moved owing to local octopi moving pieces for their nests, as well as the actions of other assorted sea life, like crabs, dolphins, and lobsters. Among those remains were 14 rams, 11 of which were found in situ (Figure 3.3). Somewhat surprisingly, at least on the basis of what Polybius has to say, the ships were all triremes (Polyb. 1.63.5–8):

FIGURE 3.3 Carthaginian Naval Ram, Egadi Islands, third century BCE, Wikimedia Commons

> Apart from all the other battles and armaments, the total naval forces engaged were, as I mentioned above, on one occasion more than five hundred quinqueremes and on a subsequent one very nearly seven hundred. Moreover, the Romans lost in this war about seven hundred quinqueremes, inclusive of those that perished in the shipwrecks, and the Carthaginians about five hundred. So that those who marvel at the great sea-battles and great fleets of an Antigonus, a Ptolemy, or a Demetrius would, if I mistake not, on inquiring into the history of this war, be much astonished at the huge scale of operations. Again, if we take into consideration the difference between quinqueremes and the triremes in which the Persians fought against the Greeks and the Athenians and Lacedaemonians against each other, we shall find that no forces of such magnitude ever met at sea.

What gives with the discrepancy? Well, Polybius likely exaggerated the size of the ships to play up the scale and scope of the battle. The reality for the Carthaginians was likely that they could perhaps no longer afford the ships bigger than 3s (i.e., triremes). That said, according to one plausible reconstruction, the course of the battle probably followed, more or less, what Polybius claimed. Specifically, the general size of the Carthaginian ships slowed them down relative to the Roman ones, and this slowing only increased with the rough seas, making their transit more challenging. The Romans were then able to ram the Punic triremes, sending many of them plunging to the bottom of the sea. The rams found showed evidence of ramming. Archaeologists also found amphorae in loose clusters, which were probably due to these items spilling from the broken hulls of their ships, which sank just as quickly. As for type of ships, it could even be that Polybius' quinqueremes were Roman only and that it was these ships that sunk the smaller Carthaginian triremes. Ultimately, too, the timber of the Punic hulls would have provided little resistance to the powerful Roman rams, and the battle as a whole was likely over rather quickly.

HANNIBAL'S MARCH ACROSS THE ALPS

As remarkable as those finds at sea are, even more so, perhaps, is Hannibal's march across southern Europe and then the Alps into

Italy at the head of a sizable Carthaginian army at the start of the Second Punic War, the most famous of the three conflicts waged between the Romans and Carthaginians. This war was fought between 218 and 201 BCE across the western Mediterranean, with far more battles fought on land than on sea, unlike in the first conflict. The opening years went exceptionally well for Carthage, so well that, if you had been a casual observer between 218 and 216 BE, you would likely have bet on the end of Rome. Rather remarkably, instead, they came back and defeated Carthage over the course of this long and brutal conflict. But let's turn to one of the most remarkable parts of this – or any ancient – war: Hannibal's march to Italy.

According to the historian Livy, the journey took five and a half months (Livy 21.38), and it covered some 1600 km or so (21.30), "from where the sun set to where it rose again". Of the initial forces that began Hannibal's march, a little less than 50% made it to the end – or at least across the Alps into Cisalpine Gaul, what is now northern Italy. By one estimate, the initial force of some 59,000 had been reduced by 33,000. In fact, if we believe Polybius, at some stages the conditions got so bad that Hannibal considered cannibalism (9.24.5–6):

> It seems that the difficulty was more than once discussed in the Council, and that one of Hannibal's friends, Hannibal surnamed Monomachus (gladiator), stated that he foresaw only one way by which it would be possible to reach Italy. When Hannibal asked him to explain himself, he said he must teach his troops to eat human flesh and accustom them to this... Hannibal had nothing to say against the boldness and usefulness of this suggestion, but he could persuade neither himself nor his friends actually to entertain it.

Though it seems unlikely that they resorted to cannibalism, there's little doubt that the march was a major logistical undertaking. The challenge involved in moving not just large bodies of soldiers and attendants but also materiel and animals, like horses, donkeys, and even elephants, over vast distances in the march to war was no mean feat. A Hellenistic world soldier might have needed about 1.8 kg of grain and 1.9 L of water per day, while a cavalry horse or pack animal (horse, mule, donkey) would have needed about

4.5 kg of forage, 4.5 kg of grain, and 30 L of water. Including just the approximate number of soldiers from the start (the number of attendants is anyone's guess) as well as the numbers, that works out to about 106,200 kg of grain and 112,100 L of water per day for the soldiers and 40,5000 kg of forage, 40,500 kg of grain, 270,000 L of water per day for the animals. Over the course of the march, here calculated by Taylor as about 165 days, and ignoring deaths, that would work out to 17,523,000 kg of grain and 18,496,5000 L of water people for people (not including attendants) and 6,682,500 kg of forage, 6,682,500 kg of grain, and 44,550,000 L of water for animals. In sum, these are staggering numbers of supplies.

Transporting wheat and barley would have been fairly easy, though flour spoiled rapidly. That said, Hannibal's army would have done a great deal of eating whatever they could find en route. Participants might also consume animals they brought with them. Those animals would have needs of their own, which could complicate matters even more. One rough estimate has it that the combat component of the Carthaginian army comprised around 20,000 men and 3,500 animals, which in turn might need 32 tonnes of wheat and 23 tonnes of barley a day. To carry food for that many people and animals for 30 days, you would need about 20,000 mules, a staggering number. As you could well imagine, it wouldn't take long for such a large force to exhaust the countryside. This could also limit the time of year when combat could take place, generally spring to fall, though there are always exceptions. Crossing the vast distance across southern Europe from Spain to Italy is a significant undertaking in and of itself. In crossing the Alps, where resources were few and far between, this would have compounded the challenges of campaigning. It wasn't until Hannibal and his entourage made it to Cisalpine Gaul (essentially northern Italy) that the process might have gotten easier.

ELEPHANTS

Hannibal didn't just march across Europe with your bog-standard infantry, cavalry, soldiers, and horses. He famously brought along several elephants, one of the more remarkable aspects of Hannibal's army, at least to modern eyes. Alexander encountered elephants in 331 BCE during his battle at Gaugamela against Persia and later in battle with Porus at the Hydaspes. The Indian elephants were generally larger than the African forest elephants, which weren't the larger bush elephants that we know today. By all accounts, the people of the Mediterranean hadn't encountered these yet. Elephants appeared in later encounters. Pyrrhus, the Greek general and king who invaded Italy early in the third century BCE, brought elephants. The Seleucids, one of the successor kingdoms from Alexander's empire, made extensive use of elephants. They used them to defeat invading Gauls. In 190 BCE, they also used them in battle against the Romans at Magnesia, who had elephants of their own, only they were so few they didn't use them. While those examples all involved one army using them against a foe who didn't wield elephants, in the battle of Raphia in 217 BCE, both the Ptolemies (Egypt) and the Seleucids (Syria) used elephants, only the former had the smaller African elephants while the latter had the larger Indian ones. The elephants used by Hannibal seem to have been different from the elephants used by the Persians.

One of the problems with using elephants is that they could be quite temperamental and unruly in combat. Some could house turrets on top, but they had to be big enough, which doesn't seem to have been the case for Carthage. In general, elephants could prove useful in warfare if they were used against troops who had not encountered them before or if they were used against horsemen whose mounts had not become accustomed to the elephant's strange appearance and smell. Not all the elephants that Hannibal included in his army made the trip across Europe and the Alps into Italy. Though, that some elephants did make it is no mean feat. One of the great unknowns of Hannibal's crossing is where exactly he did it. In trying to solve this mystery, some have sought out the remains of the perished elephants and/or their excrement, as well as all the men, horses, and more, by looking into, among other things, carbon-based material buried in the soil.

ROME'S GREATEST DEFEATS

Once Hannibal made it across, for two or so years he had incredible success against whatever armies Rome sent against them. Two battles in particular, the battles of Lake Trasimene and Cannae, had an especially marked impact on Rome, both heavy Roman defeats.

The Battle of Lake Trasimene took place on June 21, 217 BCE, with mist on the lake and Gaius Flaminius, the Roman commander, leading his army along the coast. The Romans had already suffered some big setbacks in the war and were eager to defeat Carthage once and for all. Flaminius had taken no precautions in advance, and so as soon as the Romans came upon the Carthaginian camp, Hannibal's army attacked, catching them completely by surprise. In the panic and confusion, Flaminius himself was killed, along with perhaps as few as 15,000 Romans and as many as 50,000 – to Carthage's 2,000. Another 15,000 (or so?) Romans escaped, with another sizable number taken as POWs (prisoners of war).

In the wake of this loss, the Romans themselves sought explanations in terms of Flaminius' ritual errors. Rosenstein noted that he left the city (Rome) before taking up his usual religious duties. He gave no offerings to Jupiter and ignored the accepted rites for Vesta and the Penates. Flaminius also didn't take auspices before his entry into the office and ignored repeated omens. While these might all seem trivial to us, ignoring the will of the gods was no minor matter to most republican-era Romans. Important deities like Jupiter, the head of the Roman pantheon, deserved to be propitiated not only on a regular basis but also especially before major undertakings, like going to war. Quite simply, you needed divine approval, and in their eyes, this hadn't been sought. Moreover, though you couldn't often know exactly what the gods had in mind, the Romans had all sorts of rites and rituals to try to determine what they might be thinking. You did this by taking the auspices, or observing the behaviour of birds, which provided a window into the gods' possible, even probable, actions. You ignored this at your peril, as Flaminius evidently did. Any good Roman knew that you shouldn't mess with omens and prodigies. Although we haven't discussed this at great length, it's always worth bearing in mind the extent to which religion impacted all aspects of life in the ancient Mediterranean world, even war. Looking at Roman explanations provides clear evidence of just this.

These sorts of explanations invariably came later, however. When the news first hit Rome, the fear was palpable. In Livy's own words (Livy 22.7.6–13):

At Rome the first tidings of this defeat brought the citizens into the Forum in a frightened and tumultuous throng, while the matrons wandered about the streets and demanded of all they met what sudden disaster had been reported and how it was going with the army. And when the crowd, like some vast public assembly, turned to the Comitium and the senate-house and called for the magistrates, at last, as the sun was almost going down, Marcus Pomponius, the praetor, said, "A great battle has been fought, and we were beaten." And although they learned nothing more definite from him, still they picked up a rumour here and a rumour there, and returning to their homes brought word that the consul and a great part of his soldiers had been[3] slain: that only a few survived, either dispersed as fugitives throughout Etruria or taken prisoners by the enemy.

In the immediate aftermath, the concern at Rome was obvious, as Polybius describes so well (Polybius 3.85.8–9):

On the news of the defeat reaching Rome the chiefs of the state were unable to conceal or soften down the facts, owing to the magnitude of the calamity, and were obliged to summon a meeting of the commons and announce it. When the Praetor therefore from the Rostra said, "We have been defeated in a great battle," it produced such consternation that to those who were present on both occasions the disaster seemed much greater now than during the actual battle. And this was quite natural; for since for many years they had had no experience of the word or fact of avowed defeat, they could not bear the reverse with moderation and dignity. This was not, however, the case with the Senate, which remained self-possessed, taking thought for the future as to what should be done by everyone, and how best to do it.

In the short term, Rome responded to these early disasters in the Second Punic War by appointing a dictator. In theory, a dictator was a temporary position, held for six months, that was established only in desperate times. The individual selected was a Quintus Fabius Maximus, who was chosen by the people of Rome. They also chose his lieutenant, *magister equitum* (master of horse), Marcus Minucius. Unfortunately, these two men had very different views with respect to how to approach Hannibal and Carthage. Fabius chose to shadow Hannibal and avoid a confrontation; Marcus and many (most?) soldiers wanted to meet Hannibal head on. This would cause problems later, however.

The significant and continued loss of life obviously had an impact on the groups of society who provided the bulk of Rome's soldiers. Most citizens were rural and lived and worked on small farms. They might have – or hope to have – a bit of land with a garden, maybe an orchard, and even some animals like oxen. The male members of society were either *iuniores*, unmarried younger men who were liable to military service, or *seniores*, older married men, the head of their household, and responsible for paying the state *tributum*, best thought of as a kind of tax. The loss of these unmarried young men, who worked the farms, meant there weren't enough bodies to farm, and if there weren't enough men to farm, there wouldn't be enough crops that could be used to pay the *tributum*. Soon, Rome's expenses would outstrip its income, a problem that was especially marked between the years 216 and 209 BCE, when, for the most part, they were losing a lot more than they were winning in the war. Besides the loss of life far away from the farms on the field of battle, there was the damage inflicted on the small farms themselves, usually by the Carthaginians, though it mightn't be a stretch to imagine damage caused by allied forces (Rome and their allies) too. Hunger reared its nasty head, and the devastation of crops only made matters worse. Finally, some have argued that these losses, collectively, caused big shifts in Roman society at large, such as the increased use of enslaved labour to make up for the shortfalls in free-born manpower.

As bad as the defeat at Lake Trasimene was, the defeat at Cannae was that much worse. The Romans raised a massive army in the run-up to Cannae, and some of the soldiers were battle-hardened, but many of them weren't. They also dropped their dictator, Fabius Cunctator, as the populace at large was eager to take battle back to Hannibal rather than to shadow the Carthaginian commander as he travelled the Italian countryside. So, when the Romans showed up at Cannae, a small settlement by a small river in southern Italy, they vastly outnumbered their foes, perhaps as many as 87,000 for the Romans and 45,000 for the Carthaginians (Polyb. 3.106–118, Livy 22.44–52). But it was no matter: Hannibal lured the Romans into a trap and surrounded them by backing up and giving ground while facing forward before encircling them. The Romans got hemmed in by the Carthaginian cavalry and were bombarded by missile fire (App. *Hann.* 22). By some reckoning, this was the bloodiest battle in antiquity. Besides losing a raft of their leading commanders, including one of their consuls, they lost some 50,000 or so soldiers. Another staggering number were captured. Only a comparatively small number of the whole escaped death, though that included the later general Scipio Africanus (who did not yet have that epithet). The reaction to the defeat back at home in Rome was as powerful as you might imagine. We have two complementary accounts: one from Livy, the other from Appian. Livy reports (Livy 22.56):

> a dispatch at last arrived from C. Terentius Varro. He wrote that L. Aemilius was killed, and his army cut to pieces; he himself was at Canusium collecting the wreckage that remained from this awful disaster; there were as many as 10,000 soldiers, irregular, unorganized; the Carthaginian was still at Cannae, bargaining about the prisoners' ransom and the rest of the plunder in a spirit very unlike that of a great and victorious general. The next thing was the publication of the names of those killed, and the city thrown into such universal mourning that the annual celebration of the festival of Ceres was suspended, because it is forbidden to those in mourning to take part in it, and there was not a single matron who was not a mourner during those days. In order that the same cause might not prevent other sacred observances from being duly honoured, the period of mourning was limited by a senatorial decree to thirty days.

Appian's account includes some similar language on mourning, though he also gets into the measures the Romans enacted immediately in response to this devastating loss (App. Hann. 5.27):

> When the disaster was announced in the city, multitudes thronged the streets uttering lamentations for their relatives, calling on them by name, and bewailing their own fate as soon to fall into the enemy's hands. Women went to the temples with their children and prayed that there might sometime be an end to the calamities to the city. The magistrates besought the gods by sacrifices and prayers that if they had any cause of anger, they would be satisfied with the punishment already visited. The Senate sent Quintus Fabius (the same who wrote a history of these events) to the temple of Delphi to seek an oracle concerning the present posture of affairs.

> They freed 8000 slaves with their masters' consent and ordered everybody in the city to go to work making arms and projectiles. They also made a conscription, as was allowed, even among certain of the allies.

There's no way around it: this was one of Rome's greatest defeats, and it would be remembered as such for centuries to come. What's less clear, however, is just how many men perished in the battle and even how the Romans themselves might hope to track this. What we do know is that there were frequent communications between Rome and the field in warfare, and we also know that legion lists existed. Afterall, soldiers needed to be paid and supplied, so this kind of information was important. Thus, generals tried to know the number of living and dead in the legions they commanded, and even the senate might have kept track of this sort of information. Pearson argues that the original lists of soldiers in the field were lost in battle and that the senate, anyway, was concerned with how many active soldiers they had. Fortunately, anecdotes in some of our texts provide precious insight into what this information might have looked like. In a fragment from Cato's *Origines*, we read (from Pearson, p. 82):

> While he [Q. Caedicius, a military tribune] had been wounded in many places during the battle, but he received no head wound, and they recognized him among the dead, worn out from wounds and because his blood had flowed out. They lifted him up, and he recovered.

Livy is our source for most figures from this battle, and he seems to have relied on a historian named Valerius Antias, who himself didn't make best use of the available evidence. Nevertheless, Livy provides valuable information, like this comment that gives us an idea of the kinds of material that reports might contain (Livy 35.5.14):

> Nor was the victory a bloodless one for the Romans; they and the allied contingents together lost over 5000 men, including 23 centurions, four praefects of allies and three military tribunes in the second legion: M. Genucius, Q. Marcius and M. Marcius.

Therefore, even if the exact number didn't make it down to us – or we can't determine which of those that we have is the most accurate – odds are the Romans themselves knew, and the varied authors at least knew that it was high.

As Appian's account implies, this defeat had far-reaching consequences, at least if Rome wanted to keep on fighting, which they did, a remarkable fact in and of itself. To do so would require the work of all Romans. This meant enlisting 6,000 men who were either essentially bankrupt or criminals, who might have been convicted of capital crimes (Valerius Maximus 7.6.1b, Livy 23.14). Even more remarkable, however, was the decision to enlist enslaved men, as Livy relates (Livy 22.57):

> The dearth of freemen necessitated a new kind of enlistment; 8000 sturdy youths from amongst the slaves were armed at the public cost, after they had each been asked whether they were willing to serve or no. These soldiers were preferred, as there would be an opportunity of ransoming them when taken prisoners at a lower price.

Desperate times called for desperate measures. After all, 20% of all Roman males between 18 and 50 died on that fateful day (Cannae took place August 2, 216). And yet, Rome's remarkable manpower resources proved decisive. Despite such a devastating loss of life, the number of legions in the field increased in each of the subsequent years of the conflict. In 215, Rome had 14 legions; in 214, 20 legions; in 213, 22 legions; and in 212, 26 legions. Thus, what might well have been the beginning of the end for Rome, wasn't, and within a few years Rome was taking the war to Carthage, first in their Iberian territories and then in the Carthaginian heartland itself.

BAECULA AND ILIPA

Spain was the setting for many of the wars that Rome fought in Europe during the republican era, whether the wars against the Numantines in the middle of the second century BCE, the battles against Carthage in Spain during the Second Punic War, or the conflict with Sertorius and his forces early in the first century BCE. Indeed, scholars, and archaeologists in particular, are turning increasing attention to this important theatre. A closer look at the aftermath of two Carthaginian defeats in Spain during the Second

Punic War allows us to see how scholars use texts and archaeology, where possible, to elucidate murky aspects of lesser-known battles. I start with Baecula.

In the spring of 208, the Carthaginian general Hasdrubal had encamped by a river with a ridge at the front at Baecula, near modern Santo Tomé in Spain. By this point, the war had started to turn inexorably in Rome's favour, and the Romans were regularly taking the war to their foes. Scipio Africanus, who was on the march to meet his foe, was worried that Hasdrubal would be supported with reinforcements led by the generals Gisgo and Mago. Scipio made a camp and left some troops behind. He took some *velites* (light infantry) to meet the Carthaginians in the field and sent ahead some others to block Hasdrubal's escape in the valley. The Romans launched an attack on the ridge with two forces, having split their army up into two chunks. This caught Hasdrubal by surprise, and it was only the strength of his position that prevented things from turning even worse than they already did – a Roman victory with many thousands of Carthaginian soldiers dead.

The battle is covered summarily in the works of Polybius, Livy, and Appian (Polyb. 10.34, 36–40, Livy 27.18–20, App. 6.19–23). Some remarkable finds from the battlefield itself carried out by a Spanish team (Bellón et al. 2016) have provided even more insight into how the battle unfolded. They found both the Punic and the Roman marching camps at its precise location, Cerro de las Albahacas in Spain. This illuminated a whole range of issues like the strategic position of the battlefield, its topography, and even the availability of water. Among the finds recovered were an assemblage of weapons, assorted *impedimenta* (equipment for expedition and so on), and both local and Iberian pottery. With all this material, and the aid of GIS (Geographical Information Systems), researchers were able to pinpoint troop movements in the landscape over the course of the battle. Excavators found lots of interesting things in the area. For instance, they found destroyed pottery and equipment at one of the camps. Although they acknowledged that this could have been caused by the battle itself, the absence of things like human or animal remains proved hard to reconcile. Instead, then, it looked like the pottery had been deliberately destroyed and spread round the camp in an attempt to prevent the re-use by the enemy. So, the Carthaginians destroyed their camp after losing the battle.

Despite the victory at Baecula, Scipio didn't follow-up his success, for Gisgo and Mago moved on Ilipa, near modern-day Seville, both hoping for a major factory. Despite recent setbacks against Rome, they were still able to field quite significant armies. Carthage had 50,000–70,000 infantry, 4000–4,500 cavalry, and over 30 elephants. The Romans, on the other hand, had 45,000 infantry and 3,000 cavalry. There were a few skirmishes over several days before the battle proper broke out. Scipio employed some complicated tactical manoeuvres. What ultimately brought ruin to the Punic forces, however, was that the Romans managed to rattle the elephants, which in turn wrought havoc on their own lines. As a result, the Punic lines broke and they fled. The Romans massacred the Carthaginians, and only Gisgo and some 6,000 men managed to escape. With this victory, the war in Spain was all but over (Livy 28.16).

CONCLUSION

At the start of this chapter, the Greek world was coming to grips with the death of Alexander the Great and the explosion of new kingdoms. By its end, another state entirely had emerged as arguably the most dominant player in the Mediterranean, the Roman state. Although I highlighted some of their travails against the Carthaginians, for centuries the western Mediterranean's most dominant force, the Romans were ultimately victorious. They defeated Carthage in the first Punic War, came from behind to deal them a crushing defeat in the Second Punic War, and then, effectively, wiped Carthage off the map in the misleadingly named Third Punic War. Romans aside, we got a glance at some of the better-known non-human participants in war: the elephants used by various Hellenistic powers. We also saw that for all the fame of the Classical Greek states, some of the most significant developments in war-making came during the Hellenistic military revolution. In the next chapter, we stay with Rome and look at some of the ways that a state at its peak dealt with the seemingly ubiquitous war and warfare that typified the ancient Mediterranean world.

"MORE FORTUNATE THAN AUGUSTUS, AND BETTER THAN TRAJAN"

FROM WARLORDS TO EMPERORS, 200 BCE–117 CE

This opening phrase, which comes from Eutropius' *Breviarium*, a summary of Roman history written in Latin in the fourth century CE, is said to be what the senate proclaimed at the accession of a new emperor. While we might question its historicity, it shows how later Romans looked back on two of their most famous emperors. To that end, the focus of much of this chapter will be Rome at war during the early imperial era, roughly from Augustus to Trajan. I'll begin, however, by picking up on a point that featured in the previous chapter, if in the background: Rome's remarkable manpower resources, particularly in the middle and late republic. After looking at how important it was, at least for Rome, to have more guys than the others, I'll jump ahead to Augustus and start with a battle where the Romans lost a lot of soldiers. So, although we might think of the years from Augustus to Trajan as the period when Rome was at its peak, my first discussion of the imperial era will be one of Rome's most famous disasters, Varus' defeat in the Teutoburg forest. In the middle of the chapter, I'll look at the highs and lows of Rome at war in east (Jewish War) and west (Boudica's rebellion). Where Rome was often fighting for survival in the previous chapter (at least in part), in these two wars in Judea and Britain, Rome was the imperial power, and a closer look allows us to get a sense of the impact of war on civilians in the Roman world. Where Rome's

DOI: 10.4324/9781003092636-5

subject people often had success in uprisings when they employed asymmetric tactics, a necessity when the military strength of the two belligerents diverged so much, Boudica's rebellion presents us with a situation that Rome rarely faced, a foreign entity ruled by a woman. We often think of war and the military as male spaces, but this wasn't the case. In some places, women could be at the head of armies, like Boudica. While this isn't the only place we find women in warfare, examples like this are some of the more memorable. I'll finish the chapter by closing the circle and getting back to another manpower matter, namely Rome's strategic thinking, a big reason for its success in the imperial era. Along the way, I'll illustrate how Rome used its continued demographic strengths to martial – yet again – its remarkable human resources to achieve its military ends, especially in its wars of conquest against Dacia.

MANPOWER

Before we get to the debacle in Germany, the Romans were on what must have seemed an inexorable rise. In fact, this was the subject of Polybius' much-lauded *Histories*. He wanted to tell his fellow Greeks how the Romans managed to take over what was, for him at least, much of the known world in only a few short decades. There are many reasons for Rome's success, particularly on the field of battle, but one which deserves particular attention is its remarkable manpower resources. This subject has taxed many scholars, and ancient historians, like Polybius and Livy, too.

On the surface, it might seem difficult to get precise population figures from ancient Rome. But the Romans had a regular census of Roman citizens, and yearly totals occasionally surface in our evidence. For instance, at different points in his *Ab Urbe Condita*, the historian Livy gives two different census figures, one from about 234 BCE, and the other from about 209 BCE – that is, from before the Second Punic War and when it was nearly over. Livy says (20.1), "The census was thrice taken by the censors. In the first census there were registered 270,713 citizens." Later he notes (27.36),

> This same year, for the first time since Hannibal came into Italy, the lustrum was closed by the censors Publius Sempronius Tuditanus

and Marcus Cornelius Cethegus. The citizens numbered in the census were 177,108, a number considerably smaller than before the war.

There's some debate over what these numbers represent, whether the population of free citizens are large or men of military age. The latter seems the more likely. The process of taking the census itself was well established. The censor, a prestigious political position, would take it every five years, and he would count every male citizen over 17 able to bear arms. In theory, the head of the household, the *paterfamilias*, would provide lists to streamline the process.

As for the soldiers, Polybius describes the recruitment of them as follows (Polybius 6.19–20):

> On the appointed day, when those liable to service arrive in Rome, and assemble on the Capitol, the junior tribunes divide themselves into four groups, as the popular assembly or the consuls determine, since the main and original division of their forces is into 4 legions. The 4 tribunes first nominated are appointed to the first legion, the next three to the second, the following four to the third, and the last three to the fourth. Of senior tribunes the first 2 are appointed to the first legion, the next 3 to the second, the next 2 to the third, and the 3 last to the fourth. The division and appointment of the tribunes having thus been so made that each legion has the same number of officers, those of each legion take their seats apart, and they draw lots for the tribes, and summon them singly in the order of the lottery. From each tribe they first of all select four lads of more or less the same age and physique. When these are brought forward the officers of the first legion have first choice, those of the second choice, those of the third third, and those of the fourth last. Another batch of four is now brought forward, and this time the officers of the second legion have first choice and so on, those of the first choosing last. A third batch having been brought forward the tribunes of the third legion choose first, and those of the second last. By thus continuing to give each legion first choice in turn, each gets men of the same standard. When they have chosen the number determined on — that is when the strength of each legion is brought up to four thousand two hundred, or in times of exceptional danger to five thousand — the old system was to choose the

cavalry after the 4,200 infantry, but they now choose them first, the censor selecting them according to their wealth; and three hundred are assigned to each legion.

We can go beyond Polybius and supplement what he says with what we know about the architecture and history of Rome, among other things. Pearson sets out the process as follows. These earlier republican-era levies, called the *dilectus*, would take place originally in the Area Capitolina in Rome, which could house 53,424 as a maximum. If you space them out, it would amount to 6,678. The recruits were called *assidui*, and these were the men who met the property qualifications required for service – the state provided only some of the finances needed for service. That said, there were sometimes emergency levies (as in early stages of the Second Punic War), when the qualifications were relaxed.

That gives us some idea how many individuals might show up in individual circumstances and how the process worked. But scholars have been even more interested in counting just how many free persons the Romans had to work with overall in Italy, especially during the middle republic when the manpower needs were so high. Basically, scholarship has fallen into one of two camps: the low count, who believes Rome's manpower lay on the lower end of a vast spectrum, and the high count for those who think the total was much higher. Those in favour of a low count argue the total numbered about 2,500,000, while the high count is about 8,000,000.

Much of the discussion has hinged on a select group of texts, particularly bits from Polybius, though also some numbers from Diodorus Siculus, Livy, Pliny the Elder, and two later authors: the aforementioned Eutropius and the even later (fifth century CE) Orosius. Polybius (Histories 2.24) has given us a detailed account of Italy's population, which is worth quoting in full.

> Each of the Consuls was in command of four legions of Roman citizens, each consisting of 5,200 foot and 300 horse. The allied forces in each Consular army numbered 30,000 foot and 2,000 horse. The cavalry of the Sabines and Etruscans, who had come to the temporary assistance of Rome, were 4,000 strong, their infantry above 50,000. The Romans massed these forces and posted them on the frontier of Etruria under the command of a Praetor. The levy of the

Umbrians and Sarsinates inhabiting the Apennines amounted to about 20,000, and with these were 20,000 Veneti and Cenomani. These they stationed on the frontier of Gaul, to invade the territory of the Boii and divert them back from their expedition. These were the armies protecting the Roman territory. In Rome itself there was a reserve force, ready for any war-contingency, consisting of 20,000 foot and 1,500 horse, all Roman citizens, and 30,000 foot and 2,000 horse furnished by the allies. The lists of men able to bear arms that had been returned were as follows. Latins 80,000 foot and 5,000 horse, Samnites 70,000 foot and 7,000 horse, Iapygians and Messapians 50,000 foot and 16,000 horse in all, Lucanians 30,000 foot and 3,000 horse, Marsi, Marrucini, Frentani, and Vestini 20,000 foot and 4,000 horse. In Sicily and Tarentum were 2 reserve legions, each consisting of about 4,200 foot and 200 horse. Of Romans and Campanians there were on the roll 250,000 foot and 23,000 horse; so that the total number of Romans and allies able to bear arms was more than 700,000 foot and 70,000 horse, while Hannibal invaded Italy with an army of less than 20,000 men.

Polybius' figures are tricky. Is he referring to levied and/or non-levied soldiers/people? Are there cases where he counts men twice? And how does his information compare with Livy's? Livy says the census for Rome (free Roman citizens) in Italy in 234 BCE (after the First Punic War but before the Second Punic War) was 270,713, which is awfully close to Polybius' 273,000 in 225 BCE. Rubincam shows that Polybius tends to include numbers much less often than other historians like Diodorus Siculus and classical historians Herodotus, Thucydides, and Xenophon. Diodorus is much more likely to give numbers for battles, while Polybius is more likely to be selective. Does this mean we should follow what Polybius or Diodorus says?

Perhaps, though the ultimate decision might well come down to the individual, at least until more information is brought to bear on the question. Only recently have scholars, like Launaro, started to incorporate data from archaeological excavations and surveys in Italy. Collectively, as with most things, this new material implies that the reality was somewhere in the middle: not quite the low count, not quite the high count. Regardless of how you look at it, however, Rome had a significant population base it could draw on, which helps explain how it was able to withstand Carthage during the Second Punic War after major defeats but also to wage wars of conquest in parts of Spain, the eastern Mediterranean, and beyond from the second century BCE into the first.

By the reign of Augustus (r. 27 BCE to 14 CE), the Romans had an enormous military comprising dozens of legions. In fact, at the end of the civil war with Marc Antony and Cleopatra, Rome's armies were so numerous, expensive, and potentially dangerous that Augustus chose to disband about half of the legions, with those so selected sent off into retirement. With this accomplishment and Rome at peace, at least with itself, and with Augustus as emperor, the Romans could look to continued expansion of their empire. This was going about as well as could be hoped, at least until affairs in Germany unravelled.

KALKRIESE

Early in the first century CE, the Roman Mediterranean and north ern Europe of the Germans might have seemed like different worlds. Archaeologists have identified two key cultural groups in Germany during the reign of Augustus (r. 27 BCE to 14 CE): the Jastorf people in the north and the La Tène people in the south. These peoples lived in hillforts, *oppida*, farmsteads, and assorted settlements throughout the region. These were not the villas and bustling cities of stone across the Mediterranean. In the frontier zone, where German tribes abutted the Roman Empire, the inhabitants raised cattle, sheep, pigs, horses, and some goats. They also grew cereals and often lived in longhouses, some of which had a clear separation between the living space and the production space. So far as we know, there were no places beyond the frontier into *barbaricum* with a clear military focus. Nevertheless, German military retinues grew in number, especially in the north. There's evidence for their success in battle not just at Kalkriese, the battle we are about to get to, but later, in the third century CE, at Harzhorn. But let's look more closely at Kalkriese and Varus.

In 10 BCE, the Romans were determined to push into Germany. A year later, Drusus – a Julio-Claudian (the dynasty of Julius Caesar and Augustus) prince – set out from Mainz. He got to the Elbe River, had an accident, and died. Tiberius (r. 14–37 CE), Augustus' eventual successor, rushed to Germany to take over from his brother and succeeded, celebrating a triumph back in Rome in 7 BCE.

From this early stage, the Romans had desired to extend their influence to the Elbe and then to the Vistula. These successes made it seem like Rome's march further east into Germany was inexorable. Imagine the surprise and shock back in the capital in 9 CE when they learned that the commander Quinctilius Varus and three legions were ambushed in the Teutoburg forest. Needless to say, any further designs on German expansion were shelved.

For a long time, the location of the battle site was unknown, even though we had the epitaph of at least one of the fallen Roman soldiers. The epitaph of Marcus Caelius (Figure 4.1), a centurion of the eighteenth legion, originally in Latin and found in Xanten (Germany), reads (in translation) as follows:

> To Marcus Caelius, son of Titus, of the Lemonian district, from Bologna, first centurion of the eighteenth legion. 53½ years old. He fell in the Varian War. His freedman's bones may be interred here. Publius Caelius, son of Titus, of the Lemonian district, his brother, erected (this monument).

FIGURE 4.1 Epitaph of Marcus Caelius, Wikimedia Commons

Caelius was just one of the battle's 10,000 to 15,000 deaths, at least on the Roman side. The Germans likely suffered somewhere between 500 and 1,500 deaths. Along with the deaths came all the wounds, primarily physical, though also psychological. The wounds likely consisted of punctures and slashes, though some likely suffered from shock and the loss of a lot of blood. The truth is, those who sustained wounds in ancient combat had a very real chance of succumbing to their wounds – if not initially, then not long after.

The German attackers, the Cherusci, were led by a man named Arminius, who had been a Roman officer. Many (or most?) of his soldiers might well have fought for Rome themselves and were clearly disgruntled. This could well mean that while the Romans were on the march, they hadn't expected to face enemy combatants. In fact, we do know that they were ambushed after an elaborate ruse, attacked while on the march in a narrow defile, stretched out over some distance. The attackers planned it well in advance, building ramparts to hem in the Roman forces and maximize their assault.

Although Germanicus returned to the site of the battle sometime later and managed to dispose of much of what was left of the remains, the specific location of the battle soon faded into obscurity. When it was discovered many centuries later in the late 1980s at Kalkriese (though some remain sceptical about the identification of this location with Varus' defeat), archaeologists found a number of significant and suggestive finds. These included the bones of mules and horses, a horse carcass, and even the bone fragments of humans. A wide range of military objects, including select weapons and equipment from pieces of helmet and face masks to arrowheads and swords, were recovered. A large number of coins too were found. Taken together, this material provided a good, if imperfect, indication of how the battle played out, including that it stretched out for many kilometres. The site was later visited by the Romans, after the Cherusci had had a chance to pick over the remains, which means that what's left today provides only a partial record of what transpired. The location is not quite what we find in the sources, as limited as their accounts are. The ramparts, for one, imply that this ambush was planned well in advance. That being said, the range and scale of the finds seem to support the view put forth by Roman historians like Tacitus and Cassius Dio that the loss was significant.

THE JEWISH WAR

Even if Varus' defeat and death put a stop to expansion into eastern Germany, this wasn't the end of the growth of the empire, for between Augustus and Trajan the Roman Empire continued to expand. As new regions fell under their control, however, there were often periods of significant unrest, brought on by the unsurprising and obvious discomfort – to put it mildly – experienced by those now living under Rome. While this could and sometimes did lead to single acts of violence (terror from the perspective of the Romans), there are a few instances where all-out war broke out, with the best documented being the First or Great Jewish Revolt.

The causes of the war were many. Among other things, the region was overpopulated (by some metrics), debt problems were growing, access to a temple (Jewish) in Caesarea was restricted, and the governor Florus seized money from the Temple (in Jerusalem). By war's end, the revolt had been crushed, and tens of thousands of people killed and/or enslaved. At the beginning, the rebels might have had some inkling that things could go their way. They defeated a Roman army at Beth Horon early on.

The battle is described by Josephus, our primary source for the war. The battle itself comes relatively early in the war, during the course of the withdrawal of Roman forces from Jerusalem and environs after the failed campaign of the commander, Cestius Gallus, a legate from Syria. Cestius had made insufficient plans and was unprepared for the level of organization of the rebels and their ferocity. Although he brought a sizeable army to Jerusalem, he wasn't prepared to besiege the city and, in fact, had only hoped to overawe the defenders with this display of military force. In his eyes, the mere sight of the Roman military would be enough to encourage Roman supporters to open the gates, but they didn't. Instead, Cestius was forced to march back home.

On his march back to Syria in 66 CE, his army was ambushed at Beth Horon. One of the best ways to counter Roman tactics, which at this stage tended to lean towards direct, pitched battles, was to employ surprise, as happened at Kalkriese and as sometimes happened during this war. And this battle was a good example of this, as Josephus relates (Josephus, *Jewish War*. 2.9.8):

> He [Cestius] then made his army march on as far as Bethoron. Now the Jews did not so much press upon them when they were in large open places, but when they were penned up in their descent through narrow passages, then did some of them get before, and hindered them from getting out of them, and others of them thrust the hind-most down into the lower places, and the whole multitude extended themselves over against the neck of the passage, and covered the Roman army with their darts. In which circumstances, as the footmen knew not how to defend themselves, so the danger pressed the horsemen still more, for they were so pelted, that they could not march along the road in their ranks, and the ascents were so high, that the cavalry were not able to march against the enemy; the precipices also, and valleys into which they frequently fell, and tumbled down, were such on each side of them, that there was neither place for their flight, nor any contrivance could be thought of for their defence

When given time and space, the Romans were able to bring their military might to bear in an open battle in the field, and so the circumstances could be very different indeed. That same Josephus also left us with one of the most important imperial era accounts of the functioning of the Roman military. His long and detailed digression comes in the middle of his *Jewish War* (*Jewish War* 3.5/3.70), where he marvels at the Romans' discipline and organization. He remarks on their regular training manoeuvres, which he says resemble actual warfare, so putting the Roman soldiers in good stead when war breaks out. Josephus also praises the regularity with which the Romans set up camps while on the march, so that they aren't caught off guard. Additionally, he details their varied communications, from the different trumpet calls used to communicate when to bring down the tents and when to march, to the veritable dialogue between officers and men before they head out on the march and the remarkable silence that sometimes follows. Thus, the Romans could and sometimes did get caught off guard in various military encounters, but for the most part, by this stage in their history, their military was well organized and often well disciplined. Indeed, it's accounts like these that often give rise to the notion of a Roman military machine. Though Josephus' account likely stretches the imagination at least a little – he was commissioned to write his history of the war by the very commander and later emperor who won it (Vespasian) – this efficient action is the reason that what had initially seemed like a disaster in the making soon turned into a crushing Roman victory.

By the time of the siege of Jerusalem, which took place in 70 CE, the Roman forces had been under the command of first Vespasian (under Emperor Nero's orders) and then his son Titus, who took over when Vespasian raced off to Rome to seize the throne. It was Titus who arrived in April/May of 70 outside the city and set up camp at Mount Scopus and the Mount of Olives. They cut off the city, and before too long, cannibalism had been reported. To make matters worse, not all persons within the city were on the same side, so it wasn't long before internecine fighting broke out.

The Romans attacked the outer walls first in the northern section, Bezetha. Next, they moved on to the outer walls towards the Temple. Finally, they besieged the Temple fortifications, the Temple Mount, which they destroyed. There's some debate about whether this was a conscious fear tactic employed by the Romans; Josephus, for one, argues it was a deliberate tactic. To compound matters from a Jewish perspective, they looted the temple and set up – and sacrificed to – the legionary standards, and they proclaimed Titus "imperator", or victorious general. All this was deeply sacrilegious.

The Roman siege was felt not only at the pan-Jewish level with the destruction of the Temple but also at the individual human level. Some of this comes from the remains from the so-called Burnt House, which belonged to a priestly family. Inside, they found a stone weight that was inscribed Bar Kathros. Hauntingly, archaeologists also uncovered the skeletal arm of a young woman in her twenties, who was trapped, crushed, and killed while the house burned. Those who didn't perish during the siege could expect some other potential degradations. Though there's certainly a bit of exaggeration at play, Josephus claims that, owing to a glut of enslaved persons, slavery prices dropped at the conclusion of war.

MASADA

We now come to the end of the war and the famous Siege of Masada. One of the most famous episodes from the siege is the mass suicide at the end (Jos. *BJ* 7.9.1), an alleged attempt to avoid capture by the Romans and as clear an example of the trauma brought on by Roman military might, and experienced by some of the people who lived within its empire's confines, as you're likely to see. On the other hand, more recent excavations and analysis have revealed that not everything is quite as it seemed. The trauma's likely still there, though the fate of the besieged is much murkier than the texts make it out to be.

The myth, such as we have it, goes as follows. The many rebels ensconced on the plateau of Masada, having been besieged for three to four years, decided on a course of mass suicide to avoid their inevitable capture by the Romans and all that would have entailed. Owing to strict Jewish rules about suicide and the afterlife, ten men drew lots to decide who would do the deed – that is, kill the others so that the rest wouldn't have to commit the act of suicide themselves. One man does, and he kills the rest, in some ways then succeeding in defying the Romans all while illustrating the courage of the besieged.

As it happens, however, the siege lasted only some six months, maybe even only eight weeks. It also seems that there was no mass suicide, or at least no evidence of this – the bodies we might expect in the archaeological record. But this doesn't mean that the siege itself wasn't a brutal affair for those involved or that conditions were harsh. So, while the archaeological evidence has called into question some aspects of the mythology surrounding the siege, it has revealed other aspects about the experiences of those who lived through it.

Let's start with the participants, excluding the Romans, whom we're going to leave out of this discussion. The leading group was probably the *sicarii*, the zealots responsible (from a Roman perspective at least) for much of the revolt. It comprised not only the rebels in the stronghold but also a sizeable group of refugees who had fled from other war-torn parts of the region. Masada had been home to a significant Hasmonean palace. Now, in the midst of a siege, new rooms were built into the existing structures in attempts to fit as many people and as much food as possible. Quite a few of these rooms served as food storage facilities. While the food itself is long gone, traces remain. Some of the jars used to store food and water included inscriptions which gave an indication of the food found therein. But archaeologists also found some remains, like seeds, which indicated that they had been filled with things like dried figs, berries, olives, fish, dough, meat, and various herbs. The diet of the rebels and refugee families likely consisted of bread dipped in oil, bean pastes like hummus, and even lentil stews. While these might all sound appealing and not at all unpleasant – I, for one, am a fan of all three – the reality is that their food was often (maybe eventually always) infested with pests, like bugs. Traces of insects and larvae have been found in some of these same jars.

The refugee families included women and children, details expressed by Josephus, still our principal literary source, and implied by some of the material remains. Again, some of the conditions may have seemed not unpleasant: archaeologists found jewellery and cosmetic items, like palettes, eye shadow sticks, bottles for perfume, and combs. On the other hand, some of these include hints of lice and their eggs. While pests like these might have aggravated their hosts outside of wartime, the challenging conditions – limited access to usual means of hygiene – only made things worse.

Besides the famed mass suicide, the site itself is also famous for the impressive military infrastructure put up by the Romans around the plateau. For one thing, the site was surrounded with camps. Some were more basic – housed by the lower-ranking soldiers. But archaeologists also uncovered some luxury goods (which would have been used by the officers), like a triclinium which offered views towards Masada itself. Besides the camp, there's also the massive siege ramp (Figure 4.2), which exists to this day. All the evidence points towards this ramp being constructed by Rome's soldiers and not by Jewish slaves.

Turning to the military finds, some missiles, fired by Roman artillery, including bolts which were collected and recycled, have been found on site. All in all, however, the amount of militaria, the military equipment, is comparatively small. While this might make it seem like a further downgrading of the Roman military effort, instead this is just more evidence that the Romans never left

FIGURE 4.2 Masada Siege Ramp from the Hilltop, Carole Raddato, Wikimedia Commons

any equipment behind (where possible) at the end of an operation. There are occasionally exceptions. Archaeologists have found some piles of sling bullets, some arrowheads, and even an iron sword up on the citadel, but little else. If anything, this underscores the ruthlessness and efficiency with which the Romans would carry out siege operations like this one, at least where possible.

Let's finish this subsection by going back to where we started. Was there a mass suicide, and if so, where are all the bodies? Although it's only an estimate, there were likely some 900 or so people housed in Masada in the middle of the Roman siege. What we don't have is their remains. Instead, it's likely that most were led off into captivity and ultimately a life of slavery. For those who were executed, their remains were almost certainly disposed of. For nearly 20 years after the capture of Masada, the Romans set up a garrison, and they are not likely to have left human remains inside.

It's clear, though, that this war – ultimately a convincing Roman victory – brought a lot of hardship to the people of Judea, as I mentioned above. According to Josephus, over 1,100,000 people died in Jerusalem. This is likely an exaggeration – no city outside

Rome had a population approaching a million people in the wider Mediterranean in the first century CE. That said, Josephus also claims that 97,000 people were sold into slavery, unfortunately a much more believable number. Besides the physical harm meted out to the losing side, the Romans destroyed the great Temple, carried out widespread destruction in Jerusalem, and abolished a number of Jewish institutions. In short, this war brought unspeakable trauma, both physical and psychological, to many of its participants, and the Romans deserve much, if not all (the rebels committed violent acts as well), of the blame.

BOUDICA

Shifting from the east to the west and then up to the north, we come to another significant conflict waged by Rome. In this instance, the location for the conflict was Britain, which had only recently fallen under Roman control and which contrasts, at least a little, with the situation in Judea.

After a few expeditions going back as far as Julius Caesar (died 44 BCE), it was Emperor Claudius (r. 41–54 CE) who conquered Britain. Despite this success, the island was only partially pacified. In 59 CE, C. Suetonius Paulinus was sent to Britain as governor, and he managed to capture the island of Mona, modern Anglesey. Other contentious actions include the forcible reduction of the Iceni tribe and the death of its king, King Prasutagus. To make matters worse, the procurator (man in charge), Catus Decianus, committed acts of violence (physical, sexual, and more besides) against Prasutagus' wife, Boudica (Figure 4.3), and their daughters.

In the first chapter, I highlighted some of the active roles of women in Greek warfare. The other side of the coin was the violence often suffered by women in conflict zones, and so too their children. Even if the sources don't usually document these sorts of activities, you can bet that women were regularly the victims of sexual violence, particularly if they were on the losing side and the combat itself was a siege. Polybius describes in vivid detail the sack of New Carthage back in 209 BCE during the Second Punic War. Though he doesn't highlight acts of sexual violence, both he and Livy do stress that Roman soldiers ran rampant during the sack of the city, and it's easy to surmise what this entailed. So,

FIGURE 4.3 Boudica, Boadicea Haranguing the Britons (cropped), John Opie, 1793, Wikimedia Commons

the experiences of Boudica and her daughters, many decades later, were part and parcel of the wartime experience for many women in the ancient Mediterranean.

To get back to Boudica and this unrest in Britain, the Romans also requisitioned the land of the Trinovantes. So, by 60 CE, while Suetonius was in North Wales, just across from Anglesey, Boudica, Prasutagus' widow, took control by capturing Colchester (Camulodonum), London (Londinium), and St. Albans (Verulamium). In the process, the procurator's army, which included the Ninth Legion, was defeated. Whether it disappeared is another story, though most evidence points towards its continued existence well into the second century CE.

This conflict pitted an amateur British army against a regular, standing Roman army. As we saw with the Judean rebels, the best approach in these conditions was an asymmetrical one. So, to overcome Rome's tactical and strategic advantages, Boudica's forces generally tried to stick to guerrilla tactics. Amateur though Boudica's army might have been, it seems to have been large. If we were to believe Cassius Dio, her army numbered 120,000, though he's likely exaggerating – or, at least, not aiming for precision. But the very fact that the Brits were led by a woman probably also caught the Romans off guard. Roman historians, like Tacitus and Cassius Dio, were struck by her appearance and demeanour, the latter especially. He called her appearance terrifying, her gaze fierce, and her voice harsh (Cass. Dio 62.2). Tacitus says she was deceitful, greedy, adulterous, lustful, and savage. The truth is, however, that no self-respecting Roman male could fathom going to war against a foe led by a woman, and so it's not surprising that Roman characterizations of her can be so scathing.

From the beginning, Boudica defied Roman expectations. They almost certainly hadn't expected a female commander. Boudica took advantage of her army's strengths and attacked some of the key facets of Roman rule in southern Britain, its urban centres, and in the process killed many Romans. Their targets were Camulodunum (Colchester), Londinium (London), and Verulamium (St. Albans). By this point, the principal Roman forces under the governor Suetonius Paulina (not the biographer), which had been occupied with operations on the Isle of Mona (Anglesey), had moved south to engage Boudica and the Brits. The two sides had one last, pitched battle in 60 or 61 CE at some point along Watling Street, which ran from London northwest towards Wales. The end result was the Romans were victorious. The change in tactics – shifting from asymmetric warfare (avoiding pitched battle against Rome) – was probably a significant factor in the outcome. What's less clear is the precise location of the battle and the fate of Boudica. We know the battle was fought somewhere on that street, but we don't know where. We know too that Boudica died at some stage during or after battle, but we're not sure how or when. Was it in battle? Was she poisoned? Perhaps she fell ill and died from septicaemia?

Regardless, the battle's impact was significant for the Britons, and the Romans too. Perhaps as many as 70,000 Romans died in the conflict, but maybe as many as 80,000 of their foes. Deaths aside, there were other outcomes. Two Roman legions were honoured for their success, a not-unusual procedure. The Fourteenth Legion was given the epithet Martial and Victorious, while the Twentieth Legion was given the epithet Victorius. The capital of Roman Britain was shifted westwards too, from Colchester to London. This uprising also prompted the Romans to beef up their military presence in the island. Camulodunum itself became a fortress. For the rest of Roman Britain's history, it would be one of the most militarized of provinces, even if its size and relatively distant location made it, on the surface, less important to Rome's overall security interests.

Boudica was not the first woman to lead an army, even armies, against Rome and wouldn't be the last – in the next chapter, we'll meet Zenobia, who lived some two hundred years later in Palmyra. But she's had a significant impact on contemporary British identity. Ultimately, however, she failed. Despite whatever setbacks the Romans might have experienced, uprisings like hers in no way stemmed the tide of Roman aggression. It's tempting to think that Boudica and the Britons would have had more success had they stuck to guerrilla warfare. On the other hand, the Jewish rebels' experiences in Judea suggest otherwise. The truth is, at this stage in its history, it's hard to imagine a state that was capable of challenging Rome. A big reason for this was its strategic strength.

DACIA AND ROMAN STRATEGY

I started this chapter with a Roman defeat. I want to end it by looking at a Roman victory, one which underscores the degree to which long-term planning underscored Roman success. The victory in question is the Dacian Wars, of which there were two, fought by Trajan between 101 and 102 and then 104 and 105 CE. These wars are best remembered in Rome's spectacular Column of Trajan, which provided an illustrated narrative of the two conflicts. These two wars, well documented in some respects but not in others, tell us something about how the Romans planned for major conflicts, and the significant manpower needs required to wage a war on such a large scale.

Before we look further into how Rome prepared for this conflict, I want to step back to show how it started. In the first decade of Domitian's reign (r. 81–98), the Dacians, people based in what is now Romania, raided across the Danube into Roman Moesia (roughly Bulgaria), in the process effecting major casualties on the Roman armies that they came across, which included the loss of some leading Roman government officials. Domitian was preparing for a major war against the Dacians in response at the time he was assassinated in 96 CE. So, when Trajan assumed the throne, after the short reign of Nerva, Roman forces along the lower Danube were already, more or less, on a war footing and well positioned to launch a major campaign. How do we know that Domitian was preparing for a war against Dacia? Well, if we look more closely at the abundant diploma evidence (citizenship documents which detail where auxiliary units were at any given time), we can see a clear increase in the number of troops based in the Moesisas, the provinces directly neighbouring the Dacian Kingdom (along the lower Danube), years before Trajan launched his assault.

Of course, Trajan too deserves a good deal of credit. He created two legions in the context of the war: the II Traianic Brave and the XXX Ulpian Victorious. Trajan also engaged in steady negotiations with Decebalus, the Dacian king, in the hopes, at least on the surface, of righting the wrongs his people had done to Rome. They were to no avail, however – and maybe Trajan never really intended them to be. So, in 101 CE, Trajan launched a major invasion of Dacia. By 102, the two sides had signed a treaty and the Romans had left some troops behind. Just a few years later, however, the Romans were back at war against Dacia, and among the many notable feats carried out in this second Dacian war was the construction of a remarkable bridge over the Danube, designed by the famous architect, Apollodorus. The Romans pushed into the heart of the Dacian kingdom, the capital Sarmizegethusa. Rather than be captured alive, Decebalus committed suicide in an episode that some sculptors decided to include on Trajan's Column. Dacia was made a province, the neighbouring Moesian provinces were reorganized, and the Romans left behind a heavy military presence.

So that's the war in a nutshell. But what does all this tell us about how the Romans prepared for war in the long term? Well, Roman strategy is not a topic that has been ignored by scholars. In 1976, Luttwak published an important book on Roman strategy which challenged all preconceived notions of how the Romans made war. His background was in international relations, and he applied this background to the Roman empire, so arguing that the Romans had a clear grand strategy, which shifted at different stages of its history. From Augustus to Nero, the Romans used 'economy of force';

from Vespasian to Septimius Severus, 'preclusive security'; and from the third-century crisis on, 'defence-in-depth'. The first was a more offensively minded approach that involved a prudent use of the available military resources (armies mostly) to achieve its ends, namely imperial expansion and stability. Preclusive security involved stopping potential threats to Rome before they entered Roman territory. The final strategy, defence-in-depth, was the establishment of strong fixed defensive points (fortifications and so on) to stop or slow down incursions and then a sizable mobile army to respond after the fact.

While some were persuaded by Luttwak's arguments, others were more sceptical. More recent scholarship (relatively speaking) has often taken a more measured approach. Kagan, for example, refined Luttwak's theory by proposing that grand strategy didn't necessarily involve some elaborate, far-reaching scheme to maintain, and sometimes expand, the territorial integrity of the empire. Rather, grand strategy was a question of the state, here the Roman Empire, using the resources at its disposal to achieve its ends. Her ends (Roman security) were not dissimilar from Luttwak's, but her 'strategizing' was far less elaborate. Based on her reckoning, it is much easier to see the Romans as engaging in grand strategic thinking, even if this varies over time, from emperor to emperor.

Accordingly, if we turn our attention back to Dacia, we can see this kind of grand strategic thinking in action. This is all thanks to the existence of Roman military diplomas. These bronze documents, about the size of a passport, were dated to a specific date and gave a list of all units in a province with auxiliary (usually) soldiers eligible for citizenship at a given moment in time. This sort of document provides all sorts of valuable information, least of all about family relations among Rome's auxiliary soldiers. But this list of soldiers, and the presence of diplomas from many years, means we can see how the garrison of provinces changes over time. I'll have more to say about diplomas in the next chapter. So, to get back to these wars, as far back as Domitian (r. 81–96), the Romans moved a significant number of soldiers into the lower Danube in advance of a presumed major invasion, a change we can see in the Roman military diplomas. Had Domitian not been assassinated, there's every reason to suppose that he would have attacked the Dacians himself. Trajan, in turn, built on the foundation which Domitian had carefully laid. There was a further spike in units moved into the region within a few years of his accession, which is reflected in our diplomas from 100 CE. In Moesia Superior (Upper Moesia – a province covering much of modern Serbia and the launching point for the invasion), there was a huge increase in the number of auxiliary units, with the total going from 11 to 24. Moving units into a province usually also involved moving units out of another province. In other words, this was a long and complex operation that took a good deal of planning. And planning need not have taken place over many decades to be considered grand strategy. The fact is, over a period of many years, in looking at this one conflict alone, the Romans marshalled their resources to suit their political ends: revenge against Dacia for the first-century invasions. That they could effect such change without suffering similar setbacks in other parts of the empire is a testament to the other strengths of Rome's military and the careful planning and organization that often went into its utilization.

CONCLUSION

I opened this chapter by highlighting the vast manpower resources of the Roman state. This was a big reason for their military success during the middle and late republic, and it enabled them to continue to dominate the Mediterranean world in the imperial era. The story of this chapter, however, is the story of how the vast Roman Empire dealt with ruling over a vast array of different people who often preferred to be independent. Rome dealt with problems across the empire, and by looking at some of these uprisings, we can get a glimpse of the varied ways that war impacted the ancient world's wars, some willing participants in the wars in which their worlds were embroiled, like Boudica, others perhaps less so, like the women and children hiding out on Masada. At the end, I turned to another of Rome's great strengths: its careful planning and the streamlined organization of its military. In the penultimate chapter to this book, Rome will remain the centre of attention, but I'll turn our attention to some less expected combatants.

"THEY MAKE A DESERT AND CALL IT PEACE"

THE ROMAN EMPIRE, 117–284 CE

This famous line comes from Tacitus in the *Agricola*, a biography of his so-named father-in-law. Although Tacitus describes events from the period covered by the previous chapter, the line reflects, somewhat unintentionally, how later historians have viewed at least the first part of this period – a period of sustained peace across the empire. In many ways, though, Tacitus was prescient, and while this was a period of peace in some respects, the Romans were regularly faced with new and challenging foes, which in turn triggered some significant changes in how they waged war. In this chapter, I'll look at some of the varied backgrounds of Rome's soldiers and some of the unexpected aspects of warfare, from the use of chemical weapons at Dura-Europos to the widespread raids in the Harrah, the Black Desert of Jordan and Syria, documented in innumerable Safaitic graffiti.

TACITUS AND THE ROMAN SOLDIER

Tacitus was a historian with an elite background and was friends with the author and administrator, Pliny the Younger, whose uncle famously perished during the eruption of Mt. Vesuvius in the Bay of Naples in 79 CE. He was the author of four surviving works: the *Histories*, which covers events from the year of four emperors

DOI: 10.4324/9781003092636-6

through the Flavian dynasty (c. 69–96 CE); the *Annals*, a history of Rome from the end of the reign of Augustus up to the civil war; the *Agricola*, a biography of his father-in-law, the aforementioned Agricola; and the *Germania*, an account of the Germanic people (from a Roman perspective). That biography devotes considerable space to Agricola's spell as governor of Britain, which involved military operations in the north in what is now Scotland. These actions culminated in the Battle of Mons Graupius, fought at an undetermined location and described in some detail by Tacitus.

One potential location is Mither Tap Hillfort, though we can't be sure. In fact, there are many questions surrounding this battle. The Romans might well have fielded an army 20,000 strong, which would have been fewer men than the Caledonians' 30,000-strong fighting force, though these numbers are pure speculation, albeit drawn from Tacitus' own words. But Tacitus' account, for all its detail, is short of some of the material needed to piece events together. Much space is devoted to a poignant pre-battle speech given by Calgacus and little to the tactics and manoeuvres carried out by both sides throughout its course.

What Tacitus does do, however, is argue that the Romans deployed the auxiliaries instead of the legionaries in an attempt to spare Roman blood. From the early to middle decades of the Roman imperial era, the vast majority of Rome's soldiers were either legionaries or auxiliaries. The legionaries tended to be Roman citizens, whereas the auxiliaries tended to be non-citizens, though after service they could gain citizenship for them and their families, up to a point. Even if the auxiliaries were highly regarded soldiers with abilities that complemented the legionaries, for many contemporaries these soldiers were undoubtedly more barbaric than their legionary comrades. On that note, let's turn to what Tacitus says about the two in his account of the Battle of Mons Graupius (Tac. Agr. 35, trans. Church et al.):

> While Agricola was yet speaking, the ardour of the soldiers was rising to its height, and the close of his speech was followed by a great outburst of enthusiasm. In a moment they flew to arms. He arrayed his eager and impetuous troops in such a manner that the auxiliary infantry, 8,000 in number, strengthened his centre, while 3,000 cavalry were posted on his wings. The legions were drawn up

in front of the intrenched camp; his victory would be vastly more glorious if won without the loss of Roman blood, and he would have a reserve in case of repulse. The enemy, to make a formidable display, had posted himself on high ground; his van was on the plain, while the rest of his army rose in an arch-like form up the slope of a hill. The plain between resounded with the noise and with the rapid movements of chariots and cavalry. Agricola, fearing that from the enemy's superiority of force he would be simultaneously attacked in front and on the flanks, widened his ranks, and though his line was likely to be too extended, and several officers advised him to bring up the legions, yet, so sanguine was he, so resolute in meeting danger, he sent away his horse and took his stand on foot before the colours.

These comments highlight some of the ambiguity around the presence of Roman and non-Roman soldiers in Rome's military. Rome had a long-standing practice of employing non-Romans, what many would call "barbarians", in their military. On that note, the Romans in Italy often had a negative view of soldiers, often commenting on their appearance, behaviour, and language – and in this they often referred to legionaries. The late first-century satirist Juvenal, for instance, wrote a satire about soldiers (number 16), in which he complains about them, particularly how they seem to be able to treat you (civilians) badly but get away with anything.

Most of the Latin writers were based in and around Rome and Italy – or at least had strong connections with the imperial heartland. While some types of soldier did come from Italy during much of the imperial era, namely the praetorians, most of the others came from the provinces. While many – even most – would have spoken some Latin, it's unlikely this was the Latin of those spoken by elites in Italy. Instead, we have to imagine all sorts of dialects impacted by wider local features, like local languages and religious traditions. Although we can't always see this on the ground, the names of soldiers sometimes seem to reflect these varied differences.

We do have plenty of evidence, inconsistent though it may be, for the varied origins of imperial-era Roman soldiers, some coming from texts, some from scraps of papyrus, some from citizenship documents. One particular document (*ILS* 2304), which lists some legionaries enrolled in the Legio II Traiana based in Egypt and which dates to 194 CE, gives a wide variety of different origins for the unit's soldiers. In the century of Faustino – legions were divided into centuries and different centuries could have different names – we find a trumpeter from Antioch in Syria, but also an ordinary legionary from the camp (a legionary born in the camp), and also another from Nicomedia, located in what is now Turkey. In a different century, there's a Publius Aurelius Proclion from elsewhere in Egypt, and in particular Alexandria, the region's largest city by far.

If we jump back a few decades in time to the beginning of the period under consideration, when Trajan (r. 98–117) was emperor (Figure 5.1), we find one diploma (of many) filled with insight into one province's auxiliary soldiers. Diploma is the modern name given to citizenship certificates given to some groups within the wider military in the imperial era – that is, not something an ancient Roman soldier got upon graduation, though they could get one when their term of service was at an end. The auxiliaries, the largely non-Roman component of the military which made up close to half of the total, were among the main users of these documents. But we also find those that belonged to members of the navy, among others.

FIGURE 5.1 Trajan's Column, Cichorius Plates, 1896–1900, Wikimedia Commons

As noted in the previous chapter, these diplomas would include all sorts of information. Though rather lengthy, a translation of one such diploma is given below (ILS 9034, 100 CE, Upper Pannonia (Campbell #324)):

> Emperor Caesar Nerva Trajan Augustus, Conqueror of the Germans, son of the divine Nerva, chief priest, in the fourth year of his tribunician power, father of the fatherland, consul for the third time, has granted to the cavalrymen and infantrymen who are serving in the three *alae* and twenty-one cohorts, which are called (1) first praetorian, and (2) first Claudian New, and (3) second Pannonians; and (1) first Flavian Bessians, and (2) first Thracians, Roman citizens, and (3) first Flavian milliary Spanish, and (4) first Antiochenses, and (5) first Lusitanians, and (6) first Montani, Roman citizens, and (7) first Cisipadians, and (8) first Cretans, and (9) first milliary Vindelici, Roman citizens, and (10) first Syrian Thracians, and (11) first Cilicians, and (12) second Spanish, and (13) second Macedonian Gauls, and (14) second milliary Britons, Roman citizens, Loyal and Faithful, and (15) second Flavian Commagenians, and (16) third Britons, and (17) fourth Raetians, and (18) fifth Gauls, and (19) fifth Spanish, and (20) sixth Thracians, and (21) seventh Breucians, Roman citizens, which are in Upper Moesia under the command of Gaius Cilnius Proculus, and who have been honourably discharged having completed twenty-five or more years' service, and whose names are written below, to them, their children, and their posterity, citizenship and the right of marriage *(conubium)* with the wives they had when citizenship was given to them, or, if they were unmarried, with those whom they married afterwards, limited to one wife for each man.
>
> 8 May, in the consulship of Titus Pomponius Mamilianus and Lucius Herennius Saturninus.
>
> Of the first cohort of Antiochenses which is commanded by Marcus Calpurnius Sabinus, to infantryman Sapia Anazarbus, son of Sarmosus. Recorded and authenticated from the bronze plaque which is affixed at Rome on the wall behind the temple of the divine Augustus at the statue (?) of Minerva.
>
> (Witnesses) Quintus Pompeius Homerus, Aulus Ampius Epaphroditus, Tiberius Claudius Vitalis, Gaius Julius Aprilis, Gaius Vettienus Modestus, Lucius Pullius Verecundus, Lucius Pullius Speratus.

As you can see, the diploma would include some lines about what sort of citizenship was being granted and whom it was being granted to. In this case, it was granted not only to the soldier himself but also to his wife, if he had one, and his children or other dependants, again if he had them. These rights weren't consistent across Roman history, however, for some of those rights were reduced in the second century, before Roman citizenship was extended in 212 CE during the reign of Caracalla (r. 211–217 CE).

The Roman army was a polyglot force. While some soldiers spoke Latin, some spoke Greek. One example of a soldier operating in both languages comes from Apuleius' *Metamorphoses*, or *Golden Ass*, a novel in which the main character is transformed into a donkey (but he keeps his human mind) and then goes on a series of wild adventures. In one such episode, the donkey, while being led through the Greek countryside by a farmer, stumbles across a soldier. It reads (Apuleius, *Metamorphoses* 9.39).

> On the road we met with a tall Roman, a soldier as we saw from his dress and manner, who inquired in a high and mighty voice where my master was going with that ass without a load. But my master stunned by grief, and not understanding his speech, passed him by in silence. The soldier took offence, and unable to quell his natural arrogance, thinking the gardener's silence an insult, knocked him from my back with the centurion's stick he carried. The gardener humbly explained he had no Latin, so the soldier asked him again in Greek: 'Where are you off to with that ass of yours?'

Things take a turn, and the farmer gets abused by the soldier and the donkey gets taken. While the experiences of the farmer and the donkey are unfortunate, and, most likely, all too common under imperial Rome, what's important for us in this context is the language acuity of the soldier. Although it's tempting to think of many or most soldiers as monolingual, and mostly Latin speakers at that, anecdotes like this highlight the ability of many soldiers to operate not only in the pseudo-official language of the military, Latin, but also in the local language, Greek. That this episode falls in a work of fiction, to my mind, speaks to its veracity. If the audience didn't believe this was possible, it seems less likely that Apuleius would have included this episode.

In other parts of the empire, some soldiers might speak any other of a wide variety of languages, depending on the circumstances, both the local ones and their own. In the southeast corner of the empire, roughly where modern Jordan is, some soldiers likely did speak Latin, though others spoke Greek. This was the language of administration in this part of the empire. We have papyri belonging to a woman named Babatha, and it spans the years both before and after Arabia (much of modern Jordan) became a province (between 106 and 112): previously, it had been the Nabataean Kingdom, whose famous capital was Petra. Select papyri illustrate Babatha's dealing with the local government, shifting from a form of Aramaic under the Nabataeans to Greek under the Romans. But as I was saying, there were languages besides Latin and Greek, depending on the context. In this case, there are traces of Arabic in some other, late papyri (sixth century CE) from the region, though we find traces as early as the third and fourth centuries in places like Umm el-Jimal in Jordan's Hauran. For instance, one soldier has a Greek name but a father with an Arabic name, Neon, son of Ka'ammihi. Soldiers and their family members who lived in Nessana, in the Negev in modern Israel/Palestine, seem to have spoken some (or a lot of) Arabic. Even in the late first century CE, we find soldiers from this part of the world serving far from home in Pompeii (before the eruption of Vesuvius), operating in an ancient North Arabian language related to Arabic (the script they use is called Safaitic). This is all to say the soldiers were a diverse bunch, and wherever you went you could probably find soldiers using languages besides the expected Greek and Latin.

ROMANS BESIEGED

We know the Roman military was varied in its composition, and in the previous chapter, as well as the one before that, we also saw that it was, by and large, often very successful. Among the most important collections of material from the period covered by this chapter are the remains of the frontier outpost of Dura-Europos. This Syrian locale, located along the banks of the Euphrates, seems to have started its life as a Seleucid fortification before eventually falling under the political control of the Parthians. Many decades later, the Romans conquered the city with the result that most of what remains dates to the period of Roman occupation. This came to an abrupt end during the 250s CE, when the Sasanian Persians besieged the city and eventually captured it. It was abandoned in the aftermath, and there has been virtually no settlement at the site since, and this has contributed to its excellent state of preservation.

Because of the spectacular finds and its fall during a Persian invasion, Dura provides invaluable evidence of late antique siege warfare, only here with the Romans on the defensive. Fortunately, too, this is not the only well-documented siege from late antiquity. Those same Persians besieged the city of Amida in 359 CE, and the Roman historian Ammianus Marcellinus was a firsthand witness to the events. So, I'll supplement what we have from Dura with what Ammianus has to say about his experiences in Amida, even if they do deal with events some 100 or so years later.

Ammianus Marcellinus was a Greek-speaking historian who wrote in Latin and wrote what's been called the last great Roman history, the *Res Gestae*, which survives only in part. The surviving second half (or so) includes some detailed military narratives, some of which he witnessed firsthand, like the siege of Amida in 359. That siege was launched by the Persian king Shapur II (r. 309–379 CE), or Shapur the Great, who himself participated in the conflict. Ammianus was one of the defenders based in the city when the Persian army arrived.

As we've seen, a siege was an expensive way to wage war. In general, the Romans were better than most. We saw this with Jerusalem and Masada in the Great Jewish War. But with the advent of the Sasanian Persians, Rome had met its match. Though we lack good physical evidence for the siege, we have Ammianus' sterling account of the Persian siege. There are plenty of memorable passages, but here I chose one that encapsulates some of the fear, anxiety, and drama of the final assault of a siege from the perspective of its defenders, both soldier and civilian (Ammianus Marcellinus, *Res Gestae* 19.8.2–4):

> And long did the bloody conflict last, nor was any one of the garrison driven by fear of death from his resolution to defend the city. The conflict was prolonged, till at last, while the fortune of the two sides was still undecided, the structure raised by our men, having been long assailed and shaken, at last fell, as if by an earthquake.

> And the whole space which was between the wall and the external mound being made level as if by a causeway or a bridge, opened a passage to the enemy, which was no longer embarrassed by any obstacles; and numbers of our men, being crushed or enfeebled by their wounds, gave up the struggle. Still men flocked from all quarters to repel so imminent a danger, but from their eager haste they got in one another's way, while the boldness of the enemy increased with their success. By the command of the king all his troops now hastened into action, and a hand-to-hand engagement ensued. Blood ran down from the vast slaughter on both sides: the ditches were filled with corpses, and thus a wider path was opened for the besiegers. And the city, being now filled with the eager crowd which forced its way in, all hope of defence or of escape was cut off, and armed and unarmed without any distinction of age or sex were slaughtered like sheep.

Dura-Europos offers us another example of a siege, defended by Rome, as seen not through texts but through artefact. The city had a long and complicated history, starting life when the Seleucids ruled this part of the wider Hellenistic world, though there might well have been an earlier settlement on site. Later, it was conquered by the Parthians and later still, in turn, by the Romans. At its end, in the middle of the third century CE, it was in Roman hands, and it fell to the Sasanians, who chose not to inhabit the city, though there is some debate about whether it was inhabited in the years following.

We don't have literary evidence for the city's history, even if it appears in the odd anecdote. Rather, most of what we know about the city comes from its abundant archaeological finds, which include a significant stash of papyri, primarily documents connected with the Roman units housed on site. But more on those at the end of the chapter.

Archaeologists have uncovered all sorts of interesting and varied aspects of the city, such as some breathtaking frescoes that adorn the walls of some of its buildings, like the fresco of Julius Terentius, found in the Temple of Bel, and dating to early in the third century, owing to a Latin inscription that identifies him. Julius Terenius was a tribune at Dura, and he's shown alongside a military standard and some soldiers, probably Palmyrene ones, in the context of a sacrifice, and in the presence of the *tychai* (the guardians/ spirits of cities) of Dura and Palmyra. For our purposes here, more interesting are all the finds associated with the final siege of the city, carried out by the Sasanians, in 256. We know it was 256 because of a coin found in amongst some bodies discovered in a collapsed tunnel. But how did they get there in the first place?

Sieges were a multi-staged process, and while they could be short, they could also be long, with some armies besieging sites for many long months until the defenders and their home were captured or they surrendered. Masada, as we saw, held out for a long time. Defenders could resort to several measures to defend themselves, from the physical fortifications themselves (the walls and towers), to assorted missiles (like javelins and arrows), to more opportunistic means (like rocks, boiling water, and burning oil). Being prepared, with ample food and drink, is also crucial. The more supplies you have, the longer you can hold out, and the more likely the attacking side might run into logistical challenges of their own.

Of course, attackers had all sorts of tricks of their own to take a city. Well-trained soldiers and impressive siegeworks machines could go a long way. They might bring battering rams to the walls (or gates) protected (from defenders) by hides, pieces of wicker, or something else. Artillery machines might launch missiles at the defenders and their walls. They might try to starve out those inside, to force them to surrender. In some ways, however, this was one of the most challenging ways of taking a city, as it would require enough manpower to surround a city so no one could get in or out. One final note about the length of sieges: the longer they were, the more likely, it seems, that if successful the sack of the city would be especially savage.

There were other means that attackers might employ to take a city. They might build a siege ramp, as the Romans did at Masada. The Sasanians built a ramp between towers 14 and 15 at Dura. Attackers might also try to build mines, tunnels that attempted to go under a city's walls and into the enclosure or just under the walls so that they could be brought down. As it happens, the attackers at Dura (Sasanians) built several mines of their own with the intention of getting through the defences. One of the mines was built near Tunnel 19, which lay on the city's western wall and was not far from the city's famed synagogue. This mine seems to have been built with a view to bringing down the tower, constructed as close as the mine was to the tower. The Romans discovered the mine, however, and built a countermine of their own to intercept it. But the Persians found out about the Roman efforts and prepared a defence of their own, composed of chemical weapons.

Traces of naphtha and sulfur were found, and this points to the Persian use of chemical weapons to kill the individuals found on site, 19 Romans and one Sasanian. The Persians made a fire and threw some bitumen and sulfur crystals into it. James says the chemicals combined to make a dense cloud of smoke that included carbon dioxide, carbon monoxide, and sulfur dioxide. Its impact on those exposed was lethal. Some Romans likely ran for their lives to escape from the mine, all while surrounded by black plumes of smoke. Eventually, once the smoke had cleared, the Persians piled up the bodies of dead Romans – the 19 – along a wall and gathered a host of flammable materials to try to bring down the countermine. One lone Persian was tasked with carrying this out, the one found with the Romans, only, after starting the fire, he failed to escape. Although this mining attempt and use of chemical warfare failed to bring down the tower (because it had been reinforced earlier by the Romans), they did, ultimately, succeed in taking the city. It also highlights the varied ways that besieging armies might employ to capture a location and the manifold ways that war was waged in the ancient Mediterranean world.

ASYMMETRIC WARFARE: THE RAID

So far in this book, I've focused on the pitched battles and sieges that, for many, characterize ancient warfare, though in the case of Judea and Britain, we've seen how some rebels employed asymmetrical tactics where possible. Indeed, among the people who lived in the ancient Mediterranean, the kind of warfare they were most likely to be familiar with was of the low-intensity variety, especially the raid. A big part of the relationship between the Romans and their neighbours to the north and east (that is, in the steppes) was not only through immigration but also through raids. Batty, in a book on Rome's relationship with its neighbours in the Balkans, called raids a multifaceted thing and noted the following crucial factors while considering them: their duration; the route;

the ease of return; whether families participated; wagons and provisions; the numbers involved; whether mounts were involved (horseback in his case); and the targets. For Batty, the "classic raid" in the Balkans would be of short duration, along a known route, anticipate a safe return, no families or unnecessary vehicles would be involved, the numbers would be limited, the transportation would be appropriate, and there would be suitable targets. The Romans, obviously, did what they could to counteract this, often using lightly armed cavalry and smaller attacking parties of their own and trying to maximize their own supply lines and fortifications for support.

Not all raids necessarily involved Romans and their neighbours, however. Sometimes, a group within a larger population might participate in raids against another group or groups. This is likely true for a large and diverse body of people across the wider Mediterranean world, though we are ill informed about many of the specifics owing to big gaps in the evidence. For one particular group, however, we are exceptionally well informed about their raiding habits, and to find out more we have to go to the Black Desert of southern Syria and northeastern Jordan. There, many tens of thousands of graffiti litter the landscape on the region's ubiquitous black, basalt rocks, written in a language called Ancient North Arabian, using a script called Safaitic (Figure 5.2). The inscribers practised pastoral transhumance, moving with their animals back and forth throughout the region as the conditions and seasons dictated. In fact, while most of these graffiti do little more than identify the inscribers, there are so many graffiti that discuss this movement of people and animals that scholars have been able to chart their seasonal movements over the course of the year.

Some of the graffiti even get into contemporary geo-political events, and others still discuss the subject of this section, raiding. What do they say? Well, some get into how long an individual had been raiding and where, like "'zhm son of Nbs[2] [who] raided in the Ruḥbah for two months". Sometimes it's not a specific place but something more general, like "{S¹rk} {son of} Rml [who] went on a raid in this valley". Where sometimes the raids could take place in the valleys, sometimes it was "the arable places in the plain". The authors of the graffiti sometimes even tell us why they went on the raids in the first place. "Nd' son of Ḏl son of Rbn...went on a raid in the Ḥrt to bring (back) the young she-camel(s) from Mʿn".

FIGURE 5.2 Safaitic Graffiti, Jordan, Conor Whately

"Yḫʿ son of Ḥgw son of Ksʾt son of Wmd son of Zdʾl" when on a raid because "he was poor". Somewhat more indirectly, others state that they went on raids to drive off horses or some other, sometimes unspecified, animals. Whether they were the aggressors in a raid or not, many of the persons involved recognized the dangers of raids. Some sought refuge while on a raid, whereas others despaired while looking out for raiding parties.

There are also plenty of invocations to the gods, especially Lt (Allat), to grant them security while on a raid. While the obvious threat would be their foes, it might also be the local wildlife, as was the case with "Ḥrb son of Mḥlm son of Ḥrb son of ʾdm son of Ḥdg son of Sʹwr son of Ḥmyn son of Ġddt", who asked Lt (Allat) to grant security "from the lion". Of course, while some groups would be successful after a raid, others weren't so lucky. So, in keeping with the emotional tenor of much of the graffiti as a whole, there is no shortage of those that express grief at what transpired because of a raid. Poor "Ḏhd son of Gdy son of Mty…found the traces of his raiding party buried by members of the lineage of Yẓr, and so he grieved in pain", while "'ḏnt son of 'nʿm son of 'ḏnt son of 'nʿm son of Qdm…grieved for his raiding party made captive {and} buried".

In another case, an unknown individual – his graffito is missing some elements – notes that "he was devastated by grief for his raiding party who were lost". Collectively, what this engaging epigraphic evidence shows us is that we need to be aware that, for many residents of the wider Mediterranean, the big, pitched battle or the long, drawn-out siege are only part of the story. Many experienced warfare on a smaller scale but one which was, potentially, no less impactful for those involved. Indeed, in many ways, this massive collection of graffiti gives us a much more immediate sense of the trauma of warfare as experienced by those from the lower rungs of the social ladder.

ZENOBIA

For this next section, we'll stay in western Asia but shift our focus from raids on the frontiers to the leadership of one well-known city-state. Most of the discussion of military leaders in this short book has concentrated on men, for good reason. It was a patriarchal world in which men led armies and wrote the texts and put up the inscriptions that celebrated their victories. Despite all this, we do occasionally find powerful women playing leading roles in major military operations. We've already met Boudica. Now I turn to another such notable individual, Zenobia, who led the people of Palmyra first with and then against the Romans. While the focus of the book is on warfare, in this section I want to highlight some of Zenobia's personal and political manoeuvring, for we have not yet seen how the wider context often shaped the decisions that ancient Mediterranean leaders made in making war. In the case of Zenobia, her position in Palmyrene society, her love for her children, the intrigue surrounding her husband's murder, and instability at Rome all played a role in the war between the Romans and Palmyrenes. Let's take a closer look.

Although she is better known as Zenobia, her local name, which appears on a few inscriptions, was Bathzabbai. She's also found in the odd literary source, like the Historia Augusta's *Life of Aurelian*. Physical remains, besides those of her famous city, are hard to come by. That said, there are plenty of funerary portraits from Palmyra, and they do give us some insight into the people who populated that famous city, and what we are able to glean about the lives of women can, in some respects, be applied to Zenobia. So what do we know? Well, for one thing, women covered their hair, so she likely did too. We know that descent in a family was patrilineal and that the families and wider clans, as a whole, were important – and so likely important to her.

Zenobia was born around 240 CE and was the daughter of Zabbai – hence her name, Bathzabbai (from the clan of Zabbai). Although we can't identify them in the sources, she likely had siblings. When out and about, she would have worn a long-sleeved tunic, most likely, with headbands, headscarves, or even turbans to cover her hair. In the late 250s, she married Odainath, an important military figure in the city, who eventually became its ruler. In 258, they had a son, Wahballath. Whether he was their only child, however, we cannot say, though she seems to have had some daughters.

Palmyra had a complex relationship with Rome. Most residents identified themselves as citizens of their city, which is what we find the Greeks doing across the Roman world much earlier. But there were also a demonstrable Syrian identity and Arabian customs, even if they weren't Arabs. Palmyra played an important role in Rome's relationship with Persia and the broader eastern frontier. Odainath was loyal to Rome, and after the initial, often spectacular, successes of the Persians earlier in the century, what we saw at Dura, he managed to keep Shapur I and the Persians at bay.

In the 260s, Odainath was at the peak of his success. From 262 to 263, he invaded Persia. He was so successful that the then (Roman) emperor Gallienus celebrated this with the title *corrector totius orientis*. This gave him military power, what the Romans usually termed the power of *imperium* (the right to lead an army), over Syria, Arabia, and Mesopotamia. Wahballath himself later took this title in 268 CE. Even more, Odainath was called king of kings at home and worshipped as a hero. This might have led to a possible second invasion in 267.

A year later, however, his efforts were in tatters. Both Odainath and another son, Hairan, died under suspicious circumstances. This could have come through the efforts of fellow Palmyrenes jealous of his success or even through the intrigue of the emperor Gallienus, also wary of the man's success. It's at this moment that Zenobia enters the scene in a significant way. For though the assassination attempt was successful, the attempted coup – the overthrow of the ruling family of Palmyra – failed. Zenobia and Wahballath weren't there when Odainath was assassinated, which means they survived unscathed. So, Zenobia seized control and organized an elaborate burial for her husband (though – to repeat a now familiar tune – we know little about the specifics). She also sent an embassy to Gallienus in an effort to smooth things over, but he wasn't impressed. To make matters worse, Gallienus died and his successor, Claudius II, called her a usurper. This sent the two, Rome and Palmyra, on a path to war.

In 269/270, Claudius II sent an army against Zenobia, all while casting her as a foreign despot, the sort of practice that had a long tradition in Rome: such was the case with Cleopatra VII, the famous Cleopatra, vis-à-vis her relationship with Marc Antony. But before Claudius II got very far, Zenobia responded and herself went on the offensive. In 270, she took the province of Arabia, which she saw as a springboard to taking Egypt, a much more valuable target. She sent a 70,000-strong army to Egypt to this end, which succeeded, though she didn't manage to cut off grain shipments to Rome, perhaps her ultimate target. In the midst of the war, Claudius II died, and he was succeeded by Aurelian.

Through all this, Zenobia had framed her dynasty as subordinate to, not in competition with, Rome. Around this time, she started to promote her son Wahballath on coins and more, and we even start seeing statues celebrating Zenobia and Odainath, even though he had been dead for some time. This was likely meant to emphasize her connection to her husband and perhaps stress her legitimacy. Despite all her attempts to get Rome on her side, her overtures failed, and so she decided to change her language and start referring to herself as Augusta and her son as Augustus, a serious challenge to Roman hegemony. After years of usurpers, Aurelian was keen to rein them in, and so he abandoned Dacia to concentrate his energy on a war in the east. This started in earnest in 271 with a propaganda campaign against Zenobia, perhaps not unlike that waged by Octavian against Cleopatra back in the final years of the republic.

The Romans criticized Zenobia for being masculine and oriental, again in language that would have been familiar to Boudica in the case of the former and Cleopatra in the case of the latter. Back at Palmyra, however, the locals were comfortable with a woman in charge, for she seems to have had the full (or nearly full) support of the people. When Aurelian started his invasion in 272, Zenobia attempted to negotiate with the emperor, though without success. Fighting words flew back and forth between the two sides: Aurelian stressed Zenobia's masculinity, her eastern background, and her position as a despot, while Zenobia pushed her position as Augusta as well as her virtuosity and piety. Of course, words go only so far, and such was the gravity of the situation that Aurelian sent two armies: a larger one under his authority which marched eastward from Anatolia and a smaller one which headed northward from Egypt. In response, Zenobia, who had seized control of Anatolia earlier, withdrew and ceded it to the emperor.

The sides fought two battles near Antioch in 272. The Palmyrenes made effective use of arms and soldiers familiar to those from the eastern frontier, like *clibanarii* and cataphracts. These were heavily armed shock cavalry, for which both horse and man were fully armoured. For all their fierce reputation, Aurelian managed to lure the Palmyrene cataphracts into a trap, and in this instance Zenobia only managed to escape using a trick, which entailed her faking victory. Aurelian then worked to secure the support of the reconquered inhabitants of the eastern Mediterranean by propitiating eastern deities like Elagabal. And yet, all wasn't lost for Zenobia, for it was now that she took Egypt and parts of Arabia, like Bostra. In fact, there are even hints of destruction at sites like Humayma, not far from the port at Aqaba. Zenobia then gathered a big army at Emesa along with a leading general named Zabdas. Yet another battle ensued, and yet again Rome won. Zenobia pulled back to Palmyra, but she was forced to capitulate. Two of her leading generals were killed, the aforementioned Zabdas as well as a certain Zabbai, while Zenobia managed to live out her final days, possibly with her son, possibly not, in Tibur (Tivoli), near Rome. This brought an end to Palmyra's independence and relative prosperity.

In the end, why was Rome, and Aurelian in particular, so keen on crushing Zenobia and Palmyra's revolt? On the one hand, the third century was a turbulent time for Rome, at least in some respects. There were a handful of breakaway territories, like parts of Gaul. In other words, this was a problem, and Roman rulers were undoubtedly keen on preventing any of them from going too far. In the case of the eastern Mediterranean and the Levant, this was an especially prosperous part of the empire, and the loss of this area, and Egypt in particular, was not something the Romans would be comfortable with allowing. On the other hand, as I've mentioned before (Chapter 4, for example), the Romans, like the Greeks and most of their peers and predecessors, weren't keen on states (or otherwise) ruled by women. So, for all that the loss of this fledgling Palmyrene Empire represented an economic and political threat to Rome, there was surely a sense among the powers that be that Rome couldn't be seen to be bettered by foe led by a woman, especially a foreign woman.

ROMAN PAPERWORK

So far in this chapter, we've seen a lot of action: siege warfare, waged in Roman Syria with Roman defenders staunchly holding out against seasoned Persian attackers, and lightning raids in the Black Desert in Jordan and Syria. But I started the chapter with the polyglot nature of the Roman military and even looked into some of the documents that illustrate some of this material. Here, I want to take this subject further by highlighting some of the vast paperwork that the Roman military produced and consumed, with an obvious emphasis on that which pertains more directly to warfare, even if you can argue that it all does. To simplify matters, at least a little, I'm going to focus on a collection of documents uncovered at one place we looked at above, Dura-Europos. That city is famous not only for its physical remains, from the walls and houses to the accoutrements of war, but also for an important collection of papyri, largely in Latin, that documents aspects of its resident soldiers.

The Romans are rightly famous for the mountains of paperwork that they produced for many aspects of life. Only a small fraction of all of that which once existed has survived thanks to the perishable material it was produced on, largely papyri from Egypt though also from other select sites in western Asia, like Dura-Europos. In places that didn't have papyri, wood could be used. Wooden tablets have been found in more forested parts of the empire, like Britain, Germany, and Switzerland. Some of the documents were letters between friends, like a famous letter from Vindolanda in which the wife (Claudia Severa) of a local commander (Aelius Brocchus) writes another woman (Sulpicia Lepidina, wife of Cerialis) asking Sulpicia to come to Claudia's birthday party. We even have some written by soldiers to their loved ones and vice versa. They might ask for shoes, for money, or just to find out how everyone was doing. We also have receipts for bigger or smaller purchases and assorted legal documents, whether details of a murder trial (with the bits with the outcome missing) or legal requisitions of assorted goods.

Among the vast corpus of military documents, we have receipts of the sort just mentioned. There are records of troops and their supplies, whether it's for horses that have been ordered/requisitioned or new recruits dispatched to their new headquarters. At Dura, we have a few official documents, with some of the most exciting – at least for someone like me – being the military rosters, which are just what they sound like. They are a record, from a particular time, of all the soldiers listed in a particular unit. P. Dura 100, as it is labelled, is a nearly complete roster from 219 CE of the soldiers of the 20th Cohort of Palmyrenes – remember the Palmyrene soldiers from Terentius' fresco discussed above. It's composed of 44 columns and lists soldiers by their centuries (sub-units of around 80–100 soldiers) and *turmae* (smaller sub-units of about 32). It lists those soldiers who fought as camel-riders, *dromadarii* (as they're styled here) or *dromedarii* (as we find them elsewhere). It even identifies some soldiers who provided lions, like Aurelius Lucianus, son of Themarsas (col. 36). Along the same lines, we have a guard roster (P. Dura 107), dated to 240–241 CE, which tells us where they do some of their guarding. There are also letters exchanged between commanders, with one pair discussing problems with discipline (P. Dura 55A). Another important document from Dura is the so-called *Feriale Duranum*, which, in its current state (fragmentary), includes assorted dates and who or what is celebrated on that day. For instance, January 24 is marked as the birthday of the "deified Hadrian", and soldiers (or their priests) are to mark the occasion by offering an ox to the deceased emperor. Some dates celebrate great victories, like January 28, which applauds a victory (or victories) of Septimius Severus against the Parthians. This document is the only such Roman military calendar we have, and it's easy to imagine similar calendars all across the empire. Interesting for us, the calendar even seems to celebrate some past battles, so emphasizing the role of warfare in a soldier's life, even beyond the battlefield.

In sum, this brief look at our limited record for Roman paperwork illustrates the scale and scope of Roman military administration. This, in turn, helps explain how the Romans were able to move men and materiel across the empire with relative ease, so that the planning for major campaigns, which we saw at the end of the previous chapter, was not an insurmountable task. Plus, although our direct evidence for this paperwork comes from the imperial era, recent work by scholars like Pearson shows the Romans were doing similar things for centuries.

CONCLUSION

Warfare in the ancient world wasn't just men against men in Greece and Rome. As we've now seen, for some states the most powerful war leaders were women like Boudica, as we saw in the previous chapter, or Zenobia in this one. It's also the case that war wasn't fought only in the field. It was also often fought in and around the Mediterranean world's cities, like Dura-Europos and Amida. Our surviving authors like Ammianus could leave behind the most vivid of firsthand retellings of daring escapes in the midst of brutal warfare. On the other hand, the material evidence, here the remains of men and materiel from Dura, show us just how varied the weaponry could be in this world. It wasn't just iron weapons and equipment. In fact, at some points, ancient peoples employed chemical weapons, the sort of practice usually better associated with wars in the twentieth and twenty-first centuries. In the next and final chapter, we turn to warfare at the end of antiquity.

"IF YOU WANT PEACE, PREPARE FOR WAR"

THE END OF ANTIQUITY AND THE BIRTH OF THE MEDIEVAL WORLD, 284–641 CE

THE END OF ROMAN WARFARE

I finish this little book with a quote from the author of Graeco-Roman antiquity's most famous military manual, Vegetius, whose *Epitoma Rei Militaris* was Graeco-Roman antiquity's most famous military manual and one of the most popular works in the medieval and early modern eras. Late Antiquity, the period covered by this chapter, produced some of our most important sources for ancient warfare, including Vegetius. Maurice's *Strategikon* was published around 590 CE and by some reckoning is the most accurate and valuable account of warfare from any part of antiquity. We also have at least two detailed narrative histories: the late fourth-century Latin work, called the *Res Gestae*, by Ammianus Marcellinus, and the mid-sixth-century Greek work, called the *History of the Wars of Justinian*, or *Wars* for short, by Procopius. But honourable mention should also go to two other works: Pseudo-Joshua the Stylite's *Chronicle*, a detailed account of the war between Rome and Persia in the early sixth century, written in Syriac, and Agathias' *Histories*, which was written in Greek from the end of the sixth century and which continues the story that Procopius tells. The latter two provide lengthy and detailed accounts of a few years,

DOI: 10.4324/9781003092636-7

which were marred by periods of intense warfare, often involving the Romans and the Persians.

But there are also unexpected sources, like the *Notitia Dignitatum*, or list of offices, which contains lists of commanders and regiments for both the eastern and western halves of the Roman Empire. Its date is uncertain – most accept dates between the very late fourth century and early fifth, though a recent study argued for a mid-fifth-century date – and so too are its function and purpose. The troop complement that it outlines, at least for the east, in the early fifth century seems accurate, however, and while it doesn't tell us how the Romans were fighting at that time, or even who, it does give us a good idea of what kinds of units were doing the fighting. For one thing, there are far more total units than there had been before, and while some of the names and types are familiar, even the same, there are plenty more that are new and unfamiliar, at least to those better acquainted with the early and high imperial Roman world. So, while we still find legions and auxiliaries, at least in name, we find many more new variations, like palatine auxiliaries and *comitatenses* legions, as well as cavalry units called wedges (*cunei*), vexillations (*vexillationes*), and *equites* – knights. These new monikers reflect gradual changes in the empire's troop complement that began in the late second century and continued through the fifth century when the *Notitia* was compiled. While it's tempting to imagine that the empire kept the original units to a similar size and expanded the total number of units fighting for Rome to a near-fantastical number, this would make for an enormous military far beyond the financial means of the pre-modern empire. Thus, while the total number of units had definitely gone up, the units themselves were much smaller.

One of the main divisions in the military was between the field armies, usually tasked with offensive operations, and the frontier armies, tasked with defence and internal security. While many of the units that filled their armies had the same name structures – unit number and name – the types of units could vary substantially. Some of the cavalry units were cataphracts (Figure 6.1), like the *Equites catafractarii iuniores* based in Britain, heavily armoured soldiers and horses that served as shock troops, which we'll return to below, while others were units of camel cavalry, like

FIGURE 6.1 Persian Cataphract, Taq-e Bostan, Iran, 6th century CE, Wikimedia Commons

the *Ala tertia dromedariorum*, based in Egypt. Some of the names appended to infantry units imply the continued or initial use of persons from varied regional backgrounds and possibly varied skill-types too. In other words, this was a large and diverse military with a range of specialized troops, at least at the time that the *Notitia* was compiled.

One hundred and fifty to two hundred years later, when Maurice's *Strategikon* was published (c. 590 CE), the story had changed, and this abundant specialization had been replaced by significant uniformity. If Maurice's military manual is anything to go by, all the cavalry soldiers were of more or less the same type. They were proficient, as needs be, in the use of bow or lance, in combat. Even the twelfth book of the 12-book text, on infantry, is full of infantry soldiers who are all broadly similar. This means a lot had changed in the intervening decades, and those changes are only somewhat visible in what evidence we have, some Egyptian papyri (as well as a few from Israel/Palestine and even Italy), the odd reference in a text, like Theophylact Simocatta (early seventh-century CE historian), and even an occasional inscription.

THE BATTLE OF STRASBOURG

The textual evidence, from Procopius, and a few other historians like Agathias, Procopius' successor, points to a military that was still composed of both infantry and cavalry in significant quantities, even if the proportion of cavalry had steadily increased. And while some troops, like the Herul and Hun horse archers, who made up part of the regular forces in the sixth-century military, were more specialized, there seems to have been a broad degree of uniformity in much of the military even by that day, if the evidence for the Persian, African, and Italian field armies, which fought the wars Justinian waged in northern Mesopotamia, Tunisia, and Italy, is anything to go by. In other words, where we do find pitched battles, it wasn't just on horseback, with one army of cavalry fighting against another. Procopius' description of the Battle of Dara, fought in 530 between the Romans and Persians, makes for a case in point. It's described in significant detail by the historian, enough for him to lay out the different components of big chunks of the Roman army – this is not the case for his description of the Persian forces, of which, nevertheless, cavalry made up a sizeable portion.

Although we might well characterize late antiquity as an age with fewer pitched battles involving ever-smaller armies, that's not to say there weren't any. But it's clear that war had changed in some not-insignificant ways. We can see this by looking at two battles, both waged by Rome against similar foes and described in some detail by skilled contemporary (or near contemporary historians). The first is the Battle of Strasbourg in 357 CE, when the Romans defeated the Alamanni, as described by Ammianus Marcellinus; the second is the Battle of Casilinum in 554 CE, when the Romans defeated the Franks (and the Alamanni), as described by Agathias. I'll come back to Casilinum when I turn to horse archery.

The later emperor Julian (r. 361–363, famously the last non-Christian emperor) led the Romans into battle at Strasbourg, at the head of an army of infantry and cavalry (16.12.7). This all seems familiar enough, along with the one legion named among their forces, the Legion of the Primani (*Primanorum legionem*, 16.12.49). But Ammianus includes some less familiar elements, for he notes that they also had cataphracts (16.12.7), heavily armoured cavalry, and soldiers called Cornuti and Bracchiati (16.12.43).

When Ammianus gets to battle itself, his account is full of the sort of tactical details that we might expect to find in a similar description from the early or high imperial era. When the Romans learn of the Alamanni position, they make a wedge formation, so making a solid line "like an impregnable wall" (Amm. Marc. 16.12.20). Ammianus even gets into the respective merits of infantry versus cavalry, at least in the context of this battle. He notes the contrast between the heavy Roman cavalry and the lighter German cavalry, a definite advantage for the former:

> one of their warriors on horseback, no matter how skilful, in meeting one of our cavalry in coat-of-mail, must hold bridle and shield in one hand and brandish his spear with the other, and would thus be able to do no harm to a soldier hidden in iron armour.
>
> (16.12.22)

At one stage, the Alamanni infantry even chastise their commanders for staying on horseback, which spurs their king Chnodomarius to dismount and fight on foot (16.12.34–35).

Ammianus' description is vivid and engaging, for he shifts back and forth between extreme close-ups of individuals and select groups of soldiers. In amongst that detail, we find both the familiar and the unexpected. There are references to famed figures from Rome's past, like Sulla and Mithridates. At one stage, the Romans even use a *testudo* formation, which is the famed tortoise of Rome's legionary heyday and which is so vividly illustrated on Trajan's Column (16.12.44). We even get Roman soldiers standing their ground and defending themselves like *murmillones*, gladiators known for the fish on their helmets (Ammianus 16.12.49).

But in amongst all these very traditional Roman details are some new ones, which though strange to those of us more familiar with Rome's past, would likely have seemed staunchly Roman to Ammianus' Roman present. For one, he describes his own standard, a dragon standard, which helped spur his soldiers on during a moment of panic (16.12.39). We don't know when these dragon standards were introduced. The second-century CE writer Arrian talks about dragon standards and associates them with the Scythians (*Tactics* 35.2–4). Vegetius, who's much closer in time to Ammianus, says each legionary cohort held a dragon standard (Vegetius 2.13).

Another surprising change is the word that Ammianus uses for the battle cry uttered by some of the Roman soldiers, the *barritus* (Ammianus 16.12.43). This word is just about the same as an earlier word, *barditus*, which Tacitus associated with the German people. At some point in the intervening 300 years or so, this Germanic battle cry came to be associated with the Romans. Thus, though not tactical features, per se, these two, apparently innocuous changes reflect some fundamental changes in the composition and character of the Roman army: the potential influx of people of Sarmatian and Gothic/German origin, along with assorted aspects of their backgrounds. What's more, these influences extend to not only wider aspects of Roman society but, even so, how Romans waged war.

One additional aspect of how the Romans fought that stands out in Ammianus' account of Strasbourg is the Roman employment of cataphracts. They appear not just here but in other parts of the work, especially during combat operations in assorted parts of France. When they come across some Saxons in Gaul (France) sometime later, the Romans employ cataphracts to full effect (Ammianus 28.5.6). We find units of cataphracts all throughout the *Notitia Dignitatum* in both east and west, sometimes styled as cataphracts, as in the *equites catafractarii Albigenses* serving under the Master of Soldiers for Thrace, and sometimes as clibanarii, as in the *equites sagittarii clibanarii* serving under the Master of Horse. Much like the *testudo* mentioned above, cataphracts are depicted as far back as on Trajan's Column, though their precise identity is unclear, a reflection of wider problems with identifying the soldiers on the famed architectural gem. It was in the same century when the column was erected, the second (CE), that some big changes started to emerge in Rome's cavalry. We find a unit of cataphracts on the lower Danube in the middle of the century, though they become even more numerous in the following century (CE). But they were also widely used by the Persians at this time, for we find them in other parts of Ammianus Marcellinus' *Res Gestae*. For instance, while the Romans were trying to flee Persia in the wake of Julian's disastrous invasion, they were attacked by Persian cataphracts (25.6.2). Suffice to say, the implementation of the cataphract was another sign that things had changed in Rome's army.

Shock infantry, the legions of Rome's past, hadn't disappeared, but by the fourth century, they were making much greater use of shock cavalry, at least against select foes. As it happens, we tend to see much more use of these heavily armoured cavalry troops against those opponents less familiar and capable of dealing with them, which tended to be (though wasn't always) those people in the west. The Persians already had a long tradition of employing these kinds of soldiers, as did other groups in the eastern half of the Mediterranean, like the Sarmatians and the Parthians.

THE HUNS

Why did Rome start employing mounted archers and heavy cavalry in the first place? One group seems to have played an outsized role in much of the changes in how Rome fought in late antiquity: the Huns. The Huns burst onto the scene in the late fourth century, when they appear in the works of Ammianus Marcellinus, Eunapius, and Claudian too. It was standard practice in the works of ancient historians writing in the tradition of Herodotus to include ethnographic digressions on foreign and/or exotic peoples. Herodotus did this with the Scythians. Ammianus followed suit, centuries later, with the Huns. While digressions like these contain plenty of valuable material, they often include details that leave a little to be desired. On that note, while there's some truth scattered in Ammianus' detailed ethnographic digression, which comes near the end of his history and in the build-up to his climactic account of the Battle of Adrianople, much of it, like their supposed furrowed cheeks, is questionable. He claims too that they participated in cranial deformation, where they flattened the fronts of their skulls. Fortunately, we have plenty of evidence for their customs and history. We know, for instance, that they hailed from the Altai mountains of Inner Asia, between Mongolia and Kazakhstan. Some argue that they should be connected to the earlier Xiongnu Empire, very active in China against the Han dynasty in last few centuries BCE (third century BCE to first century CE).

In terms of the Roman Empire, so much of the contact between the Romans and steppe peoples took place in the Pontic-Danubian area, in part due to widespread migration between the Pontic Steppe and Danubian basin. Among the many people who moved across the region in antiquity were the Alans, Bastarnae, Carpi, Costoboci, Dacians, Goths, Sarmatians, and Taifali. Greek and Roman writers generally had a negative view of people from the steppes, many of whom were nomadic or semi-nomadic. As – or when (for not all did) – these groups became more closely integrated into wider Mediterranean society, opinions tended to shift, a tendency you can see when you read about the depictions of the Huns that Ammianus gives in the fourth century, Priscus in the fifth, and then Procopius in the sixth.

The fourth century CE is when the Huns entered the Romans' geopolitical sphere. One possible – maybe even plausible – reconstruction, following Ammianus, runs like this. The Huns in Central Asia were forced westwards owing to significant environmental challenges in their traditional homeland, drought in particular. As this mass of Huns – men, women, and children – migrated west, they eventually encountered the Alans, whom they ultimately defeated in battle. In turn, the Alans were pushed up against the neighbouring Goths, who fled further west and south, finally coming upon the outskirts of Roman territory. The Goths pleaded with the Romans to be allowed inside their vast and prosperous empire – in this case, the south bank of the Danube River in what is today Bulgaria. The Romans agreed, on a few conditions, though a Roman governor turned duplicitous, which triggered a major conflict between the two. This culminated in the worst defeat the Romans had faced since Cannae, way back in 216 BCE, when tens of thousands of republican Roman soldiers succumbed to Hannibal and the Carthaginians. In this case, on a hot day in August 378 CE, tens of thousands of Roman soldiers, including the eastern emperor Valens, were crushed by their Gothic allies-turned-foes. The significant losses experienced by the Roman armies in this battle led to the increasing use of non-Romans, like those Goths, because of the recruitment challenges this defeat offered. That, then, is one (probable/possible) early dimension to the movement of the Huns to the west.

As engaging as that tale is, the Huns are probably best known for their later forays in the fifth century under Attila. Aetius, a late Roman general known by some as "the last of the Romans", fought with the Huns against other peoples in Europe, like the Burgundians, in 436. That relationship had soured not long after, and, by 441, the Romans faced simultaneous attacks by the Huns and Persians, which they managed to bring to an end. At this point in time, the Huns were ruled in part by their engaging king, Attila, later conceived of as the scourge of God for the terror he wrought on some Western European populations. In 445, Attila killed his co-ruler, his brother Bleda, and assumed sole rule of the Huns.

There are fierce debates among scholars over the exact character of this Hunnic force: was it a mixed body comprising infantry and cavalry from across Europe and beyond, or was it primarily a Hunnic cavalry force that relied on horse archery and hit-and-run tactics? Whatever the composition and precise character of the army, the Huns eventually ran afoul of Rome, threatening first the eastern empire of Theodosius II (r. 408–450 CE) and later the west, then ruled by Valentinian III (r. 425–455 CE). Early in the fifth century CE, what had once been one empire was now two, an eastern and a western empire. This change was not sudden; rather, it had slowly gathered steam over the course of the fourth century as successive emperors made administrative changes to make the management of such a vast territory more streamlined, particularly in an era of increased foreign threats. To get back to the Huns, the eastern empire was able to pay them off, owing in no small part to the booming economy of the eastern Mediterranean. The west was in a rather more precarious state, and the Hunnic incursions led to war. For some late antique authors and later scholars, this culminated in 451 with the Battle of Catalaunian Plains, fought somewhere in what is now France between the Romans under Aetius and the Huns under Attila. For the later sixth-century Latin writer Jordanes, the outcome, which he describes in epic language, was a Roman victory. Some scholarship has sought to temper Jordanes' boasting, in the odd case going so far as to reframe the battle as a Hunnic victory. Regardless of the outcome of this battle, just a few years later, Attila was dead, and his empire dissolved. In the sixth century, we find Huns fighting in Roman ranks during Justinian's famed conquests of Africa and Italy, perhaps as clear a sign as any of the eventual 'victory' of the Romans in a somewhat long and drown-out period of conflict.

Although I touched on it above, it's worth coming back to one of the big questions surrounding the Huns, namely why they moved into Roman territory in the first place. Students of migration studies have looked at lots of different variables to try to determine the movements of groups of people, big and small, in the ancient world. The remains of burials and their attendant cemeteries have provided some clues, particularly the goods buried with the deceased, which have been used to chart the arrival of new people. The artefacts studied include pottery and metalwork, though also weapons and armour. The results of these studies have been mixed, however, with serious questions raised about whether everyone (or anyone) buried with weapons was a soldier and whether the presence of non-local items really meant the arrival of foreigners. Whereas some have homed in on burial goods, others have looked for evidence of migration in coins. The Goths captured the imperial treasury in the third century at Abritus, on the Danube. The coins were cut up and re-used in other contexts for other purposes. We find them used for arm rings and finger rings and in general as symbols of power in *barbaricum*, or the barbarian world. Others had holes and loops and were defaced in various ways.

As noted earlier, the Huns migrated into eastern, central, and then Western Europe in the first half of late antiquity. The why is more difficult to discern. It might be due to environmental pressures, a refrain that should be familiar to modern readers. Drought afflicted the Altai Mountains of Mongolia in the fourth century. This was the region where the Huns seem to have been from. As a result of this, they pushed west, particularly in the years between 338 and 377. By the 370s, they had reached the Don River, which is the approximate area where they came across the Goths, whom they attacked. In turn, the Goths pushed further west and south, before finally coming up against Roman territory, all of which culminated in Adrianople.

As much as the Huns were a problem for the Romans, they were also a problem for the Persians. There is perhaps no better illustration of this than in the impressive Great Wall of Gorgan, built in northeastern Iran to the southeast corner of the Caspian Sea. In the words of Howard-Johnston (2012: 103), it was "the largest single investment in military infrastructure made by Iran in classical antiquity or the Middle Ages". This wall was constructed in the fifth and/or sixth century and was close to 200 km in length. What's less clear is exactly how many soldiers were stationed along its length. Some have looked at the evidence of its barracks to determine the number of soldiers, whereas others have questioned whether we should see a correlation between the size of the barracks and the number of soldiers, a point which I readily endorse. There's no doubt that some of the bases, rather more fleeting campaign bases, were substantial and potentially able to house massive armies. It's possible that during individual campaigns these bases housed upwards of tens of thousands of soldiers, potentially an entire campaign army. We get hints at the character of some of these armies, including the names of the ranks, from scattered sources like the late antique and medieval Armenian texts. Therein, we read about officers like the *spahbed, marzban*, and *hazarbed*. There were also four big regional commanders. These significant investments in infrastructure, which are finally getting the attention that they deserve, helped to keep Persian territory secure from Hunnic incursions, at least from the Caucasus, for some time. Indeed, just as the Persians weren't the only foe faced by the Romans, so too were the Romans not the only foe faced by the Persians.

HORSE ARCHERY

We can see evidence of the Huns' arrival in Central Europe in some of the burials unearthed in central Poland, especially between the Oder and Vistula rivers. In this context, archaeologists have found isolated burials and stray finds – there had been large cemeteries in use earlier, but they seem to have gone out of use. These more recent isolated burials are the ones associated with the presence of nomadic peoples, like the Huns. Indeed, whether the Huns were wholly or partially a nomadic force remains somewhat unresolved and is tied to arguments about the character of its armies. Getting back to the archaeology, at one particular site, Jakuszowice in Poland, archaeologists have found human remains along with a horse and some impressive grave goods, some of which were gold, some silver. Among these finds was a bow encased in gold. Bows, in general, are hard to find as they're often made with perishable materials, so few survive. Its presence here, in a burial involving a human and a horse, points to the deceased as a nomadic horse archer.

Those archers started to become more widespread in the second and third century (CE). By the sixth century, when Agathias was writing, they were a widespread and important part of Rome's military.

They employed them in many theatres of war – Rome was engaged in wars in the Balkans, North Africa, Italy, and Mesopotamia – though especially Italy, which is where the Battle of Casilinum was fought, between the Romans and Franks, in 554 CE.

Just as at Strasbourg, Agathias comments on the stark differences between the Roman and non-Roman forces, here Frankish. They use axes and spears (Agathias 2.5.4); in fact, he goes into considerable detail about those spears, *angones*, and how they're used in combat, both for throwing and as thrusting weapons. Of note in this discussion of mounted archers, Agathias claims the Franks mostly use infantry, and only limited numbers of cavalry, and even artillery (here, think arrows and more). This is in stark contrast to the Romans, who place their cavalry on the wings and who are equipped with short spears, shields, bow and arrows, and a sword. The Romans have other lightly armed soldiers, including slingers (Agathias 2.8.5).

Agathias spends a good amount of time on the formations and spacing employed by the two sides. He claims the Romans formed a phalanx (Agathias 2.85) – we're to understand this as a tightly packed formation and not a classical Greek phalanx – with a gap for one of their principal allied groups, the Heruls. On the other side, Agathias says the Franks lined up in a wedge formation like a triangular delta, with a compact mass of shields that gave the appearance of a boar's head (Agathias 2.8.8), a description that has puzzled scholars. Besides comments like those on the general shape of the formations, he also gets into how they're to be used, with much attention given to the important role of the Roman army's mounted archers, who are to fire arrows crosswise onto the backs of the enemy.

One of the significant features, at least for many, of Hunnic warriors was their penchant for riding into battle on horseback and their skill at archery. Horse archers were the stock in trade of nomadic armies for a long time. Indeed, at the opposite end of antiquity, the Iron Age, or better the tail end of Archaic Greece, the Scythians were famed for their mounted archers. Archery in general became so closely associated with the Scythian people that classical Athens had a police force that comprised Scythian archers. Although there are good arguments that the Huns weren't entirely nomadic, or at least not for the period under consideration here, late antiquity

FIGURE 6.2 Plate with a Hunting Scene from the Tale of Bahram Gur and Azadeh, Iran, 5th century CE, MET

finds, like the deceased man and horse from Jakuszowice, point to the continued presence of horse-based nomads among the Huns.

Rome's great foe, the Persians, had long been adept at mounted warfare. To that end, there are plenty of silver plates from the Persian Empire, which depict Sasanian warriors/elites on horseback with bows, often engaged in hunting (Figure 6.2). To the uninitiated, then, it might come as a bit of a surprise to find, at the start of the sixth-century historian Procopius' *Wars*, a detailed exposition of the Roman mounted archer. According to Procopius, in this oft-discussed part of this work, the archers of his day were far superior to the archers of Homer's day. We'll never know why Procopius included this comparison exactly, despite all the scholarship on just this topic (and I'm part of the problem), but the fact that he made mounted archers an important part of his big history of Justinian from the beginning deserves our attention.

This was no longer a world where only Rome's neighbours excelled in mounted archery. Rather, this was a staple of Rome's own approach to war. It's not just the preface to Procopius' *Wars* that we find these horse archers. They play a pivotal role in the long and detailed description of the siege of Rome, which took place in 537 and 538, lasted a little more than a year, and involved the besieged "Romans" under Belisarius locked in the city against the Gothic assault. At Casilinum too, mounted archers were being used very effectively by Roman armies in combat.

To some degree, the presence of mounted archers could be attributed to an influx of Hunnic soldiers in Roman armies. Procopius' digression implies that they were more widespread. Indeed, by the end of the sixth century, Maurice (the author of the *Strategikon*, unlikely the emperor himself) could write this about Roman cavalry (Maurice Strat. 1.2.28–32):

> Apart from foreigners, all the younger Romans up to the age of forty must definitely be required to possess bow and quiver, whether they be expert archers or just average. They should possess two lances so as to have a spare at hand in case the first one misses.

Maurice includes all sorts of other comments about wider steppe influences (i.e., not just the Huns). The Avars, a people who entered Roman consciousness in the sixth century, both for good and for bad (they did go to war with each other), also left their mark on Roman soldiers and war-making on some level. He notes: "cavalry lances of the Avar type" (Maurice Strat. 1.2.19), "round neck pieces of the Avar type" (1.2.20), "the horses…should have…breast or neck coverings such as the Avars use" (1.2.35–39), "men's clothing…should be…cut according to the Avar pattern" (1.2.46–47), and "it is well to have tents of the Avar type" (1.2.60–61).

However, arguably the most significant adaptation from the Avars was the stirrup, which gave some mounted soldiers even greater stability on the saddle in combat. Some, in fact, have gone so far as to argue that the lack of a stirrup prevented cavalry from functioning correctly, with them operating as little more than mounted infantry – hence all the examples of soldiers dismounting to fight on foot. This seems to understate the effectiveness of the cavalry used by Parthians, Persians, Scythians, and more. Perhaps the best way to understand the importance of the stirrup is that it allowed those less skilled at riding to fight on horseback more effectively than they would otherwise.

In the end, the people of the steppes had a measurable impact on war-making in the late antique Mediterranean world. Their impact on tactics and troop types across the Roman and Persian Empires was measurable. It even extended to parts further east (China). The steppe peoples provided not only troop types, tactics, and equipment but manpower too. The Romans, for one thing, had Hunnic soldiers by the sixth century. Of course, it wasn't all positive. The Persians were defeated by the Hephthalites in combat in the fifth century. The great wall of Gorgan was built in response to the threat posed by those same Hephthalites in the sixth century. In short, the impact of the people of the steppes on the settled empires of the Mediterranean basin lasted for centuries in manifold ways.

THE LAST GREAT WAR OF ANTIQUITY

We finish with the "Last Great War" in antiquity, waged by the Persians and Romans in the first quarter or so of the seventh century CE. Many have argued, even recently, that the Persians had carried out some major military reforms during the reign of Khusro I, who reigned from 531 to 579. These reforms included the creation of a permanent, standing, cavalry, likely of heavily armed cataphracts. On the other hand, many have commented on how sophisticated the military likely was beforehand. It might not have been a professional military, but it was state-funded. The point is, the Persians were in a good position to take on the Romans, as they had been throughout their history. In fact, ever since the Sasanians overthrew the Arsacids, who had ruled the Parthian Empire for centuries back in the early third century CE, Rome and Persia had been to war on several occasions. We already got a taste of this one chapter ago, when we discussed the exploits of Zenobia and the siege of Dura-Europos. Both of those stories come from the early days of Roman–Persian relations. By the sixth century, the cities of the eastern Roman Empire closer to the frontier were well fortified, with towering fortifications, in part, a response to Persia's proclivity at siege warfare (Figure 6.3). The two states fought several times over the course of that century, with the record perhaps a draw.

FIGURE 6.3 Walls of Halabiye, Syria, 3rd century CE (?), Wikimedia Commons

A long history of conflict is one explanation for why the two went to war again at the end of the sixth century. That said, there are more specific reasons germane to this war: Persia went to war with Rome ostensibly as revenge on the then shahanshah's part, Khusro II (r. 591–628), against the emperor Phocas (r. 602–610) for his coup against Maurice (r. 582–602). However, there were likely a host of other motives, like past grievances and designs on territorial aggrandisement. For the first half of the war at least, the Persians managed to occupy a large swath of Roman territory in the Levant from Syria south to Egypt, some traces of which appear in the Pahlavi papyri produced during the period of Persian rule. Ultimately, thanks to the leadership of Heraclius, who overthrew Phocas and also had to contend with an Avar invasion in East Rome's core, in and around the capital Constantinople, the Romans managed to come back and defeat Persia and in the process regain their lost territory.

The conflict has been the subject of some exciting recent work, with Howard-Johnston's *Last Great War* especially notable. The amount of evidence is also reasonable, with a fair number of ancient accounts, from the poetry of George of Pisidia to the later chronograph of

Theophanes. Although debate has raged on what sort of impact this war had on the occupied territories of the Roman Empire, the fact remains that an entire generation of "Romans" grew up across the Levant under Persian rule. We get hints of this in some of the Pahlavi papyri from Egypt.

Foreign occupation aside, those who first had to face the Persians suffered to a varying degree as well. While some Levantine residents may have little noticed the replacement of some rulers with another, some Persian attacks on Roman sites were demonstrably violent and destructive. In fact, we also have some evidence for this sort of destruction in the case of Jerusalem, where scores of civilians were massacred between the years 610 and 615. Antiochus Strategius, a seventh-century monk of Mar Saba, wrote a sermon on the 614 sack of Jerusalem:

> The Persians however beleaguered the entire city, and surrounded it for the combat; and hourly they questioned the monks in regard to the city, whether God would deliver it or not into their hands. And the first day they asked them the same question afresh. Then the monks consulted one with the other and said: ' If we lie, 'tis evil; but if we tell the truth, woe to us. Rather) whether we tell or whether we conceal the truth, it cannot but be that this city be laid waste. So it is right that we should not conceal the truth.' Then the monks sighed from the depths of their hearts, and smiting themselves on the face, and shedding tears, as if in a flood from their eyes, they replied: 'For our sins God hath delivered us into your hands.'
>
> (tr. Conybeare)

While this passage sets up the anguish felt by certain Christian participants, later Antiochus sought to quantify the suffering by giving figures for the number of persons who perished during the siege.

> For we found in the court of the government 6228 persons. In the cisterns we found of the slain 275 (250) persons. In front of the gates of Holy Sion we found 2270 persons. At the altar of the Holy New 64 we found 600 (290) souls. In the church of St. Sophia we found 477 (369) souls. In the church of Saints Cosmas and Damian we found 2212 (2112) souls. In the Book room 65 of Holy New 70 souls. And we found in the monastery of Holy Anastasis 212 souls. And we found in the market place 38 souls. In front of the Samaritan

temple 66 we found 919 (723) souls. In the lane of St. Kiriakos we found 1449 (1409) souls. And we found on the western side of Holy Sion 196 (197) souls. At the gate Probatike we found 2107 souls. In the passage of St. Jacob we found 308 (1700) souls. In the flesher's row we found 921 souls. And we found at the spring of Siloam 2818 (2318) souls. And we found in the cistern of Mamel 24, 518 souls. In the Gerakomia of the patriarch *e found 318 souls. In the place called the Golden City 1202 souls. In the monastery of Saint John we found 4219 (4250) souls. In the imperial Gerakomia 780 (167) souls. We found on the Mount of Olives 1207 souls. On the steps 69 of the Anastasis we found 300 (83) souls. In the place of Little Assembly we found 202 (102) souls. In the place of Large Assembly we found 317 (417) souls. In the church of Saint Serapion we found 338 souls. We found in front of Holy Golgotha 80 souls. We found in the grottos, fosses, cisterns, gardens, 6917 (6907) souls. At the Tower of David we found 2210. Within the city we found 265 souls Just where the enemy overthrew the wall of the city we found 9809 (1800) souls. And in Jerusalem we buried many others in addition that were massacred by the Persians beside these saints. The total number of all was 66,509 souls...

(tr. Conybeare)

Antiochus' account, by virtue of its detail and concrete data, paints a grim picture of the violence incurred during one phase of the long, drawn-out war. But as plausible as that image is, do we have any independent evidence to corroborate Antiochus' account? As it turns out, we do. On the one hand, archaeologists have uncovered a hoard of 264 gold coins, which date to the conflict. There is also evidence of damage to some of the city walls, including hints at some fire. Also of significance is the discovery of a cave, called the Mamilla Cave, which is connected specifically with the Persian massacre of Christians during war. Therein they found 1388 vertebrae. The victims were relatively young, and their remains differed from those of the nomadic people found nearby. Collectively, even if they do deal with somewhat different circumstances, contexts, and events, this literary and archaeological evidence illuminates much of the human cost of warfare in the ancient Mediterranean world, especially among non-combatants. For all that notions of war and warfare in the ancient world concentrate on the combatants and soldiers who carry out much of the violence, it's always worth keeping in mind the civilians caught up in these conflicts.

As these anecdotes illustrate, Jerusalem (and more places beside) suffered in this conflict. These Roman territories would fall under Persian control for close to a generation, so a number of persons grew up knowing only Persian rulers. Eventually, however, the Roman emperor Heraclius (r. 610–641) turned the tide in Rome's favour and took back this territory. Although, ultimately, Rome could claim victory over Persia, things soon turned against them both. Scholars debate the impact of this war, but Howard-Johnston's assertion that it was the last one from the ancient world is probably not far off the mark. It marks the last time these two historic enemies, Rome and Persia, would meet in combat. This would also mark the last time that Rome would have full possession of the Levant, parts of which they had controlled since the late republic. For as the Romans and Persians were recovering from this long, brutal conflict, a new threat emerged from the Arabian Peninsula, originally led by an enigmatic figure named Muhammad and a growing new religion, Islam.

It was Muhammad's successor, the first caliph, Abu Bakr, who pushed the expansion of Arab forces north into Rome and Persia, and he transformed a series of raids into a larger campaign. His route took him north to Tabuk, and close to what had been the southern terminus of Roman territory, and then upwards to Aqaba. By all accounts, they seem to have followed the spice routes north from Yemen and the Himyarite Kingdom, perhaps in part onwards from Aqaba along the coast and perhaps in part up the west side of the Jordan valley up to the Hauran. By 634, they were in the former capital of Roman Arabia, Bostra (now a UNESCO World Heritage site in southern Syria). In 636, they fought the Roman forces at Yarmuk, in northwest Jordan, in a battle in which the second caliph, Umar ibn al-Khaṭṭāb, defeats Heraclius and Rome. With this victory, the Levant fell into Arab hands, and it would leave Rome after close to 600 years. The Persians would suffer a similar defeat of their own to the Arabs in the same year, the Battle of Qadisiyya, in Mesopotamia (modern Iraq in this case).

Jerusalem fared poorly again, and Sophronius of Jerusalem, a seventh-century patriarch of Jerusalem and later saint, gives some details. Christian items, by this point in a Christian empire important to Romans' very identity and more, were shipped to Constantinople for safe keeping. Heraclius withdrew Roman forces westwards as well. Caesarea, a famed city on the Mediterranean coast, held out for a few years until December of 640 (or early in 641). The Arabs brought 72 siege engines to bear and killed perhaps 7,000 Roman soldiers, whom the commander Mu'awiya made an example of. The third caliph, Uthman ibn Affan, reigned from 644 to 656 CE, and he was from the Umayyad family back in Mecca. His family was one of the only ones to support Muhammad back in 622, the time of the Hijra, Muhammad's migration from Mecca to Medina and the start of the Islamic calendar. Uthman and his family also gave their name to the Umayyad Caliphate, which lasted from 661 to 750 CE and, for me at least, marked the end of the ancient world.

CONCLUSION

It's perhaps fitting to finish this book with a discussion of what's known as the last great war of antiquity. We started with a world where much of the fighting was direct and involved closely arrayed and serried men lined up against similarly deployed foes. Now, we've entered a world where many of the combatants fought on horseback in lightning strikes. Infantry weren't gone, but their role had unquestionably been minimized. That being said, the end point for this book is just as arbitrary as any other potential endpoint. Afterall, for some residents of the Levant, which includes parts of modern Syria, Lebanon, Israel/Palestine, and Jordan, little might have changed, at least initially, in their lives. Many continued to practise Christianity, to speak Arabic, and to depict scenes from Greek myth in their art. Plus, the early Islamic Umayyad armies and many of those of early medieval China employed similar tactics: mounted archers. In other words, whenever we put the beginning of the Medieval period (and it varies significantly from region to region), there was no sudden change in how people fought. Nevertheless, the loss of the Levant, which was followed by the loss of Egypt and later North Africa, makes as fitting a stopping point as any.

CONCLUSION

We've finally reached the end of this short book on ancient warfare. In this introduction to the subject, I've tried to emphasize all the splendours of the varied types of evidence. I want readers to see how we know what we know about how the Greeks, Romans, and their neighbours fought and to appreciate that new discoveries continue to be made which have transformed our understanding of all this. In other words, writing a new introduction is not just a case of rehashing the works of Thucydides or Caesar, as the case may be. New readings of well-known authors do appear often enough, and these provide added nuance to our understanding of warfare. But scholars have also been turning their attention increasingly to little-used authors or texts, like Aristophanes' *Birds*. Aristophanes' *Lysistrata*, by contrast, has attracted no shortage of attention. Sometimes there's a disconnect between those who work primarily on texts and those who work primarily on the material culture. To that end, as someone with more training in the texts, I have included as many good examples of exciting new excavations as possible, whether it be the mass burials from fifth-century BCE Sicily, the shipwrecks off the Egadi Islands, or the siege mines of Dura-Europos.

At the same time, I've tried to centre this book on the experiences of the people who engaged in the fighting and those who fell victim to it. This reflects a longstanding interest of mine in how war impacted regular people (i.e. non-elites). Material like epitaphs and graffiti, though often invisible in the works of some ancient authors, can give readers a glimpse of how war impacted these people, like the fallen soldier Marcus Caelius from the Teutoburg Forest. Along those lines, I have tried to draw attention not just to regular people but to the unexpected from among those groups, like all those nomads who inscribed the graffiti about raids in the Black Desert or the women and children who were besieged by the Romans at Masada. Or the female commanders who led armies both with and against Rome, like Boudica and Zenobia. As much as we like to think it was the male leaders like Cimon or Alexander who led the armies of the ancient world, it's worth remembering that there were exceptions, and very successful ones at that.

Besides all those things I did cover, there are all those subjects I left out. The remit for this book was limited, both by the publisher and by my own skills and experiences. The book was to be relatively short; on the other hand, as a scholar of late antiquity, I had to fit in as much late antique content as possible. To that end, I have tried to split the book into three chunks: a Greek chunk, a Roman chunk, and a late antique chunk. I'll add that I drew a great deal from classes that I've taught here at the University of Winnipeg, over the past sixteen years, and three in particular: Greek Warfare, the Punic Wars, and Romans and Barbarians. The students who got previews of much of this material deserve my thanks.

Despite the end of the ancient world, its impact on warmaking, whether direct or indirect, continued. Two of the most prominent military authors from the ancient world, Vegetius and Maurice, both authors of military manuals, had a huge influence on later military thinking. By some measures, Vegetius was the most popular author from the ancient world in the medieval. Indeed, in the medieval west, there was a relative dearth of new military manuals owing, in no small part, to the popularity of Vegetius. Conversely, in the Byzantine east, views on originality differed from our own, and Byzantine authors regularly adopted and adapted pre-existing texts into new works, such that a mark of a good author was not how new their work was but how well it used pre-existing material. Such was the case with the Leo V's *Tactica*, which was closely modelled on Maurice's *Strategikon*. So, while the ancient world came to an end, by some reckoning, in the seventh century, its legacy lasted for centuries after.

GLOSSARY

Achaemenids The ruling dynasty of Persia between 553 and 330 BCE.

Achilles In the mythical Trojan War, Achilles, a Greek warrior, was widely regarded a s the best fighter on either side (Greek or Trojan).

Adrianople, Battle of Arguably the second worst loss in Roman history, it occurred on August 9, 378 CE, and was fought between the Romans and the Goths.

Agathias One of the last Roman historians, he wrote a continuation of the *Wars* of Procopius set during the reign of Justinian in the late sixth century CE, in Greek.

Alexander III (the Great) Famed Macedonian general and king who conquered the Achaemenid Persian Empire starting in 336 BCE but who died, prematurely, in 323 BCE.

Ammianus Marcellinus Widely regarded as the last great Roman historian to write in Latin, who described events between 96 and 378 CE in his *Res Gestae*, though only his account of the final few decades survives.

Antigonos the One-Eyed A Macedonian general and one of the successors of Alexander the Great, he went on to control much of the Greek world following Alexander's death in the fourth century BCE.

Appian Historian, who wrote in Greek, who was active in the second century CE and wrote accounts of Rome's foreign wars and civil wars.

Apuleius A North African Latin author and neo-Platonist philosopher who is perhaps best known for his *Metamorphoses* or *Golden Ass*, in which the main character is transformed into a donkey and goes on a series of adventures – and misadventures.

Aristophanes Arguably Athens' best known comedic playwright, Aristophanes was active in the fifth century BCE and wrote several plays, including *Birds*, *Lysistrata*, *Peace*, and more besides, not all of which survive.

Asymmetric warfare Warfare waged between two parties in which one has decided advantages, whether in terms of capabilities, strategy, tactics, or something else, and which might involve the use of atypical tactics.

Attila Hunnic warlord who managed to expand Hunnic territory, if briefly, westwards into central Europe in the fifth century CE, so wreaking havoc on what was left of Roman territory in the process, even if his impact was fleeting.

Augustus By most measures Rome's first emperor (d. 14 CE), Augustus is also remembered by both ancients and moderns alike as one of its best due, in large part, to the significant mark he left on the city of Rome and its empire.

Auxiliaries (Roman) Rome's allied soldiers who, in the imperial era, would be divided up either into infantry cohorts (*cohortes*), which usually numbered about 500 men, and cavalry wings (*alae*), which usually numbered about the same. Over time, these units were increasingly composed of Roman citizens.

Babatha Jewish woman who lived in and around the southern coast of the Dead Sea in the late first and early second century CE, first as a resident of the Nabataean kingdom, later the Roman province of Arabia. A well-off landowner, while fleeing unrest during the Bar Kochkba revolt, she left behind a cache of papyri that provides invaluable insight into life in this corner of the empire.

Baecula, Battle of Battle fought between the Romans and Carthaginians in the Second Punic War in 208 BCE in southern Spain, which the Romans won. The battle is significant, in large part (in my eyes) owing to the remarkable finds recovered during excavations.

Barbaricum The Latin name given to the lands beyond Roman territory, primarily in Europe, but generally applicable empire-wide, owing to the presence of barbarians (i.e. non-Romans).

Bronze Age A period in human development in which the primary (and for humans first) metal used to make tools was bronze and which runs from around 3500 BCE down to 1200 BCE, though it is not the same across the globe.

Caesar, Julius One of Rome's most famous generals, Caesar fought off several rivals to become emperor in all but name in the first century BCE, along the way conquering Gaul (among other things), which he described in his *Bellum Gallicum* (one of a few works he wrote). He was famously assassinated in 44 BCE on the Ides of March (March 15th).

Cannae, Battle of Rome's most famous defeat came in this battle with Hannibal and the Carthaginians in 216 BCE in the Second Punic War. On this day, the Romans lost many tens of thousands of soldiers, and their very existence, by some measures, seemed in doubt in the immediate aftermath.

Carthaginians Based in modern Tunisia, for in the first millennium BCE, they were the most powerful entity in the western Mediterranean. They eventually expanded northwards into Sicily and Spain and east and west across north Africa. Probably (or possibly) settled by people from the Levant, they fought Rome in three wars between 264 BCE and 146 BCE, losing each one.

Casilinum, Battle of Battle which was fought between the Romans and the Franks and their allies in the aftermath of Rome's conquest of Italy, in 554 CE, which the Romans won, and which was described by the historian Agathias.

Cassius Dio Roman historian who wrote in Greek and who provided a long and detailed history of Rome from the republican period right up to his own day in the third century CE. His history survives only in part, with many significant chunks only extant thanks to later Byzantine excerpts and summaries.

Catalaunian Plains, Battle of A celebrated battle between the Romans and their allies and the Huns and their allies in 451 CE, which the Romans won, though its impact on wider history is now disputed.

Cataphracts In the ancient Mediterranean world, cataphracts were heavily armoured cavalry, initially found amongst the Parthians, Sasanians, and Sarmatians, though some are later found in Roman armies.

Chaeronea, Battle of Battle which was fought between allied Greek city states and Macedon and which ended Greek independence in 338 BCE and ushered in a period of Macedonian supremacy in the Greek world and beyond.

Claudia Severa The literate wife of a Roman commander, active in the late first and early second century CE, based in the north of England, best known for the birthday invitation she sent to her friend Sulpicia Lepidina, wife of the commander at Vindolanda.

Column of Trajan A nearly 40-metre-tall column found in Rome which contains illustrations – sculptural friezes – of Rome's two Dacian wars fought in the early second century CE.

Combined Arms The integrated use of the varied components of an army or military, like infantry, cavalry, and artillery in any context, ancient, medieval, or modern.

Corvus, crow A somewhat mysterious tool developed by the Romans used to aid the boarding of Carthaginian ships during the First Punic War, it probably involved some sort of ramp which could latch on to enemy ships.

Dacian Wars Two wars, fought back-to-back in the early second century CE (101–102, 105–106 CE), between Rome and Dacia, in large part in response to earlier Dacian aggression during the reign of Domitian (d. 96 CE). In the end, Dacia was defeated and became the Roman province of Dacia (roughly modern Romania).

Darius III The last Achaemenid Persian king, he was on the throne when Alexander conquered the Persian Empire in the fourth century BCE.

Decebalus The Dacian king who was defeated by the Romans in the two Dacian wars and who took his own life rather than fall into Roman captivity in a scene illustrated on Trajan's Column.

Demetius the Besieger (Macedonian King) The son of Antigonos the one-eyed, this Macedonian king is, for our purposes, most important for his contributions to siege warfare, which, though fleeting, included things like the creation of the monstrous *helepolis*, an enormous mobile siege tower.

Diploma (Roman military) A diploma (the name is modern) was a citizenship certificate given to Roman soldiers, primarily auxiliaries, who could gain this benefit upon retirement. Many hundreds survive in whole or in part from across the Roman empire.

Dromedarii **(camel-riders)** Camel cavalry used sparingly by the Romans and others across the Mediterranean world. The term, however, is Latin (i.e. Roman).

Dura-Europos In its final period of occupation, a Roman city on the Euphrates that was besieged and taken by the Sasanians in the 250s CE, it is best known for the spectacular finds left behind after its capture, like many hundreds of papyri, the equipment of Roman and Persian soldiers and their animals, and even some impressive frescoes on its buildings.

Egadi/*Aegates* Islands, Battle of A naval battle fought by Rome and Carthage that came near the end of the First Punic War in 241 BCE and that resulted in a Roman victory. This battle is best known now for the spectacular remains left behind by the two sides, which were found at the bottom of the Mediterranean Sea off the coast of Sicily.

Epaminondas Theban general and politician best known for his role in helping bringing Thebes to prominence in the fourth century BCE, he ultimately died in battle at Mantinea in 362 BCE despite Thebes' coalition managing to defeat the Spartans.

Euripides One of Classical Greece's three most celebrated tragic playwrights, active in the fifth century BCE, and best known for his plays like the *Electra*, the *Suppliants*, and many more.

Eutropius Fourth-century Roman (Latin) author of an abbreviated history of Rome, the *Brevarium*.

***Face of Battle* (John Keegan)** This book by John Keegan is well regarded in military history for putting the emphasis on the rank-and-file and their experiences when analysing combat. Its approach was later applied to other areas like ancient military history.

Gorgan, Great Wall of Large wall constructed by the Sasanians primarily in the sixth century CE in the Caucasus to the east of the Caspian Sea, which is nearly 200 km in length and which was meant to keep their steppe neighbours in check.

Goths A central European (or eastern European or even central Asian) people of unknown origins who migrated into Roman territory in late antiquity and who sometimes went to war against Rome, as they did, for example, in the conflict that culminated in the Battle of Adrianople in 378 CE. Some Goths went on to establish kingdoms of their own, like Theoderic and the Ostrogothic Kingdom in Italy (sixth century CE).

Hannibal One of the greatest generals from the ancient world, the Carthaginian general managed to push Rome to the brink in the Second Punic War before ultimately being undermined by a lack of Carthaginian support and an improvement in Rome's fortunes.

Helots Indentured residents of Laconia and Messenia in the Peloponnesus whose efforts, primarily in agriculture, supported Sparta's elite citizens, the Spartiates.

Heraclius Roman emperor at the end of antiquity (d. 641 CE), he first managed to fight back against Persia in the "Last Great War" of antiquity and reclaim all lost land by 628 CE before succumbing to the advancing Muslim forces inspired by Muhammad who claimed a decisive victory at Yarmuk (in Jordan) in 636 CE.

Herodotus The "father of history," Herodotus described the wars waged by the Greeks and Persians in the early fifth century BCE. While his account is filled with many astonishing stories, many of the miraculous elements are proving to be increasingly accurate through the passage of time.

Hittites A people from Anatolia who rose to prominence in the Bronze Age and who feature in what few records we have of a potential historical conflict involving Wilusa (Troy) from the late twelfth century BCE.

Hoplite Heavily armoured infantry soldier from the Archaic and Classical Greek world, usually associated with a particular panoply, the term came to be associated with heavy infantry in general.

Homer The name associated with two of the most famous works of literature from any period of human history: the epic poems the *Iliad* and the *Odyssey*. The former, (slightly) more relevant to this book, details a few weeks in the ten-year-long Trojan War from the end of the Bronze Age. Homer himself, or the poems associated with him, are usually dated to the eighth or even seventh centuries BCE, even if the events they described are set in the twelfth century BCE.

Horse archer Cavalry soldiers who focus on archery.

Huns Originally, if not entirely, nomadic and semi-nomadic steppe people from central Asia who eventually warred against Rome (and Persia) but who eventually served as valuable soldiers in Rome's military.

Jewish War (First/Great) The war fought between the Romans and Judeans in the first century CE (66–73 CE) in significant parts of the modern Levant. The Romans were victorious with major victories coming in the sieges of Jerusalem and Masada, both of which are described by Josephus.

Josephus Jewish author who also fought against Rome during the First Jewish War, he later befriended the Flavians and wrote a detailed history of the war, in Greek (*The Jewish War*).

Legion The best known of Rome's military units, from the republican to the imperial era, it numbered close to 5000 citizen soldiers and was composed primarily of infantry. In late antiquity, the number of legions increased but their size decreased to between 1000 and 1500 men.

Leuctra, Battle of Battle which was fought between Thebes and its allies and Sparta and its allies in 371 BCE and which ushered in a brief period of Theban dominance in Greece following Thebes' victory (in this battle).

Linear B Term which is used to describe the script used for the Greek used by the Mycenaeans in the Bronze Age and which survives in several tablets from that period.

Marathon, Battle of A battle which was fought in 490 BCE between Athens and its allies against the Achaemenid Persians and which was a major Greek victory.

Marcus Caelius One of the fallen from the Battle of the Teutoburg Forest. His family left behind a tombstone commemorating his life.

Maurice (pseudo, author) Name given to the author of the *Strategikon*, the best regarded Byzantine (late Roman) military manual, which was composed in the late sixth century CE and which provides an accurate account of warfare, particularly involving cavalry, from the end of antiquity.

Mons Graupius, Battle of Battle which was fought between the Romans under Agricola, father-in-law of Tacitus (the historian), and the indigenous Caledonian people then living in Scotland, in 83 or 84 CE, and which the Romans won.

Mycenae Greek city in the Peloponnesus, Mycenae reached prominence in the Bronze Age and features regularly in the Greek myths surrounding Trojan War thanks, in large part, to the significant role played by its king, Agamemnon.

Myrmidons The soldiers led by Achilles in the Trojan War.

Nabataea/Nabataeans Ancient kingdom occupying much of modern Jordan and parts of northern Saudi Arabia, southern Syria, and parts of Israel/Palestine, it was centred on its capital Petra. Its wealth was driven from its extensive trade networks, though it ultimately succumbed to Roman expansion and became the Roman province of Arabia.

Notitia Dignitatum A late fourth- and early fifth-century CE late Roman list (in Latin) of offices, with one list comprising civil and military ranks for the western empire, the other the same sorts of information for the eastern empire.

Othismos The literal or figurative shove (perhaps akin to a rugby scrum) that accompanied the clashing of two phalanxes in Archaic and Classical Greek warfare, its existence is the subject of fierce debate.

Pahlavi (papyri) Middle Persian, or Pahlavi, was the primary literary language used by the Sasanian Persians, and it appears in many papyri from Egypt that date to the Sasanian occupation in the seventh century CE.

Palmyra At its peak, Palmyra was an independent city-state that was allied to Rome found in modern Syria and that was famed for its trading network and its third-century queen, Zenobia, who fought a war against Rome during a period of increased tension.

Parthians Originally from around the Caucasus, the Parthians (and Arsacid dynasty in particular) conquered the Seleucids, so forming a Persian empire of their own beginning in the third century BCE. They were eventually overthrown by the Sasanians in the third century CE (224 CE) after successive defeats at the hands of the Romans.

Paterfamilias In Roman society, the *paterfamilias* was the head of the Roman household.

Peloponnesian War One of the best-known wars from Greek antiquity, this war was fought between Athens and its allies and Sparta and its allies from 431–404 BCE, with Sparta ultimately emerging as the victor. The war itself is described in detail by Thucydides, even though his *History* ends before the war finished.

Pericles A famous Athenian statesman who rose to prominence in the 450s BCE and who played a significant role in Athens' building programme in the 440s and 430s BCE. He died of plague (Athenian) long before the Peloponnesian War ended in 429 BCE.

Periokoi Those who lived "round about". Though in the context of Sparta they were recognized as full-fledged Spartans (Lacedaemonians) and served in the military, they lacked the ability to participate fully in running the state.

Phalanx Tightly packed formation composed of hoplites usually associated with the armies of the Greek city-states of the Archaic and Classical periods, the term also came to be used by historians working in Greek to describe any generic, tightly organized battle formation.

Philip II One of Macedon's most famous kings, he is credited with transforming their military and ushering in many of the changes that enabled Alexander's later conquests, like the phalanxes filled with sarissa-bearing professional soldiers.

Polybius Greek historian living during the second century BCE who became a prisoner of the Romans, befriended the Scipiones, and described Rome's rise, particularly during the Punic Wars.

Pompeii Italian city (in the Bay of Naples) which was buried by the eruption of Mt. Vesuvius in 79 CE and which, as a result, has provided remarkable insight into daily life in the Roman world.

Procopius Sixth-century CE historian who described the wars waged by Justinian in the *Wars* but who also wrote two other works: the panegyrical *Buildings* and the biting invective known as the *Secret History*.

Ptolemies The ruling dynasty in Egypt from a few years after the death of Alexander the Great in 305 BCE down to the death of Cleopatra VII in 30 BCE, Ptolemies is named after Alexander's general Ptolemy, who became satrap of Egypt in 323 BCE.

PTSD Post-traumatic stress disorder, in the context of this book, often refers to the psychological trauma experienced by soldiers in the aftermath of combat, though it could just as well apply to all those impacted by war in the ancient world. Some, however, question its prevalence in the ancient world.

Punic Wars Three wars fought between Rome and Carthage, with Rome successful in each case. The first was fought between 264 and 241 BCE, the second 218 to 201 BCE, and the third between 149 and 146 BCE.

Qadisiyya, Battle of The battle between the Sasanians and Muslims in Iraq that brought an end to the Sasanian dynasty in 636 CE.

Sacred Band An elite heavy infantry unit of, by some measures, professional soldiers at Thebes comprising pairs of lovers and numbering 300 men.

Safaitic Name of the script (the language is ancient North Arabian) used in many thousands of graffiti inscribed by pastoral nomads in the Black Desert (Syria, Jordan, Saudi Arabia) and environs in the first few centuries CE.

Sasanians The Persian Empire that succeeded the Parthians, led by the House of Sasan, and that for four centuries matched the Romans and fought them regularly.

Scipio (Africanus) Roman mid-republican general who fought off Hannibal and defeated the Carthaginians at Zama in 202 BCE, hence the epithet Africanus.

Scythians Nomadic or semi-nomadic people, at least originally, from the Eurasian steppe, who over time became more sedentary. They might have served, in part, as the inspiration for the later Amazons due to the presence of grave sites of both male and female warriors.

Septimius Severus Founder of the Severan dynasty, this soldier emperor (d. 211 CE) had success militarily against the Parthians and increased the pay and position of Rome's soldiers.

Shapur I (King, *Shahanshah*) First Sasanian Persian king to take the title *shahanshah* (d. 270 CE), who also, famously, captured the Roman emperor, Valerian.

Shapur II (King, *Shahanshah*, the Great) One of Sasanian Persia's most successful kings (d. 379 CE), who ruled in the fourth century CE and who successfully fended off Julian's invasion.

Single combat One-on-one battles, often fought before regular fighting began, in open battle, or potentially in the course of a siege.

Sophocles One of Classical Athens' three great tragedians, active in the fifth century BCE, who wrote plays such as *Antigone*, *Electra*, and *Oedipus Rex*.

Spartiates Spartiates were full elite citizens at Sparta and members of the ruling class.

Tacitus One of the most famous of Roman Latin historians, who was active in the late first and early second century CE, he is the author of at least four works: the *Agricola*, the *Annals*, the *Germania*, and the *Histories*.

Testudo Roman formation formed by locking shields together to create something that looked like a tortoise shell, hence the English meaning of *testudo*, tortoise.

Teutoburg Forest, Battle of Significant defeat suffered by the Romans at the hands of the Cherusci, erstwhile allies, in 9 CE, which resulted in the loss of three legions and the end of Roman expansion into Germany.

Thermopylae, Battle of Battle fought between Xerxes I of Persia and Leonidas I of Sparta and their Greek allies in 480 BCE at a narrow pass near some hot springs. The Persians won the battle, but the Spartans and their allies were long remembered for their bravery.

Thucydides By most accounts, the best Greek historian, he established the war monograph by means of his vividly written *History of the Peloponnesian War* documenting said conflict.

Trajan Widely regarded, by ancient Romans, as one of its two best emperors (the other being Augustus), Trajan (r. 98–117 CE) conquered Dacia in the early second century CE in addition to Parthia, though his success there was fleeting.

Trireme An ancient kind of boat used in the ancient Mediterranean that got its name from its three rows of oars.

Trojan War Legendary war between the Greeks and Trojans which was said to have been fought in the late twelfth century BCE and which ultimately resulted in a Greek victory. This war has been the subject of countless works of literature, art, and much more besides. The earliest, and perhaps best known, of these works is Homer's *Iliad*.

Tyrtaeus Spartan elegiac poet writing in the seventh century BCE, whose work survives only in part.

Varus, Quinctilius Roman general who was ambushed along with his legions while campaigning in what is now Germany in 9 CE.

Vegetius One of the most popular authors from the ancient world in the Medieval and Early Modern eras, Vegetius wrote the *Epitoma Rei Militaris*, a handbook detailing how to reform the Roman military in the fifth century CE.

Vindolanda Site in northern England, just to the south of Hadrian's Wall, famed for its spectacular finds, like thousands of shoes and hundreds of wooden tablets.

Western Way of War The belief, largely discredited, that there is a distinctive means of waging war in the western hemisphere which entails open and direct warfare.

Xenophon Greek author, writing in the late fifth to early fourth century BCE, of several works, including the *Anabasis*, a firsthand account of his escape from Persian territory with thousands of other Greek mercenaries following defeat during an attempted usurpation.

Xiongnu A confederation of nomadic and semi-nomadic people from the Eurasian steppe in Asia who regularly interacted with the Chinese (including the Han Dynasty) and might be connected with the later Huns.

Yarmuk, Battle of This battle, won by the Rashidun Caliphate in 636 CE, ended Roman rule in the Levant at the end of antiquity.

Zama, Battle of This battle, won by the Romans against the Carthaginians in 202 BCE, brought the Second Punic War to an end.

FURTHER READING

Scholarship on ancient warfare is some of the most voluminous out there, fuelled in part by the incredible demand for work on the subject by the general public, and this little book is a good example of this. Although the select bibliography that I included below might seem to be extensive, it provides only the barest of samples of this vast material. Obviously, a little book like this can't hope to include all works published on a subject like this. For one thing, tracking them all down is likely beyond the scope of even the most seasoned scholar. For another thing, I've come to this book as a specialist on imperial Roman and late antique military things. This didn't mean that the warfare of the Greek and republican worlds was unknown territory to me; rather, I just didn't know it (and still don't) to the same degree that the specialists named below would. One other point before I get into some recommendations. Despite the prevalence of scholarship in English, the discipline (Classics and/or ancient history) is international, and a huge body of material has been published in other languages, like French, German, and Italian, and much more besides. For example, some of the most exciting research on Roman republican era warfare has been carried out by archaeologists working on shipwrecks off Sicily connected to the First Punic War and Spanish sites connected to the Second Punic War. I would encourage any of those in the early stages of an academic career coming at this with English as their first language to do their best to get some grasp of at least a couple of these other languages. On to the suggestions.

Thanks to the proliferation of companions and handbooks from a range of publishers, like Brill/de Gruyter, Cambridge University Press, Oxford University Press, Routledge, and Wiley, there are a few relevant volumes on related topics. For instance, Heckel (2021) and others edited a volume on Greek warfare, and Erdkamp (2007) edited a volume on the Roman army, both published by Wiley. Oxford published a handbook that covers both the Greek and Roman worlds (Campbell and Trite 2013). Cambridge, on the other hand, has published a handful of collected volumes on specific time periods covered by this book, like their companion to the Archaic Greece (Shapiro, listed with Krentz 2007), the Hellenistic world (Bugh, listed with Bugh 2006), or the Age of Attila (Maas 2015). Although the books will be priced out of the range of most, the volumes published (and forthcoming) in Brill/de Gruyter's series "Warfare in the Ancient Mediterranean World" are full of useful material. Just a few are listed below, like Konijnendijk and others' (2021) book on land warfare beyond the phalanx, Kvapil and Shelton's (2023) book on Bronze Age warfare, Armstrong and Trundle's (2019) book on sieges, or my and Mark Hebblewhite's (2022) book on bodyguards. Other volumes in the series cover everything from war in ancient Iran and war in the ancient world on film, to military defeats and logistics. Plus, new volumes continue to appear, and each one tends to include both new and established scholars and a wide range of diverse subjects. On the subject of useful series, Oxford has one entitled "Women in Antiquity", which contains well-written, up-to-date, and informed treatments of leading women, like Gillespie's (2018) book on Boudica or Andrade's (2018) on Zenobia. More recently, Greene and Brice's (2024) book explores the role of women in Roman warfare more broadly.

For those looking to delve more deeply into the archaeology of warfare, there is no shortage of good papers and books on the subject. Dura-Europos in Syria, discussed at a few points in this book, has been the subject of several important studies, particularly recently. Simon James has published book-length reports (James 2004) and studies (James 2019) on the finds as well as many shorter contributions. Baird wrote both a short introduction (2018) and a more detailed study of its remarkable houses (2014). More recently – and here I stray outside the world of archaeology – Iovine (2023) has published all the military papyri from Dura. Shifting to the Greek world, a number of recent studies examined the osteological remains from Himera, connected to the war fought between Sicily and Carthage (Kyle et al. 2018). To my mind, they highlight some of the potential of DNA evidence, which to this point has proven only limited for the subject of ancient warfare owing in large part to a limited body of material to work with. Liston's (2020) work on the remains from Chaeronea are eye-opening and have been used with great profit to reveal not only some of the experiences of the victims' last moments but also how the battle was fought (Sears and Willekes 2016).

There are many great books on Greek warfare. For a good, concise overview, Sears' (2019) introduction is well worth reading. Two edited collections investigate the hoplite battle experience from a variety of perspectives. Hanson's (1991) older but still useful book along with Kagan and Viggiano's (2013) more recent one cover topics like the brutality of the battle to the types of equipment the soldiers used. There are also plenty of chapters between the two on the origins of the hoplites. For more wide-ranging overviews of Greek warfare, Van Wees' (2004) book is a standout, though Rawlings' (2007) is also worth reading. Konijnendijk's (2018) book on classical Greek tactics, building on the work of scholars like Echeverría, reframed the debate on the origins of the phalanx, pushing it forward to the classical era (i.e. after the Persian invasions of mainland Greece). Some books look at particular aspects of Greek warfare, like Alexander's logistics (Engels 1978) or Xenophon's march of the 10,000 (Lee 2007). There are also studies of the psychology and experience of warfare, before, during, and after war (Tritle 2000, Crowley 2012, Rees 2022), or individual conflicts, like the Peloponnesian war (Tritle 2010, Roberts 2019). See too the exhibition and catalogue from Chaeronea exhibition at the Cycladic Museum in Athens (Iossif and Fappas 2024).

Warfare in ancient Rome is also well-served. The best, recent, overview of warfare across the Roman world is Lee's (2020) small book. Its breadth of coverage, both chronologically and thematically, helps make it standout. On the subject of wide-ranging overviews of war and Rome, Bishop and Coulston's (2006) book on Roman military equipment is also noteworthy. It's been through a few editions, with a new, updated one not far off – perhaps it will be available by the time this book sees the light of day. I also wrote an introduction to the Roman military in the imperial era, aimed at university students and a general audience, which frames the military through the perspective of three historical soldiers (Whately 2021a). There are studies of specific eras of Roman history. Armstrong's (2016a) first monograph focuses on the Roman army/ies of early Rome (up to the early fourth century BCE and the sack of Rome), while his latest book (2025) charts the rise of Rome over that same period. Erdkamp (1998), Taylor (2020), and Pearson (2021), among others, tackle aspects of the republican era armies. Goldsworthy (1996), Gilliver (1999), and Le Bohec (2000) look at aspects of the imperial era armies. For late antiquity, among the many standouts, there are the books by Elton (1996), Nicasie (1998), Richardot (2005), and Le Bohec (2006). Petitjean's (2022) book on Roman cavalry covers the gamut of Roman history from the republican age through the reign of Justinian. The end of antiquity, the reign of Justinian in particular, has a few standalone studies, like Ravegnani's (1988, 2004), Heather's (2018), Koehn's (2018), and Whitby's (2021). There are even studies of individual ranks or units, like Bingham's (2013) book on the praetorian guard (there are more now) or Emion's (2023) book on the protectors. We also have plenty of books on individual conflicts, like the Punic Wars (Fronda 2010, Hoyos 2015), the Jewish War (Mason 2016), Rome's Gothic wars (Kulikowski 2006), or Rome's later wars with Persia (Whitby 1988, Greatrex 1998, Howard-Johnston 2021).

Several studies approach combat more generally, that is not specifically Greek or specifically Roman. Though not specifically about battle in the ancient world, Keegan's (1976) landmark study paved the way for all sorts of research and launched the now ubiquitous "face of battle" approach to ancient combat. His book influenced some later papers and books, like Hanson's (1989) on the Greek experience and Goldsworthy's (1996), Sabin's (1996, 2000), Daly's (2000), and Lenski's (2007) on the Roman. Partially as a response to this, Lendon's (2005) eminently readable book on battle looks at the relationship between combat and culture in the Greek and Roman worlds. My own little book (Whately 2021b), aimed at a general audience, tries to apply a sensory approach to ancient combat (i.e. framed around how one's senses were impacted by combat), though many readers will find that it bears many of the hallmarks of Keegan's face of battle. Some scholarship uses some of the approaches adopted by those looking at contemporary armies. One recent edited volume looks at how unit cohesion, how units stay and work together, impacted ancient armies and how they made war (Hall et al. 2023). Wrightson's (2019) monograph examines how combined arms, how the different components in a military work together, impacted how Greek armies fought.

The previous survey gives only a glimpse of some of the vast scholarship out there. Finally, the items listed below informed my discussion in the pages above, some more than others. As I've already implied, however, the literature is vast, and so it represents only a small fraction of what's out there.

All translations quoted in the pages above are drawn from the most common, freely available versions found online on sites like Perseus and Lacus Curtius, unless otherwise stated. We are fortunate to live in an age when the works of many Greek and Roman authors are now freely available and easily accessible.

SELECTED BIBLIOGRAPHY

Adams, C. 1995. "Supplying the Roman Army: O. Petr. 245," *ZPE* 109: 119–126.

Adamson, G. 2012. "Letter from a Soldier in Pannonia," *BASP* 49: 79–94.

Adler, E. 2011. *Valorizing the Barbarians*. Austin: Texas University Press.

Allason-Jones, L. 1999. "Woman and the Roman Army in Britain," in A. Goldsworthy and I. Haynes (eds.), *The Roman Army as Community*. Portsmouth, RI: Journal of Roman Archaeology, pp. 41–51.

Allison, P. 2011. "Soldiers' Families in the Early Roman Empire," in B. Rawson (ed.), *A Companion to Families in the Greek and Roman Worlds*. Malden, MA: Wiley, pp. 161–182.

Allison, P. 2013. *People and Spaces in Roman Military Bases*. Cambridge, UK: Cambridge University Press.

Allyón-Martin, R., González, J., and J. Rodríguez. 2019. "Olive Oil at the Border of the Roman Empire. Stamps on Baetican Dressel 20 Found on the Tyne-Solway Isthmus," *Marburger Beiträge zur antiken Handels-, Wirtschafts- und Sozialgeschichte* 36: 167–215.

Alofs, E. 2014a. "Studies on Mounted Warfare in Asia I," *War in History* 21: 423–444.

Alofs, E. 2014b. "Studies on Mounted Warfare in Asia II," *War in History* 22: 4–27.

Alofs, E. 2015a. "Studies on Mounted Warfare in Asia III," *War in History* 22: 132–154.

Alofs, E. 2015b. "Studies on Mounted Warfare in Asia IV," *War in History* 22: 275–297.

Alston, R. 1994. "Roman Military Pay from Caesar to Diocletian," *JRS* 84: 113–123.

Alston, R. 1995. *Soldier and Society in Roman Egypt*. London: Routledge.

Anders, A. 2015. "The Face of Roman Skirmishing," *Historia* 64: 263–300.

Andrade, N. 2018. *Zenobia*. Oxford/New York: Oxford University Press.

Andrete, G., Bartell, S., and A. Aldrete. 2013. *Reconstructing Ancient Linen Body Armor*. Baltimore: Johns Hopkins University Press.

Anson, E. 2010. "The General's Pre-Battle Exhortation in Graeco-Roman Warfare," *G & R* 57: 304–318.

Armstrong, J. 2016a. *War and Society in Early Rome: From Warlords to Generals*. Cambridge, UK: Cambridge University Press.

Armstrong, J.(ed.). 2016b. *Circum Mare: Themes in Ancient Warfare*. Leiden: Brill.

Armstrong, J. 2025. *Children of Mars. The Origins of Rome's Empire*. Oxford/New York: Oxford University Press.

Armstrong, J., and M. Fronda (eds.). 2020. *Romans at War. Soldiers, Citizens, and Society in the Roman Republic*. London: Routledge.

Armstrong, J., and M. Trundle (eds.). 2019. *Brill's Companion to Sieges in the Ancient Mediterranean*. Leiden: Brill.

Arnould, D. 1981. *Guerre et paix dans le poésie grecque: De Callinos à Pindare*. New York: Arno Press.

Atkinson, J., and R. Hendriks. 2021. "The Skull of Philip II of Macedon and the Mind of His Assassin," *Acta Classica* 64: 29–47.

Avni, G. 2010. *The Byzantine-Islamic Transition in Palestine*. Oxford: Oxford University Press.

Azarnouche, S., and M. Petitjean. 2022. "Sasanian Warriors in Context: Historical and Religious Commentary on a Middle Persian Chapter on Artēštārān (Dēnkard VIII.26)," *HiMA* 11: 331–384.

Baird, J. 2014. *The Inner Lives of Ancient Houses: An Archaeology of Dura-Europos*. Oxford: Oxford University Press.

Baird, J. 2018. *Dura-Europos*. London: Bloomsbury.

Baitinger, H. 2019. "Commemoration of War in Archaic and Classical Greece. Battlefields, Tombs and Sanctuaries," in Giangiulio et al. (2019), pp. 131–145.

Baker, G. 2020. *Spare No One*. Lanham, MD: Rowman and Littlefield.

Ball, J. 2014. "Small Finds and Roman Battlefields: The Process and Impact of Post-Battle Looting," in H. Platts, J. Pearce, C. Barron, J. Lundock, and J. Yoo (eds.), *TRAC 2013: Proceedings of the Twenty-Third Annual Theoretical Roman Archaeology Conference, King's College, London*. Oxford: Oxbow, pp. 90–104.

Ball, J. 2016. *Collecting the Field: A Methodological Reassessment of Greek and Roman Battlefield Archaeology*. PhD dissertation, University of Liverpool.

Barber, C. 2020. "Uncovering a "Lost Generation" in the senate: Demography and the Hannibalic War," in Armstrong and Fronda (2020), pp. 154–170.

Bartsiokas, A., Arsuaga, J.-L., Santaos, E., and A. Gómez-Olivencia. 2015. "The Lameness of King Philip II and Royal Tomb I at Vergina," *PNAS* 112: 9844–9848.

Batty, R. 2007. *Rome and the Nomads. The Pontic-Danubian Realm in Antiquity*. Oxford: Oxford University Press.

Beard, M. 2007. *The Roman Triumph*. Cambridge, MA: Harvard University Press.

Beckmann, M. 2011. *The Column of Marcus Aurelius*. Chapel Hill: University of North Carolina Press.

Bellón, J. P., Rueda, C., Lechuga, M. A., and María Isabel Moreno. 2016. "An Archaeological Analysis of a Battlefield of the Second Punic War: The Camps of the Battle of Baecula," *JRA* 29: 73–104.

Bellón Ruiz, J. P., Rueda Galán, C., Lechuga Chica, M. A., Rodríguez, R. A., and Molinos, M. M. 2017. "Archaeological Methodology Applied to the Analysis of Battlefields and Military Camps of the Second Punic War: Baecula," *Quarternary International* 435: 81–97.

Bellucci, N., and L. Bortolussi. 2016. "Thetati in the Roman Military Papyri: An Inquiry on Soldiers Killed in Battle," *Aegyptus* 94: 75–82.

Ben-Ami, D., Tchekhanovets, Y., and G. Bijovsky. 2010. "New Archaeological and Numismatic Evidence for the Persian Destruction of Jerusalem in 614 CE," *Israel Exploration Journal* 60: 204–221.

Bergmann, B. 2019. "Beyond Victory and Defeat. Commemorating Battles prior to the Persian Wars," in Giangiulio et al. (2019), pp. 111–129.

Bettalli, Marco. 2011. "Guerre tra polemologi: Dodici anni di studi sulla guerra nel mondo greco antico, 1998–2009." *Quaderni di Storia* 73: 235–308.

Bingham, S. 2013. *The Praetorian Guard: A History of Rome's Elite Special Forces*. Waco, TX: Baylor University Press.

Bishop, M. C. 2010. "Roman Military," in *Oxford Bibliographies Online*. https://www.oxfordbibliographies.com/display/document/obo-9780195389661/obo-9780195389661-0148.xml?rskey=uxqppv&result=5&q=warfare#firstMatch. Accessed November 28, 2024.

Bishop, M. C., and J. Coulston. 2006. *Roman Military Equipment: From the Punic Wars to the Fall of Rome*. Oxford: Oxbow.

Bivar, A. D. H. 1972. "Cavalry Equipment and Tactics on Euphrates," *DOP* 26: 273–291.

Blockley, R. C. 1977. "Ammianus Marcellinus on the Battle of Strasburg: Art and Analysis in the *History*," *Phoenix* 31: 218–231.

Blome, D. 2020. *Greek Warfare Beyond the Polis*. Ithaca: Cornell University Press.

Bonner, M. 2020. *The Last Empire of Iran*. London: Gorgias Press.
Börm, H. 2007. *Prokop und die Perser: Untersuchungen zu den römischen-sasanidischen Kontakten in der ausgehenden Spätantike*. Stuttgart: Franz Steiner.
Bosworth, A. B. 1988. *Conquest and Empire: The Reign of Alexander the Great*. Cambridge, UK: Cambridge University Press.
Breccia, G. 2004. "L'arco e la spada. Procopio e il nuovo esercito bizantino," *Rivista di ricerche bizantinistiche* 1: 73–99.
Brennan, P. 1996. "The *Notitia Dignitatum*," in C. Nicolet (ed.), *Les Littératures Techniques dans l'Antiquité Romaine*. Geneva: Fondation Hardt, pp. 147–178.
Brennan, P. 1998. "The User's Guide to the *Notitia Dignitatum*: The Case of the *Dux Armeniae* (*ND Or.* 38)," *Antichthon* 32: 34–49.
Brennan, P. 2015. "Units in the *Notitia Dignitatum*," in Y. Le Bohec (2015), pp. 1049–1054.
Brice, L. 2011. "Philip II, Alexander the Great, and the Question of a Macedonian 'Revolution in Military Affairs (RMA)," *Ancient World* 42: 137–147.
Brice, L. (ed.). 2020. *New Approaches to Greek and Roman Warfare*. Malden, MA: Wiley.
Brouwers, J. 2021. "The Anatolian Roots of Archaic Greek Warfare," in Konijnendijk et al. (2021), pp. 64–82.
Brunt, P. 1971. *Roman Manpower*. Oxford.
Bruun, C., and J. Edmondson (eds.). 2015. *The Oxford Handbook of Roman Epigraphy*. New York: Oxford University Press.
Bugh, G. 2006. "Hellenistic Military Developments," in G. Bugh (ed.), *The Cambridge Companion to the Hellenistic World*. Cambridge, UK: Cambridge University Press, pp. 265–294.
Bugh, G. 2020. "Greek Cavalry in the Hellenistic World: Review and Reappraisal," in Brice (2020), pp. 65–80.
Burckhardt, L. A. 1999. "Katalogos," in H. Cancik and H. Schneider (eds.), *Der neue Pauly*. Stuttgart: Franz Steiner, Volume 6, col. 337.
Burn, T. 2003. *Rome and the Barbarians, 100 B.C. – A.D. 400*. Baltimore: Johns Hopkins University Press.
Bursche, A., Hines, J., and A. Zapolska (eds.). 2020. *The Migration Period between the Oder and the Vistula*. Leiden: Brill.
Bursche, A., and K. Myzgin. 2020. "The Gothic Invasions of the Mid-3rd c. A.D. and the Battle of Abritus: Coins and Archaeology in East-central Barbaricum," *JRA* 33: 195–229.
Burton, P. 2011. *Friendship and Empire*. Cambridge, UK: Cambridge University Press.
Butera, J., and M. Sears. 2019. *Battles and Battlefields of Ancient Greece*. Barnsley: Pen & Sword.

Cameron, A. (ed.). 1995. *The Byzantine and Early Islamic Near East III: States, Resources and Armies*. Princeton: Gerlach Press.

Campbell, B. 1984. *The Emperor and the Roman Army*. Oxford: Oxford University Press.

Campbell, B. 1994. *The Roman Army, 31 BC to AD 235: A Sourcebook*. London: Routledge.

Campbell, B. 2002. *War and Society in Imperial Rome, 31 BC to AD 235*. London: Routledge.

Campbell, B. 2017. "The Jewish Revolt, 66," in M. Whitby and H. Sidebottom (2017), pp. 1004–1010.

Campbell, B., and L. Tritle (eds.). 2013. *The Oxford Handbook of Warfare in the Classical World*. New York: Oxford University Press.

Carney, E. 2021. "Women and War in the Greek World," in Heckel et al. (2021), pp. 329–338.

Carrié, J.-M. 1995. "L'État à la recherche de nouveaux modes de financement des armées (Rome et Byz- ance, IVe–VIIIe siècles)," in A. Cameron (1996), pp. 31–53.

Carrié, J.-M. 2002. "Fournitures militaires, recrutement et archéologie des fortifications," *AntTard* 10: 427–442.

Carrié, J.-M. 2004. "Le système de recrutement des armées romaines de Dioclétien aux Valentiniens," in Y. Le Bohec et C. Wolff (eds.), *L'armée romaine de Dioclétien à Valentinien Ier*. Paris: de Boccard, pp. 71–87.

Cartledge, P. 2020. *Thebes*. New York: Pan Macmillan.

Chaniotis, A. 2005. *War in the Hellenistic World*. Malden, MA: Wiley.

Charles, M. 2002. "The Flavio-Trajanic Miles: The Appearance of Citizen Infantry on Trajan's Column," *Latomus* 61: 666–695.

Charles, M. 2016. "Elephant Size in Antiquity. DNA Evidence and the Battle of Raphia," *Historia* 65: 53–65.

Chlup, J., and C. Whately (eds.). 2020. *Greek and Roman Military Manuals: Genre, Theory, Influence*. London: Routledge.

Christ, M. 2006. *The Bad Citizen in Classical Athens*. Cambridge, UK: Cambridge University Press.

Christ, M. 2019. "The Conscription of Cavalrymen in Classical Athens," *Phoenix* 73: 313–332.

Clark, J. 2014a. "Roman Optimism Before Cannae: The Vow of the Ver Sacrum (Livy 22.10)," *Mnemosyne* 67: 405–422.

Clark, J. 2014b. *Triumph in Defeat. Military Loss and the Roman Republic*. New York: Oxford University Press.

Cline, E. 2014. *1177 BC. The Year Civilization Collapsed*. Princeton: Princeton University Press.

Clunn, T. 2005. *The Quest for Rome's Lost Legions: Discovering the Varus Battlefield*. New York: Savas Beatie.

Coello, T. 1996. *Unit Sizes in the Late Roman Army*. Oxford: Tempus Reparatum.

Colombo, M. 2009. "La forza numerica e la composizione degli eserciti campali durante l'alto impero: legion e *auxilia* da Cesare Augusto a Traiano," *Historia* 58: 96–117.

Cooley, A. 2012. *The Cambridge Manual of Latin Epigraphy*. Cambridge, UK: Cambridge University Press.

Cosmo, N., and M. Mass (eds.). 2018. *Empires and Exchanges in Eurasian Late Antiquity*. Cambridge, UK: Cambridge University Press.

Coulston, J. 1986. "Roman, Parthian and Sassanid Tactical Developments," in P. Freeman and D. Kennedy (eds.), *The Defence of the Roman and Byzantine East*. Oxford: BAR Publishing, pp. 59–75.

Coulston, J. 1989. "The Value of Trajan's Column as a Source for Military Equipment," in C. van Driel-Murray (ed.), *Roman Military Equipment: The Sources of Evidence. Proceedings of the Fifth Roman Military Equipment Conference*. Oxford: BAR Publishing, pp. 31–44.

Coulston, J. 2005. "Military Identity and Personal Self-identity in the Roman Army," in L. de Ligt, E. A. Hemelrijk, and H. W. Singor (eds.), *Roman Rule and Civic Life: Local and Regional Perspectives*. Amsterdam: J. C. Geiben, pp. 133–152.

Coulston, J. 2008. "The Enemies of Rome," *Journal of Roman Military Equipment Studies* 16: 17–30.

Crowley, J. 2012. *The Psychology of the Athenian Hoplite*. Cambridge, UK: Cambridge University Press.

Crowley, J. 2014. "Beyond the Universal Soldier: Combat Trauma in Classical Antiquity," in Meineck and Konstan (2014), pp. 105–130.

Culham, P. 1989. "Chance, Command, and Chaos in Ancient Military Engagements," *World Futures* 27: 191–205.

Cunliffe, B. 1988. *Greeks, Romans, and Barbarians*. London: Metheun.

Cuomo, S. 2007. *Technology and Culture in Greek and Roman Antiquity*. Cambridge, UK: Cambridge University Press.

Czermak, A. 2020. "Human Remains and What They Can Tell Us about Status and Identity in the Merovingian Period," in B. Effros and I. Moreira (2020), pp. 139–163.

Daly, G. 2000. *Cannae: The Experience of Battle in the Second Punic War*. London: Routledge.

Davenport, C. 2019. *A History of the Roman Equestrian Order*. Cambridge, UK: Cambridge University Press.

Davies, G. 2006. *Roman Siege Works*. Stroud: Tempus.

De Groote, K. 2022. "A Core Difference! The Varying Hoplite Shield Designs and their Effects on Economic Value, Performance and Combat Effectiveness," *International Journal of Military History and Historiography* 42: 267–299.

de la Vaissière, E. 2014. "The Steppe World and the Rise of the Huns," in M. Maas (ed.), *The Cambridge Companion to the Age of Attila*. Cambridge, UK: Cambridge University Press, pp. 175–192.
De Light, L. 2012. *Peasants, Citizens and Soldiers: Studies in the Demographic History of Roman Italy 225 BC-AD 100*. Cambridge, UK: Cambridge University Press.
De Souza, P. 2007. "Naval Forces," in P. Sabin, H. Van Wees, and M. Whitby (2007), Volume 1, pp. 357–367.
De Vivo, J. 2014. "The Memory of Greek Battle: Material Culture and/as Narrative of Combat," in Meineick and Konstan (2014), pp. 163–184.
Decker, M. 2022. *The Sasanian Empire at War*. Yardley, PA: Westholme.
Dillon, S., and K. Welch (eds.). 2006. *Representations of War in Ancient Rome*. Cambridge, UK: Cambridge University Press.
Domaszewski, A. 1967. *Die Rangordnung des Römischen Heeres*, 2nd edition. Cologne: Graz-Böhlau.
Dridi, H. 2019. "Early Carthage: From Its Foundation to the Battle of Himera," in López-Ruiz and Doak (eds.), pp. 141–154.
Eadie, J. W. 1967. "The Development of Roman Mailed Cavalry," *JRS* 57: 161–173.
Echeverría, F. 2011a. "Greek Military," in *Oxford Bibliographies Online*. https://www.oxfordbibliographies.com/display/document/obo-9780195389661/obo-9780195389661-0128.xml?rskey=V92n1U&result=1&q=warfare#firstMatch. Accessed November 28, 2024.
Echeverría, F. 2011b. "Taktikè technè. The Neglected Element in Classical Hoplite Battles," *Ancient Society* 41: 45–82.
Echeverría, F. 2012. "Hoplite and Phalanx in Archaic and Classical Greece: A Reassessment," *CP* 107: 291–318.
Echeverría, F. 2021. "The Nature of Hoplite Warfare," in Heckel et al. (2021), pp. 75–87.
Eckstein, A. 2005. "Bellicosity and Anarchy: Soldiers, Warriors, and Combat in Antiquity," *International History Review* 27: 481–497.
Eckstein, A. 2006. *Mediterranean Anarchy, Interstate War, and the Rise of Rome*. Berkeley: University of California Press.
Eckstein, A. 2008. *Rome Enters the Greek East*. Malden, MA: Wiley.
Effors, B., and I. Moreira (eds.). 2020. *The Oxford Handbook of the Merovingian World*. Oxford/New York: Oxford University Press.
Effros, B. 2003. *Merovingian Mortuary Archaeology and the Making of the Early Middle Ages*. Berkeley: University of California Press.
Elton, H. 1996. *Warfare in Roman Europe AD 350-425*. Oxford: Oxford University Press.
Elton, H. 2007. "Military Forces [The Later Roman Empire]," in P. Sabin, H. Van Wees, and M. Whitby (2007), pp. 270–309.

Emion, M. 2023. *Les protectores Augusti (IIIe-VIe s. a.C.)*. Bordeaux: Ausonius.

Engels, D. 1978. *Alexander the Great and the Logistics of the Macedonian Army*. Berkeley: University of California Press.

Erdkamp, P. 1998. *Hunger and the Sword: Warfare and Food Supply in Republican Wars*. Leiden: J. C. Geiben.

Erdkamp, P. (ed.). 2002. *The Roman Army and the Economy*. Amsterdam: J. C. Geiben.

Erdkamp, P. (ed.). 2007. *A Companion to the Roman Army*. Malden, MA: Wiley.

Erdkamp, P. 2011. "Manpower and Food Supply in the First and Second Punic Wars," in D. Hoyos (ed.). *A Companion to the Punic Wars*. Malden, MA: Wiley, pp. 58–76.

Fan Chiang, S.-C. 2018. "Between Facts, Contexts, and Traditions: Procopius' Description of Women's Suffering During Wartime," in Greatrex and Janniard (2018), pp. 229–247.

Fear, A. 2007. "War and Society," in P. Sabin, H. Van Wees, and M. Whitby (2007), pp. 424–458.

Febre-Serris, J., and A. Keith (eds.). 2015. *Women and War in Antiquity*. Baltimore: Johns Hopkins University Press.

Finley, M. 1971. *The World of Odysseus*. New York: The Viking Press.

Flower, M. 2012. *Xenophon's Anabasis or the Expedition of Cyrus*. Oxford/New York: Oxford University Press.

Forni, G. 1953. *Il reclutamento delle legioni da Augusto a Diocleziano*. Milan and Rome: Bocca.

Fox, R. L. (ed.). 2004. *The Long March: Xenophon and the Ten Thousand*. New Haven: Yale University Press.

Foxhall, L. 2013. "Can We See the 'Hoplite Revolution' on the Ground? Archaeological Landscapes, material Culture, and Social Status in Early Greece," in Kagan and Viggiano (2013), pp. 194–221.

Fronda, M. 2010. *Between Rome and Carthage: Southern Italy during the Second Punic War*. Cambridge, UK: Cambridge University Press.

Fuhrmann, C. 2012. *Policing the Roman Empire: Soldiers, Administration, and Public Order*. Oxford/New York: Oxford University Press.

Gabriel, R., and K. Metz. 1991. *From Sumer to Rome: The Military Capabilities of Ancient Armies*. Westport, CT: Greenwood Press.

Gaca, K. 2011. "Girls, Women, and the Significance of Sexual Violence in Ancient Warfare," in E. Heineman (ed.), *Sexual Violence in Conflict Zones*. Philadelphia: University of Pennsylvania Press, pp. 73–88.

Garlan, Y. 1975. *War in the Ancient World: A Social History*. London: Chatto & Windus.

Garland, R. 2017. *Athens Burning: The Persian Invasion of Greece and the Evacuation of Attica*. Baltimore: Johns Hopkins University Press.

Georganas, I. 2018. "'Warrior Graves' vs. Warrior Graves in the Bronze Age Aegean," in Horn and Kristiansen (2018), pp. 198–212.
Gersbach, J. 2020. *The War Cry in the Ancient Mediterranean World.* London: Routledge.
Giangiulio, M., Franchi, E., and G. Proietti (eds.). 2019. *Commemorating War and War Dead. Ancient and Modern.* Stuttgart: Franz Steiner.
Giles, R. 2012. *The Roman Soldier and the Roman Army.* Oxford: BAR Publishing.
Gillespie, C. 2018. *Boudica: Warrior Woman of Roman Britain.* Oxford/ New York: Oxford University Press.
Gilliver, C. M. 1996. "Mons Graupius and the Role of Auxiliaries in Battle," *G & R* 43: 54–67.
Gilliver, C. M. 1999. *The Roman Art of War.* Stroud: Tempus.
Gilliver, C. M. 2007. "Battle [The Late Republic and the Principate]," in Sabin, Van Wees, and Whitby (2007), pp. 122–157.
Goffart, W. 2006. *Barbarian Tides.* Philadelphia: University of Pennsylvania Press.
Goldsworthy, A. 1996. *The Roman Army at War 100BC to AD 200.* Oxford: Oxford University Press.
Goldsworthy, A. 2007. "War [The Late Republic and the Principate]," in P. Sabin, H. Van Wees, and M. Whitby (2007), pp. 76–121.
Graells i Fabregat, R. 2021. "Greek Archaic Panoplies: An Archaeo-Iconographic Diachronic Approach," in (ed.), *Ancient Weapons. New Research Perspectives on Weapons & Warfare.* Mainz: Verlag des Römisch-Germanischen Zentralmuseums, pp. 161–190.
Graff, D. 2016. *The Eurasian Way of War.* London: Routledge.
Greatrex, G. 1998. *Rome and Persia at War, AD 502-532.* Leeds: Francis Cairns.
Greatrex, G., and S. Janniard (eds.). 2018. *The World of Procopius/Le Monde de Procope.* Paris: de Boccard.
Greene, E. 2015. "*Conubium cum uxoribus*: Wives and Children in the Roman Military Diplomas," *JRA* 28: 125–159.
Greene, E., and L. Brice (eds.). 2024. *Women and the Army in the Roman Empire.* Cambridge, UK: Cambridge University Press.
Grillo, L. 2012. *The Art of Caesar's Bellum Civile.* Cambridge, UK: Cambridge University Press.
Grossman, D. 1995. *On Killing.* Boston: Little, Brown.
Grossman, D. 2004. *On Combat.* Millstadt, IL: PPCT Research Publications.
Gruen, E. 1984. *The Hellenistic World and the Coming of Rome.* Berkeley: University of California Press.
Gruen, E. 2010. *Rethinking the Other in Antiquity.* Princeton: Princeton University Press.

Haldon, J. 1975. "Some Aspects of Byzantine Military Technology from Sixth to the Tenth Centuries," *BMGS* 1: 11–47.

Haldon, J. 1979. *Recruitment and Conscription in the Byzantine Army c. 550-950*. Vienna: Österreichischen Akademie der Wissenschaften.

Haldon, J. 1993. "Administrative Continuities and Structural Transformations in East Roman Military Organisation c. 580-640," in F. Vallett and M. Kazanski (eds.), *L'Armée romaine et les barbares du 4e au 7e siècle*. Paris: de Boccard, pp. 45–51.

Haldon, J. 1999. *Warfare, State and Society in the Byzantine World, 565-1204*. London: Routledge.

Haldon, J. 2001. *The Byzantine Wars*. Stroud: Tempus.

Haldon, J. 2002. "Some Aspects of Early Byzantine Arms and Armour," in D. Nicolle (ed.), *A Companion to Medieval Arms and Armour*. Woodbridge: Boydell Press, pp. 65–79.

Hall, J., Rawlings, L., and G. Lee (eds.). 2023. *Unit Cohesion and Warfare in the Ancient World. Military and Social Approaches*. London: Routledge.

Halsall, G. 2007. *Barbarian Migrations and the Roman West, 376-568*. Cambridge, UK: Cambridge University Press.

Halsall, G. 2020. "Gender in Merovingian Gaul," in B. Effros and I. Moreira (2020), pp. 164–185.

Handley, M. A. 2011. *Dying on Foreign Shores. Travel and Mobility in the Late-Antique West*. Portsmouth, RI: Journal of Roman Archaeology.

Hansen, M. 1993. "The Battle Exhortation in Ancient Historiography: Fact or Fiction?" *Historia* 42: 161–180.

Hansen, M. 2001. "The Little Grey Horse: Henry V's Speech at Agincourt and the Battle Exhortation in Ancient Historiography," *C & M* 52: 95–116.

Hansen, M. 2006. *Polis. And Introduction to the Ancient Greek City-State*. Oxford: Oxford University Press.

Hanson, V. D. 1989. *The Western Way of War*. Berkeley: University of California Press.

Hanson, V. D. (ed.). 1991. *Hoplites: The Classical Greek Battle Experience*. London: Routledge.

Hanson, V. D. 1995. *The Other Greeks*. Berkeley: University of California Press.

Harl, O. 1996. "Die *Kataphraktarier* im römischen Heer – Panegyrik und Realität," *JRGZM* 43: 601–627.

Harris, W. V. 1979. *War and Imperialism in Republican Rome 327-70BC*. Oxford: Oxford University Press.

Haynes, I. 2013. *Blood of the Provinces: The Roman Auxilia and the Making of Provincial Society from Augustus to the Severans*. Oxford: Oxford University Press.

Heather, P. 2015. "The Huns and Barbarian Empire," in Maas (2015), pp. 209–229.
Heather, P. 2018. *Rome Resurgent*. Oxford/New York: Oxford University Press.
Hebblewhite, M. 2017. *The Emperor and the Army in the Later Roman Empire, AD 235-395*. London: Routledge.
Hebblewhite, M., and C. Whately (eds.). 2022. *Brill's Companion to Bodyguards in the Ancient Mediterranean*. Leiden: Brill.
Heckel, W. 2008. *The Conquests of Alexander the Great*. Cambridge, UK: Cambridge University Press.
Heckel, W., Naiden, F. S., Garvin, E., and J. Vanderspoel (eds.). 2021. *A Companion to Greek Warfare*. Malden, MA: Wiley.
Heidenreich, S., and J. Roth. 2020. "The Neurophysiology of Panic on the Ancient Battlefield," in Brice (2020), pp. 127–138.
Heinrichs, J. 2021. "Bronze Age and Early Greek Wars," in Heckel et al. (2021), pp. 9–20.
Hin, S. 2013. *The Demography of Roman Italy*. Cambridge, UK: Cambridge University Press.
Hölscher, T. 2004. *Language of Images in Roman Art*. Cambridge, UK: Cambridge University Press.
Hölscher, T. 2018. *Visual Power in Ancient Greece and Rome. Between Art and Social Reality*. Berkeley: University of California Press.
Hope, V. 2003. "Trophies and Tombstones: Commemorating the Roman Soldier," *World Archeology* 35: 79–97.
Hope, V. 2015. "Bodies on the Battlefield: The Spectacle of Rome's Fallen Soldiers," in V. Hope and A. Bakogiannia (eds.), *War as Spectacle. Ancient and Modern Perspectives on the Display of Armed Conflict*. London: Bloomsbury, pp. 157–178.
Horn, C., and K. Kristiansen (eds.). 2018. *Warfare in Bronze Age Society*. Cambridge, UK: Cambridge University Press.
Howard-Johnston, J. 1995. "The Two Great Powers in Late Antiquity: A Comparison," in A. Cameron (1995), pp. 157–226.
Howard-Johnston, J. 2010. *Witness to a World Crisis*. Oxford: Oxford University Press.
Howard-Johnston, J. 2012. "The Late Sasanian Army," in T. Bernheimer and A. Silverstein (eds.), *Late Antiquity: Eastern Perspectives*. Edinburgh: Edinburgh University Press, pp. 87–127.
Howard-Johnston, J. 2021. *The Last Great War in Antiquity*. Oxford: Oxford University Press.
Howe, T., and L. Brice (ed.). 2016. *Brill's Companion to Insurgency and Terrorism in the Ancient Mediterranean World*. Leiden: Brill.
Hoyland, R. 2015. *In God's Path*. Oxford: Oxford University Press.

Hoyos, D. 2007. "The Age of Overseas Expansion (264-146 BCE)," in P. Edrkamp (ed.), *A Companion to the Roman Army*. Malden, MA: Wiley, pp. 63–79.

Hoyos, D. (ed.). 2011. *A Companion to the Punic Wars*. Malden, MA: Wiley.

Hoyos, D. 2015. *Mastering the West*. New York/Oxford: Oxford University Press.

Hoyos, D. 2019. "Classical-Hellenistic Carthage before the Punic Wars (479-265 BCE)," in López-Ruiz (2019), pp. 155–168.

Humfries, M. 2017. "The Fourth-Century Roman Empire: West," in Whitby and Sidebottom (2017), pp. 1110–1117.

Hunt, P. 2007. "Military Forces [Archaic and Classical Greece]," in P. Sabin, H. Van Wees, and M. Whitby (2007), pp. 108–146.

Iossif, P., and I. Fappas (eds.). 2024. *Chareonea, 2 August 338 BC: A Day that Changed the World*. Athens: Museum of Cycladic Art.

Iovine, G. 2023. *Latin Military Papyri of Dura-Europos (P.Dura 55-145)*. Cambridge: Cambridge University Press.

Isaac, B. 1992. *Limits of Empire*. Oxford: Oxford University Press.

Isaac, B. 2004. *The Invention of Racism in Classical Antiquity*. Princeton: Princeton University Press.

James, S. 2004. *The Excavations at Dura-Europos conducted by Yale University and the French Academy of Inscriptions and Letters 1928 to 1937. Final Report VII: The Arms and Armour and other Military Equipment*. Oxford: Oxford University Press.

James, S. 2006. "The Impact of Steppe Peoples and the Partho-Sasanian World on the Development of Roman Military Equipment and Dress, 1st to 3rd Centuries AD," in M. Mode, J. Tubach, and G. Sophia Vashalomidze (eds.), *Arms and Armour as Indicators of Cultural Transfer: The Steppes and the Ancient World from Hellenistic Times to the Early Middle Ages*. Weisbaden: Reichert, pp. 357–392.

James, S. 2010. "The Point of the Sword: What Roman-era Weapons Could Do to Bodies—And Why they Often Didn't," in A. W. Busch and H. J. Schalles (eds.), *Waffen in Aktion. Akten der 16. Internationalen Roman Military Equipment Conference*. Xanten: Van Zabern, pp. 41–54.

James, S. 2011a. *Rome and the Sword*. London: Thames and Hudson.

James, S. 2011b. "Stratagems, Combat, and "Chemical Warfare" in the Siege Mines of Dura-Europos," *AJA* 115: 69–101.

James, S. 2013. "The Archaeology of War." In Campbell and Tritle (2013), pp. 91–127.

James, S. 2019. *The Roman Military Base at Dura-Europos, Syria*. Oxford: Oxford University Press.

James, S., and S. Krmnicek (eds.). 2020. *Oxford Handbook of the Archaeology of Roman Germany*. Oxford/New York: Oxford University Press.

Janniard, S. 2008. "Végèce et les transformations de l'art de la guerre aux ive et ve siècles," *AnTard* 16: 19–36.
Janniard, S. 2011. *Les Transformations de l'Armée Romano-Byzantine (IIIe – VIe Siècles apr. J.-C.): Le Paradigme de la Bataille Rangée*. Unpublished PhD dissertation, L'Atelier du Centre de Recherches Historiques.
Janniard, S. 2015. "Les adaptations de l'armée romaine aux modes de combat des peuples des steppes (fin IVe-début VIe siècle apr. J.-C.)," in U. Roberto and L. Mecella (eds.), *Governare e riformare l'impero al momento della sua divisione: Oriente, Occidente, Illirico*. Paris: École Française de Rome, pp. 1–34.
Jensen, E. 2018. *Barbarians in the Greek and Roman World*. Cambridge, MA: Hackett Publishing.
Johstono, P. 2020. *The Army of Ptolemaic Egypt 323-204 BC*. Barnsley, UK: Pen & Sword.
Kaegi, W. 1981. *Byzantine Military Unrest, 471-843: An Interpretation*. Amsterdam: Hakkert.
Kagan, D., and G. Viggiano (eds.). 2013. *Men of Bronze*. Princeton: Princeton University Press.
Kagan, K. 2006a. *The Eye of Command*. Ann Arbor: University of Michigan Press.
Kagan, K. 2006b. "Redefining Roman Grand Strategy," *JMH* 70: 333–362.
Keegan, J. 1976. *The Face of Battle*. New York: Viking.
Keegan, J. 1987. *The Mask of Command*. New York: Viking.
Kelly, C. 2015. "Neither Conquest Nor Settlement: Attila's Empire and Its Impact," in Maas (2015), pp. 193–208.
Kennedy, D. 2004. *The Roman Army in Jordan*. London: Council for British Research in the Levant.
Keyser, P. G Irby-Massie. 2006. "Science, Medicine, and Technology," in G. Bugh (ed.), *The Cambridge Companion to the Hellenistic World*. Cambridge, UK: Cambridge University Press, pp. 241–264.
Kim, H. Y. 2016. *The Huns*. London: Routledge.
King, A. 1999a. "Animals and the Roman Army: The Evidence of Animal Bones," in A. Goldsworthy and I. Haynes (eds.) *The Roman Army as a Community*. Portsmouth, RI: Journal of Roman Archaeology, pp. 139–150.
King, A. 1999b. "Diet in the Roman World: A Regional Inter-site Comparison of the Mammal Bones," *JRA* 12: 168–202.
Koehn, C. 2018. *Justinian und die Armee des frühen Byzanz*. Boston/Berlin: de Gruyter.
Konijnendijk, R. 2018. *Classical Greek Tactics: A Cultural History*. Leiden: Brill.
Konijnendijk, R. 2019. "Commemoration through Fear: The Spartan Reputation as a Weapon of War," in Giangiulio et al. (2019), pp. 257–269.

Konijnendijk, R., Kucewicz, C., and M. Lloyd (eds.). 2021. *Brill's Companion to Greek Land Warfare Beyond the Phalanx*. Leiden: Brill.

Koon, S. 2011. "Phalanx and Legion: The "Face" of Punic War Battle," in D. Hoyos (2011), pp. 77–94.

Krentz, P. 1985. "The Nature of Hoplite Battle," *CA* 4: 50–61.

Krentz, P. 2007. "Warfare and Hoplites," in H. A. Shapiro (ed.), *The Cambridge Companion to Archaic Greece*. Cambridge, UK: Cambridge University Press, pp. 61–84.

Krentz, P. 2010. *The Battle of Marathon*. New Haven: Yale University Press.

Kucewicz, C. 2021. *The Treatment of the War Dead in Archaic Athens*. London.

Kucewicz, C., Lloyd, M., and R. Konijnendijk. 2021. "'Not Many Bows'? Light-Armed Fighters of the Tenth through Fourth Centuries," in Konijnendijk et al. (2021), pp. 205–235.

Kuhrt, A. 2007. *The Persian Empire: A Corpus of Sources of the Achaemenid Period*. London: Routledge.

Kulikowski, M. 2000. "The *Notitia Dignitatum* as a Historical Source." *Historia* 49: 358–377.

Kulikowski, M. 2006. *Rome's Gothic Wars from the Third Century to Alaric*. Cambridge, UK: Cambridge University Press.

Kvapil, L., and K. Shelton (eds.). 2023. *Brill's Companion to Warfare in the Bronze Age Aegean*. Leiden: Brill.

Kyle, B., Reitsema, L., Tyler, J., Fabbri, P., and S. Vassallo. 2018. "Examining the Osteological Paradox: Skeletal Stress in Mass Graves versus Civilians at the Greek Colony of Himera (Sicily)," *American Journal of Physical Anthropology* 167: 161–172.

Laforse, B. 2013. "Fighting the Other Part 1: Greeks and Achaemenid Persians," in Campbell and Tritle (2013), pp. 570–588.

Latacz, J. 1977. *Kampfparänese, Kampfdarstellung und Kampfwirkichkeit in der Ilias, bei Kallinos und Tyrtaios*. Munich: H. C. Beck.

Latacz, J. 2004 [1977]. *Troy and Homer*. Oxford: Oxford University Press.

Launaro, A. 2011. *Peasants and Slaves*. Cambridge, UK: Cambridge University Press.

Lavan, M. 2016. "The Spread of Roman Citizenship," *P & P* 230: 3–46.

Lavan, M. 2019. "The Army and the Spread of Roman Citizenship," *JRS* 109: 27–69.

Lazenby, J. 1991. "The Killing Zone," in Hanson (ed.). London: Routledge, pp. 87–109.

Le Bohec, Y. 2000. *The Imperial Roman Army*. Trans. R. Bate. London: Routledge.

Le Bohec, Y. 2006. *L'armée romaine sous le Bas-Empire*. Paris: de Boccard.

Le Bohec, Y. (ed.). 2015. *The Encyclopedia of the Roman Army*. Malden, MA: Wiley.

Le Bohec, Y., and C. Wolff (eds.). 2000. *Les Légions de Rome sous le Haut-Empire*. Paris: de Boccard.

Le Roux, P. 1995. "Le ravitaillement des armée romaines sous l'Empire," in R. Etienne (ed.), *Du Latifundium au Latifondo*. Paris: de Boccard, pp. 403–424.

Lee, D. 1993. *Information and Frontiers*. Cambridge, UK: Cambridge University Press.

Lee, D. 1996. "Morale and the Roman Experience of Battle," in A. B. Lloyd (ed.), *Battle in Antiquity*. Swansea: Classical Press of Wales, pp. 199–217.

Lee, D. 2005. "The Army at War," in M. Maas (ed.), *The Cambridge Companion to the Age of Justinian*. Cambridge, UK: Cambridge University Press, pp. 113–133.

Lee, D. 2007a. *War in Late Antiquity: A Social History*. Oxford: Blackwell.

Lee, D. 2007b. "Warfare and the State [the Later Roman State]," in P. Sabin, H. Van Wees, and M. Whitby (2007), pp. 379–423.

Lee, D. 2020. *Warfare in the Roman World*. Cambridge, UK: Cambridge University Press.

Lee, J. 2007. *A Greek Army on the March*. Cambridge, UK: Cambridge University Press.

Lendon, J. E. 2005. *Soldiers and Ghosts*. New Haven: Yale University Press.

Lendon, J. E. 2006. "Contubernalis, Commanipularis and commilito in Roman Soldier's Epigraphy," *ZPE* 157: 270–276.

Lendon, J. E. 2017a. "Battle Description in the Ancient Historians, Part I: Structure, Array, and Fighting," *G & R* 64: 39–64.

Lendon, J. E. 2017b. "Battle Description in the Ancient Historians, Part II: Speeches, Results, and Sea Battles," *G & R* 64: 145–167.

Lenski, N. 2007. "Two Sieges of Amida (AD 359 and 502-503) and the Experience of Combat in the Late Roman East," in A. S. Lewin and P. Pellegrini (eds.), *The Late Roman Army in the Near East from Diocletian to the Arab Conquest*. Oxford: BAR Publishing, pp. 219–236.

Lenski, N. 2015. "Captivity Among the Barbarians and Its Impact on the Fate of the Roman Empire," in Maas (2015), pp. 230–246.

Levene, D. S. 2010. *Livy on the Hannibalic War*. Oxford: Oxford University Press.

Levithan, J. 2013. *Roman Siege Warfare*. Ann Arbor: University of Michigan Press.

Lewin, A. S., and P. Pellegrini (eds.). 2007. *The Late Roman Army in the Near East from Diocletian to the Arab Conquest*. Oxford: BAR Publishing.

Lintott, A. 1999. *The Constitution of the Roman Republic*. Oxford: Oxford University Press.

Lissarrague, F. 1990. *L'autre guerrier: Archers, peltastes, cavaliers dans l'imagerie attique.* Rome: École française de Rome.

Liston, M. 2020. "Skeletal Evidence for the Impact of Battle on Soldiers and Non-Combatants," in Brice (2020), pp. 81–94.

Llewellyn-Jones, L. 2022. *Persians. The Age of Great Kings.* London.

Lloris, F. B. 2015. "The 'Epigraphic Habit' in the Roman World," in Bruun and Edmondson (2015), pp. 131–148.

Lloyd, M. 2021. "Men of Iron. Pre-Archaic Greek Warfare in Context," in Konijnendijk et al. (2021), pp. 17–63.

Loman, P. 2004. "No Woman No War: Women's Participation in Ancient Greek Warfare," *G & R* 51: 34–54.

Lonis, R. 1985. "La guerre en Grèce: Quinze années de recherche, 1968–1983," *Revue des Études Grecques* 98: 321–379.

Lonoce, N., Palma, M., Viva, S., Valentino, M., Vassallo, S., and P. F. Fabbri. 2018. "The Western (Buonfornello) Necropolis (7th to 5th BC) of the Greek Colony of Himera (Sicily, Italy): Site-specific Discriminant Functions for Sex Determination in the Common Burials Resulting from the Battle of Himera (ca. 480 BC)," *International Journal of Osteoarchaeology* 28: 766–774.

López-Ruiz, C. 2019. "Phoenician Literature," in López-Ruiz and Doak (2019), pp. 257–269.

López-Ruiz, C., and B. Doak (eds.). 2019. *Oxford Handbook of the Phoenician and Punic Mediterranean.* Oxford/New York: Oxford University Press.

Loreto, L. 2011. "Roman Politics and Expansion, 241-219," in Hoyos (2011), pp. 184–203.

Lorimer, H. 1947. "The Hoplite Phalanx with Special Reference to the Poems of Archilochus and Tyrtaeus," *Annual of the British School of Athens* 42: 76–138.

Lucas, T. 2022. "Early Greek Catapults and 'First-Generation Artillery Towers'," *Historia* 71: 130–149.

Luttwak, E. N. 2016. *The Grand Strategy of the Roman Empire from the First Century A.D. to the Third, revised edition.* Baltimore: Johns Hopkins University Press.

Maas, M. (ed.). 2015. *Cambridge Companion to the Age of Attila.* Cambridge, UK: Cambridge University Press.

MacDonald, E. 2015. *Hannibal: A Hellenistic Life.* New Haven: Yale University Press.

Machajewski, H., and J. Schuster. 2020. "Cemeteries and Burials," in Bursche et al. (2020), pp. 333–369.

MacMullen, R. 1963. *Soldier and Civilian in the Later Roman Empire.* Cambridge, MA: Harvard University Press.

MacMullen, R. 1982. "The Epigraphic Habit in the Roman Empire," *AJP* 103: 233–246.
Madadh, R. 2019. "Inscriptions," in López and Doak (2019), pp. 223–240.
Magness, J. 2019. *Masada: From Jewish Revolt to Modern Myth*. Princeton: Princeton University Press.
Maher, M., 2017. *The Fortifications of Arkadian City States in the Classical and Hellenistic Periods*. Oxford: Oxford University Press.
Mann, J. C. 1979. "Power, Force, and the Frontiers of the Roman Empire," *JRS* 69: 175–183.
Manning, S. 2020. *Armed Force in the Teispid-Achaemenid Empire*. Stuttgart: Franz Steiner.
Marincola, J. 2018. "*Omerikwtatos*? Battle Narratives in Herodotus," in E. Bowie (ed.), *Herodotus: Narrator. Scientist. Historian*. Berlin/Boston: de Gruyter, pp. 3–24.
Marsden, E. W. 1969. *Greek and Roman Artillery*. Oxford: Oxford University Press.
Martinez Morales, J. 2019. "Women on the Walls? The Role and Impact of Women in Classical Greek Sieges," in J. Armstrong and M. Trundle (2019), pp. 150–168.
Martinez Morales, J. 2021. "Women, Diversity, and War off the Battlefield in Classical Greece," in Konijnendijk et al. (2021), pp. 122–144.
Mason, S. 2016. *A History of the Jewish War*. Cambridge, UK: Cambridge University Press.
Mattern, S. P. 1999. *Rome and the Enemy: Imperial Strategy in the Principate*. Berkeley: University of California Press.
Matthew, C. 2016. *An Invincible Beast: Understanding the Hellenistic Pike Phalanx in Action*. Barnsley, UK: Pen & Sword.
Matthews, J. F. 1989. *The Roman Empire of Ammianus*. London: Duckworth.
Mattingly, D. 2011. *Imperialism, Power and Identity Experiencing the Roman Empire*. Princeton: Princeton University Press.
Mayor, A. 2003. *Greek Fire, Poison Arrows and Scorpion Bombs*. New York: Overlook.
Mayor, A. 2015. *The Amazons: Lives and Legends of Warrior Women Across the Ancient World*. Princeton: Princeton University Press.
McCall, J. B. 2002. *The Cavalry of the Roman Republic: Cavalry Combat and Elite Reputations in the Middle and Late Republic*. London: Routledge.
McCarty, M. 2019. "The Tophet and Infant Sacrifice," in López-Ruiz and Doak (2019), pp. 311–325.
Mederos Martín, A. 2019. "North Africa: From the Atlantic to Algeria," in López-Ruiz and Doak (2019), pp. 627–643.

Meineck, P., and D. Konstan (eds.). 2014. *Combat Trauma and the Ancient Greeks*. New York: Palgrave Macmillan.

Meyer, A. 2013. *The Creation, Composition, Service and Settlement of Roman Auxiliary Units Raised on the Iberian Peninsula*. Oxford: BAR Publishing.

Millender, E. 2019. "The Greek Battlefield: Classical Sparta and the Spectacle of Hoplite Warfare," in Reiss and Fagan (2019), pp. 162–194.

Millington, A. 2021. "Worshipping Violence," in Konijnendijk et al. (2021), pp. 145–168.

Milne, K. 2020. "The Middle Republican Solider and the Systems of Social Distinction," in Armstrong and Fronda (2020), pp. 134–153.

Mitford, T. 2018. *East of Asia Minor*. Oxford: Oxford University Press.

Mitthof, F. 2001. *Annona Militaris: Die Heeresversorgung im spätaniken Ägypten*. Florence: Edizioni Gonnelli.

Molloy, B. 2010. "Swords and Swordsmanship in the Aegean Bronze Age," *AJA* 114: 403–428.

Moore, R. 2013. "Generalship: Leadership and Command," in Campbell and Tritle (2013), pp. 457–473.

Murdoch, A. 2006. *Rome's Greatest Defeat. Massacre in the Teutoburg Forest*. Stroud: Sutton.

Muth, S. 2008. *Gewalt im Bild: Das Phänomen der medialen Gewalt im Athen des 6. und 5. Jahrhunderts v. Chr*. Berlin: de Gruyter.

Nagar, Y., Taitz, C., and R. Reich. 1999. "What Can We Make of These Fragments? Excavation at 'Mamilla' Cave, Byzantine Period, Jerusalem," *The International Journal of Bioarchaeology* 9: 29–38.

Naiden, F. S. 2021. "Religion and Warfare," in Heckel et al. (2021), pp. 127–146.

Nappi, M. 2015. "Women and War in the Iliad," in Fabre-Serris and Keith (2015), pp. 34–51.

Nevin, S. 2022. *The Idea of Marathon: Battle and Culture*. London: Bloomsbury.

Nicasie, M. J. 1998. *Twilight of Empire: The Roman Army from the Reign of Diocletian until the Battle of Adrianople*. Amsterdam: J. C. Geiben.

Noguera, J., Asensio, D., Ble, E., and R. J. Niella. 2014. "The Beginnings of the Roman Conquest of Hispania. Archaeological Evidence of the Assault and Destruction of the Iberian City of Castellet de Banyoles (Tivissa, Tarragona)," *JRA* 27: 60–81.

Ober, J. 1994. "The Rules of War in Classical Greece," in M. Howard, G. Andreopoulos, and M. Shulman (eds.), *The Laws of War: Constraints of Warfare in the Western World*. New Haven: Yale University Press, pp. 12–26.

Onur, F. 2017. "The Anastasian Military Decree from Perge in Pamphylia: Revised 2nd Edition," *Gephyra* 14: 133–212.

Owens, E. 2017. "The Second Punic War. 220-202 BC," in Whitby and Sidebottom (2017), pp. 668–796.

Parnell, D. 2012. "A Prosopographical Approach to Justinian's Army," *Medieval Prosopography* 27: 1–75.

Parnell, D. 2015. "Barbarians and Brothers-in-Arms: Byzantines on Barbarian Soldiers in the Sixth Century," *BZ* 108: 809–826.

Parnell, D. 2017. *Justinian's Men*. London: Palgrave Macmillan.

Paul, G. 1982. "*Urbs Capta*: Sketch of a Literary Motif," *Phoenix* 36: 144–155.

Payne, R. 2015. "The Reinvention of Iran: The Sasanian Empire and the Huns," in Maas (2015), pp. 282–299.

Pearson, E. 2019. "Decimation and Unit Cohesion: Why Were Roman Legionaries Willing to Perform Decimation?" *JMH* 83: 665–688.

Pearson, E. 2021. *Exploring the Mid-Republican Origins of Roman Military Administration*. London: Routledge.

Perez, E. 2020. "Children's Lives and Deaths in Merovingian Gaul," in B. Effros and I. Moreira (2020), pp. 186–213.

Petersen, L. R. 2013. *Siege Warfare and Military Organization in the Successor States (400-800 AD)*. Leiden: Brill.

Petitjean, M. 2022. *Le combat de cavalerie dans le monde romain*. Leuven: Brepols.

Phang, S. 2001. *The Marriage of Roman Soldiers (13 BC – AD 235)*. Leiden: Brill.

Phang, S. 2007. "Military Documents, Languages, and Literacy," in P. Erdkamp (2007), pp. 286–305.

Pollard, N. 2000. *Soldiers, Cities, and Civilians in Roman Syria*. Ann Arbor: University of Michigan Press.

Pollard, N. 2013. "*Imperatores castra dedicaverunt*: Security, Army Bases, and Military Dispositions in Later Roman Egypt (Later Third-Fourth Century)," *JLA* 6: 3–36.

Poma, G. 2015. "Religions: Republic," in Le Bohec (2015), pp. 820–822.

Pritchard, D. 2015. *Public Spending and Democracy in Classical Sparta*. Austin: Texas University Press.

Pritchard, D. 2019. *Athenian Democracy at War*. Cambridge, UK: Cambridge University Press.

Pritchett, W. K. 1979. *The Greek State at War, Part III: Religion*. Berkely: University of California Press.

Pritchett, W. K. 1985. *Greek State at War Volume IV*. Berkeley: University of California Press.

Pritchett, W. K. 1994. "The General's Exhortations," in *Essays in Greek History*. Amsterdam: J. C. Geiben, pp. 111–144.

Pritchett, W. K. 2002. *Ancient Greek Battle Speeches and a Palfrey*. Amsterdam: J. C. Geiben.

Przybyla, M. 2020. "Migration Studies in Archaeology: Building a Circumstantial Case," in Bursche (2020), pp. 15–64.

Quaesada Sanz, F. 2006. "Not so Different: Individual Fighting Techniques and Small Unit Tactics of Roman and Iberian Armies within the Framework of Warfare in the Hellenistic Age," *Pallas* 70: 245–263.

Quinn, J. 2019. "Phoenicians and Carthaginians in Greco-Roman LIteratuer," in López-Ruiz and Doak (2019), pp. 671–683.

Raaflaub, K. 2008. "Homeric Warriors and Battles: Trying to Resolve Old Problems," *CW* 101: 469–483.

Raaflaub, K. 2014. "War and the City: The Brutality of War and Its Impact on the Community," in Meineck and Konstan (2014), pp. 15–46.

Rance, P. 2004. "The *fulcum*, the Late Roman and Byzantine *testudo*. The Germanisation of Roman Infantry Tactics," *GRBS* 44: 265–326.

Rance, P. 2007. "Battle [The Later Roman Empire]," in P. Sabin, H. Van Wees, and M. Whitby (2007), pp. 342–378.

Rankov, B. 2007. "Military Forces [The Late Republic and the Principate]," in P. Sabin, H. Van Wees, and M. Whitby (2007), pp, 30–75.

Rankov, B. 2017. "Ancient Naval Warfare, 700 BC to AD 600," in Whitby and Sidebottom (2017), pp. 3–41.

Ravegnani, G. 1988. *Soldati di Bisanzio in età giustinianea*. Rome: Jouvence.

Ravegnani, G. 2004. *I Bizantini e la Guerra*. Rome: Jouvence.

Rawlings, L. 2007. *The ancient Greeks at war*. Manchester: Manchester University Press.

Rees, O. 2018. "Dogs of War, or Dogs in War? The Use of Dogs in Classical Greek Warfare," *G & R* 67: 230–246.

Rees, O. 2022. *Military Departures, Homecomings and Death in Classical Athens*. London: Bloomsbury.

Reeves, J. 2020. "Making the List: Coercion, Co-operation, and Competition in the Hoplite Katalogos," *Historia* 69: 128–153.

Reid, J., and A. Nicholson. 2019. "Burnswark Hill: The Opening Shot of the Antonine Reconquest of Scotland?" *JRA* 32: 459–477.

Reinberger, K., Reitsema, L., Kyle, B., Vassallo, S., Kamenov, G., and J. Krigbaum. 2021. "Isotopic Evidence for Geographic Heterogeneity in Ancient Greek Military Forces," *PLOS One* 16: 1–18.

Reiss, W., and G. Fagan (eds.). 2019. *The Topography of Violence in the Greco-Roman World*. Ann Arbor: University of Michigan Press.

Reitsema, L. J. et al. 2022. "The Diverse Genetic Origins of a Classical Period Greek Army," *PNAS* 119: 41.

Rhodes, P. J., and R. Osborne. 2007. *Greek Historical Inscriptions, 404-323 BC*. Oxford: Oxford University Press.

Rich, J. 2013. "Roman Rituals of War," in Campbell and Tritle (2013), pp. 542–568.

Rich, J., and G. Shipley (eds.). 1993. *War and Society in the Roman World.* London: Routledge.

Richardot, P. 2005. *La Fin de l'Armée Romaine 284-476.* Paris: Economica.

Richmond, I. A. 1935. "Trajan's Army on Trajan's Column," *Papers of the British School at Rome* 13: 1–40.

Riggsby, A. 2006. *Caesar in Gaul and Rome.* Austin: Texas University Press.

Ripat, P. 2006. "Roman Omens, Roman Audiences, and Roman History," *G & R* 53: 155–174.

Roberts, J. 2019. *The Plague of War.* Oxford/New York: Oxford University Press.

Rodzińska-Nowak, J. 2020. "Early Migration Period Nomadic Finds," in Bursche et al. (2020), pp. 370–410.

Roisman, J. 2017. *The Classical Art of Command.* Oxford: Oxford University Press.

Rop, J. 2019a. *Greek Military Service in the Ancient Near East, 401-330 BCE.* Cambridge, UK: Cambridge University Press.

Rop, J. 2019b. "The Phocian Betrayal at Thermopylae," *Historia* 68: 413–435.

Roselaar, S. 2015. "Battle Formation in the Roman Republic: Parade Show or Practical Purpose?" *Revue Internationale d'histoire militaire ancienne* 2: 23–53.

Rosenstein, A. 1990. *Imperatores Victi: Military Defeat and Aristocratic Competition in the Middle and Late Republic.* Berkeley: University of California Press.

Rosenstein, A. 2004. *Rome at War: Farms, Families, and Death in the Middle Republic.* Chapel Hill: University of North Carolina Press.

Roth, J. 1994. "The Size and Organization of the Roman Imperial Legion," *Historia* 43: 346–362.

Roth, J. 1999. *The Logistics of the Roman Army at War (264 B.C. – A.D. 235).* Leiden: Brill.

Rover, T. 2020. "The Combat Archaeology of the Fifth-Century BC Kopis: Hoplite Swordsmanship in the Archaic and Classical Periods," *International Journal of Military History & Historiography* 40: 7–49.

Royal, J., and S. Tusa. 2019. *The Site of the Battle of the Aegates Islands at the End of the First Punic War.* Rome: "L'Erma" di Bretschneider.

Rubin, Z. 1995. "The Reforms of Khusro Anushirwan," in A. Cameron (2015), *The Byzantine and Early Islamic Near East Volume III: States, Resources,* pp. 227–297.

Rubincam, C. 2021. *Quantifying Mentalities.* Ann Arbor: University of Michigan Press.

Sabin, P. 1996. "The Mechanics of Battle in the Second Punic War," in T. Cornell, B. Rankov, and P. Sabin (eds.), *The Second Punic War. A Reappraisal.* London: Institute of Classical Studies, pp. 59–79.

Sabin, P. 2000. "The Face of Roman Battle," *JRS* 90: 1–17.
Sabin, P. 2007. *Lost Battles: Reconstructing the Great Clashes of the Ancient World*. London: Bloomsbury.
Sabin, P., Van Wees, H., and M. Whitby (eds.). 2007. *The Cambridge History of Greek and Roman Warfare Volume 1: Greece, the Hellenistic World and the rise of Rome/Volume 2: Rome from the late Republic to the late Empire*. Cambridge, UK: Cambridge University Press.
Sage, M. 1996. *Warfare in Ancient Greece: A Sourcebook*. London: Routledge.
Salazar, C. 2000. *The Treatment of War-Wounds in Graeco-Roman Antiquity*. Leiden: Brill.
Salazar, C. 2013. "*Treating the Sick and Wounded*," in Campbell and Tritle 2013), pp. 294–311.
Sarantis, A. 2016. *Justinian's Balkan Wars*. Cambridge, UK: Francis Cairns.
Scharf, R. 2001. *Foederati. Von der völkerrechtlichen Kategorie zur byzantinischen Truppengattung*. Vienna: Holzhauser.
Scheidel, W. 2007. "Marriage, Families, and Survival: Demographic Aspects," in Erdkamp (2007), pp. 417–443.
Scheidel, W. 2011. "The Roman Slave Supply," in K. Bradley and P. Cartledge (eds.), *The Cambridge World History of Slavery*. Cambridge, UK: Cambridge University Press, Volume 1, pp. 287–310.
Schmitt, O. 1994. "Die buccellarii," *Tyche* 9: 147–174.
Schwartz, A. 2009. *Reinstating the Hoplite. Arms, Armour and Phalanx Fighting in Archaic and Classical Greece*. Stuttgart: Franz Steiner.
Schwartz, A. 2013. "Large Weapons, Small Greeks: The Practical Limitations of Hoplite Weapons and Equipment," in Kagan and Viggiano (2013), pp. 157–175.
Sears, M. 2010. "Warrior Ants: Elite Troops in the *Iliad*," *Classical World* 103: 139–155.
Sears, M. 2019. *Understanding Greek Warfare*. London: Routledge.
Sears, M., and C. Willekes. 2016. "Alexander's Cavalry Charge at Chaeronea, 338 BCE," *JMH* 80: 1017–1035.
Sekunda, N. 2007. "Military Forces [The Hellenistic World and the Roman Republic]," in P. Sabin, M. Whitby, and H. Van Wees (2007), pp. 325–357.
Shay, J. 1994. *Achilles in Vietnam: Combat Trauma and the Undoing of Character*. New York: Simon and Schuster.
Shean, J. 1996. "Hannibal's Mules: The Logistical Limitations of Hannibal's Army and the Battle of Cannae, 216 BC," *Historia* 45: 159–187.
Sidebottom, H. 2004. *Ancient Warfare*. Oxford: Oxford University Press.
Sidebottom, H. 2017. "Ancient Siege Warfare, 700 BC – AD 645," in Whitby and Sidebottom (2017), pp. 42–82.
Silver, M. 2016. "Public Slaves in the Roman Army: An Exploratory Study," *Ancient Society* 46: 203–240.

Snodgrass, A. 1965. "The Hoplite Reform and History," *JHS* 85: 110–122.
Snodgrass, A. 2013. "Setting the Frame Chronologically," in Kagan and Viggiano (2013), pp. 85–94.
Southern, P. 1989. "The Numeri of the Roman Imperial Army," *Britannia* 20: 81–140.
Southern, P. 2007. *The Roman Army: A Social and Institutional History*. Oxford: Oxford University Press.
Spaul, J. 1994. *Ala2*. Andover: Nectoreca.
Spaul, J. 2000. *Cohors2*. Oxford: BAR Publishing.
Spaul, J. 2002. *Classes Imperii Romani*. Andover: Nectoreca.
Speidel, M. A. 1996. *Die römischen Schreibtafeln von Vindonissa*. Brugg: Gesellschaft Pro Vindonissa.
Speidel, M. A. 2009. *Heer und Herrschaft im Römischen Reich der Hohen Kaiserzeit*. Stuttgart: Franz Steiner.
Speidel, M. A. 2015. "The Roman Army," in Bruun and Edmondson (eds.). Oxford, pp. 319–344.
Speidel, M. P. 2006. *Emperor Hadrian's Speeches to the African Army – A New Text*. Mainz: Verlag des Römisch-Germanischen Zentralmuseums.
Spiciarich, A., Gadot, Y., and Sapir-Hun, L. 2017. "The Faunal Evidence from Early Roman Jerusalem: The People behind the Garbage," *Tel Aviv* 44: 98–117.
Sprawski, S. 2017. "Campaigns of Thebes, 379-362 BC," in Whitby and Sidebottom (eds.). Malden, MA, pp. 447–466.
Stallibrass, S., and R. Thomas (eds.). 2008. *Feeding the Roman Army: The Archaeology of Production and Supply in NW Europe*. Oxford: Oxbow.
Stanfill, J., and A. Schneider. 2017. "Gothia Submerged: The Impacts of Severe Flooding on Valens's First Gothic War," *Journal of Late Antiquity* 10: 351–371.
Starr, C. 1960. *The Roman Imperial Navy: 31 BC to AD 324*. Cambridge, UK: Cambridge University Press.
Stathopoulos, P. 2017. "Did King Philip II of Ancient Macedonia Suffer a Zygomatico-Orbital Fracture? A Maxillofacial Surgeon's Approach?" *Craniomaxillofac Trauma Reconstruction* 10: 183–187.
Stefan, A. S. 2005. *Les guerres daciques de Domitien et de Trajan: architecture militaire, topographie, images et histoire*. Rome: École française de Rome.
Stewart, M. 2016. *The Soldier's Life*. Leeds: Kismet Press.
Stewart, R. 2011. "Did Greek and Roman Soldiers 'Aim High'? Toward a Psychological Profile of Combat Soldiers, Ancient and Modern," *Ancient World* 42: 34–51.
Stoll, O. 2007. "The Religions of the Roman Armies," in Erdkamp (2007), pp. 451–477.

Strauss, B. 2006. *The Trojan War*. New York: Simon and Schuster.
Strauss, B. 2013. *Masters of Command*. New York: Simon and Schuster.
Syon, D. 2002. "Gamla — City of Refuge," in A. M. Berlin and J. A. Overman (eds.), *The First Jewish Revolt: Archaeology, History and Ideology*. London: Routledge, pp. 134–153.
Syvänne, I. 2004. *The Age of Hippotoxotai*. Tampere: Tampere University Press.
Tan, J. 2017. *Power & Public Finance at Rome*. Oxford: Oxford University Press.
Taylor, M. 2014. "Roman Infantry Tactics in the Mid-Republic: A Reassessment," *Historia* 63: 301–322.
Taylor, M. 2020. *Soldiers & Silver*. Austin: Texas University Press.
Teytelbaum, E. 2024. "Land Battles in Polybius' *Histories*: General Characteristics and the Determinants of Success," in O. Devillers and B. B. Sebastiani (eds.), *Sources et modèles des historiens anciens, 3*. Bordeaux: Ausonius, pp. 125–136.
Thomas, C. 2004. "Claudius and the Roman Army Reforms," *Historia* 53: 424–452.
Thompson, E. A. 1958. "Early Germanic Warfare," *P&P* 14. 2–27.
Tomlin, R. 1972. "*Seniores-Iuniores* in the Late Roman Field Army," *AJP* 93: 253–278.
Tomlin, R. 2000. "The Legions in the Late Empire," in R. J. Brewer (ed.), *Roman Frontiers and Their Legions*. London/Cardiff: Society of Antiquaries of London, pp. 159–178.
Treadgold, W. 1995. *Byzantium and its Army, 284-1081*. Stanford: Standford University Press.
Treadgold, W. 2005. "Standardized Numbers in the Byzantine Army," *War in History* 12: 1–14.
Tritle, L. 2000. *From Melos to My Lai: War and Survival*. London: Routledge.
Tritle, L. 2010. *A New History of the Peloponnesian War*. Malden, MA: Wiley.
Tritle, L. 2014. "'Ravished Minds' in the Ancient World," in Meineck and Konstan (2014), pp. 87–103.
Tritle, L. 2021. "Battle Trauma in Ancient Greece," in Heckel et al. (eds.). Malden, MA, pp. 309–321.
Trundle, M. 2017. "The *Anabasis* and the Ten Thousand, 401-399 BCE," in Whitby and Sidebottom (2017), pp. 408–416.
Trundle, M. 2020. "Wealth and the Logistics of Greek Warfare: Food, Pay, and Plunder," in Brice (2020), pp. 17–28.
Tully, G. D. 1998. "The Stratarkhes of Legio VI Ferrata and the Employment of Camp Prefects as Vexillation Commanders," *ZPE* 120: 226–232.

Tully, G. D. 2002. "The *Vexillarii* in Pseudo-Hyginus' *De Munitionibus Castrorum* and Some Observations on the Strengths and Structure of Legionary Vexillations," *AHB* 16: 127–134.

Tully, G. D. 2004. "Did Centurions Lead Detachments of their Legions in Wartime?" *AClass* 47: 139–150.

Tuplin, C., and J. Ma (eds.). 2020. *Arsāma and His World*. Oxford: Oxford University Press.

Turner, B. 2013. "War Losses and Worldview: Re-examining the Roman Funerary Altar at Adamclisi," *AJP* 134: 277–304.

Tusa, S., and J. Royal. 2012. "The Landscape of the Naval Battle at the Egadi Islands (241 B.C.)," *JRA* 25: 7–48.

Van Lommel, K. 2013. "The Recognition of Roman Soldiers' Mental Impairment," *AClass* 56: 155–184.

Van Lommel, K. 2015. "Heroes and Outcasts: Ambiguous Attitudes towards Impaired and Disfigured Roman Veterans," *CW* 109: 91–117.

Van Wees, H. 1988. "Kings in Combat: Battles and Heroes in the Iliad," *CQ* 38: 1–24.

Van Wees, H. 1992. *Status Warriors: Violence and Society in Homer and History*. Amsterdam: J. C. Geiben.

Van Wees, H. 1994. "The Homeric Way of War: The Iliad and the Hoplite Phalanx (I) and (II)," *G & R* 41: 1–18, 131–155.

Van Wees, H. 1996. "Heroes, Knights and Nutters: Warrior Mentality in Homer," in A. B. Lloyd (ed.), *Battle in Antiquity*. Swansea: Classical Press of Wales, pp. 1–86.

Van Wees, H. 2004. *Greek Warfare: Myths and Realities*. London: Duckworth.

Van Wees, H. 2021. "The First Greek Soldiers in Egypt. Myths and Realities," in Konijnendijk et al. (2021), pp. 293–344.

von Carnap-Bornheim, C. 2020. "The Germani and the German Provinces of Rome," in James and Krmnicek (2020), pp. 409–436.

Waebens, S. 2012a. "Imperial Policy and Changed Composition of the Auxilia: The 'change in AD 140' Revisited," *Chiron* 42: 1–23.

Waebens, S. 2012b. "Reflecting the 'Change in A.D. 140': The Veteran Categories of the *Epikrisis* Documents Revisited," *ZPE* 180: 267–277.

Ward, G. 2016. "The Roman Battlefield: Individual Exploits in Warfare of the Roman Republic," in Reiss and Fagan (2016), pp. 299–324.

Wells, P. 2003. *The Battle that Stopped Rome*. New York: W. W. Norton.

Whately, C. 2016a. *Battles and Generals: Combat, Culture, and Didacticism in Procopius' Wars*. Leiden: Brill.

Whately, C. 2016b. *Exercitus Moesiae: The Roman Military in Moesia from Augustus to Severus Alexander*. Oxford: BAR Publishing.

Whately, C. 2021a. *An Introduction to the Roman Military from Marius (100 BCE) to Theodosius II (450 CE)*. Malden, MA: Wiley.

Whately, C. 2021b. *A Sensory History of Ancient Warfare*. Barnsley, UK: Pen & Sword.

Whately. C. 2021c. "Was There a Military Revolution at the End of Antiquity?" *Journal of Ancient History* 9: 203–220.

Wheeler, E. 1979. "The Legion as a Phalanx," *Chiron* 9: 303–318.

Wheeler, E. 1991. "The General as Hoplite," in V. D. Hanson (ed.), *Hoplites: The Classical Greek Battle Experience*. London: Routledge, pp. 121–170.

Wheeler, E. 1993a. "Methodological Limits and the Mirage of Roman Strategy: Part I," *JMH* 57: 7–41.

Wheeler, E. 1993b. "Methodological Limits and the Mirage of Roman Strategy: Part II," *JMH* 57: 215–240.

Wheeler, E. 2001. "Firepower: Missile Weapons and the 'Face of Battle'," *Electrum* 5: 169–184.

Wheeler, E. 2007. "Battle: A. Land Battles [Archaic and Classical Greece]," in P. Sabin, H. Van Wees, and M. Whitby (2007), pp. 186–223.

Wheeler, E. 2010. "Rome's Dacian Wars: Domitian, Trajan, and Strategy on the Danube, Part I," *JMH* 74: 1185–1227.

Wheeler, E. 2011a. "Greece: Mad Hatters and March Hares," in L. Brice, and J. Roberts (eds.), *Recent Directions in the Military History of the Ancient World*. Claremont, CA: Regina Books, pp. 53–104.

Wheeler, E. 2011b. "Rome's Dacian Wars: Domitian, Trajan, and Strategy on the Danube, Part II," *JMH* 75: 191–219.

Wheeler, E. 2012. "The General's *Metier*: The Lists of 'Great Captains' and Criteria for Selection," in C. Wolff (ed.), *Le métier de soldat dans le monde romain*. Paris, pp. 416–449.

Whitby, M. 1988. *The Emperor Maurice and His Historian*. Oxford: Oxford University Press.

Whitby, M. 2004a. "Emperors and Armies, AD 235-395," in S. Swain and M. Edwards (eds.), *Approaching Late Antiquity*. Oxford: Oxford University Press, pp. 156–186.

Whitby, M. 2004b. "Xenophon's Ten Thousand as a Fighting Force," in R. L. Fox (ed.), *The Long March: Xenophon and the Ten Thousand*. New Haven: Yale University Press, pp. 215–242.

Whitby, M. 2021. *The Wars of Justinian I*. Barnsley, UK: Pen & Sword.

Whitby, M., and H. Sidebottom (eds.). 2017. *The Encyclopedia of Ancient Battles*. Malden, MA: Wiley.

Whitehead, D. 1990. *Aineias the Tactician, How to Survive a City Under Siege*. Oxford: Oxford University Press.

Whitehead, D. 2016. *Philo Mechanicus, On Sieges*. Stuttgart: Franz Steiner.

Whittaker, C. R. 1994. *Frontiers of the Roman Empire: A Social and Economic Study*. Baltimore: Johns Hopkins University Press.

Worthington, I. 1999. "How 'great' was Alexander?" *Ancient History Bulletin*, 13: 39–55.

Worthington, I. 2017. "Campaigns of Alexander the Great, 336-323 BC," in Whitby and Sidebottom (2017), pp. 503–573.

Wrightson, G. 2019. *Combined Arms Warfare in Ancient Greece*. London: Routledge.

Zhmodikov, A. 2000. "Roman Republican Heavy Infantrymen in Battle (IV–II Centuries B.C.)," *Historia* 49: 67–78.

Ziolkowski, A. 1993. "*Urbs direpta*, or How the Romans Sacked Cities," in J. Rich and G. Shipley (1993), pp. 69–91.

Zuckerman, C. 1998. "Two Reforms of the 370s: Recruiting Soldiers and Senators in the Divided Empire," *REByz* 56: 79–139.

INDEX

Pages in *italics* refer to figures

Achaeans 11
Achaemenids 44–46, 53, 145
Achilles 6–7, 52–53, 145
Adrianople, Battle of 129, 132, 145
Aeneas Tacticus: *How to Defend a City* 62
Aeschylus 24
Aetius 130–131
Agathias 123, 126, 133–134, 145
Agesilaus II (of Sparta) 42, 50
Alans 130
Alcibiades 24, 39
Alexander III (the Great) 37, 46, 48–57, 60, 63, 65, 70–71, 145
Altai Mountains 129, 132
Alps (Hannibal's march) 68–70
Amida 110
Ammianus Marcellinus 110, 126–129, 145
Antiochus Strategius 139–140
Antigonos the One-Eyed 63, 145
Aphrodite 6
Apollo 7, 43
Apollodorus 99
Appian 59, 75, 77–78, 146

Apuleius: *Metamorphoses* (*Golden Ass*) 108, 146
Arabia 109, 114, 117–119, 141
Arabic (language) 109, 142
Aramaic 44, 109
Arcadia 41–42, 62
Archimedes 61
Aristophanes 24–25, 28, 38, 60; *Birds* 24, 143; *Lysistrata* 24, 28, 143; *Peace* 38
Aristotle 11
Arrian 127
Artemisium, Battle of 63
Artillery 46, 63, 66, 93, 112, 134
Asclepiodotus: *Tactica* 62
Assidui 84
Asymmetric warfare 82, 96–97, 113–116, 146
Athenaeus: *Deipnosophistae* 63
Athenaeus Mechanicus 62
Athens 15, 20, 24, 30–31, 38–40, 46, 49–50, 60, 62, 65
Attila 130–131, 146
Augustus (emperor) 81, 86, 146
Aurelian 118–119

Auxiliaries (Roman) 99–101, 104, 106, 124, 146

Babatha 109, 146
Baecula, Battle of 77–79, 146
Band of Brothers 1
Barbaricum 86, 132, 147
Barritus/barditus 128
Beth Horon, Battle of 89–90
Biton: *Construction of War Machines and Catapults* 62
Black Desert (Harra–Syria, Jordan, Saudi Arabia) 114, 120, 144
Boeotia 41–43
Boeotian Helmet 19
Bostra 119, 141
Boudica 82, 95–98
Bracchiati 126
Britain/Britons 95–98, 104, 124
Bronze Age 6, 7, 9–12, 20, 147
Bulgaria 98, 130
Burnt House (Jerusalem) 91

Caesar, Julius 86, 95, 147
Caledonians 3, 104
Cannae, Battle of 34, 72, 74–75, 77, 130
Caracalla 108
Carthaginians 34, 61, 65–67, 67, 68–75, 77–79, 85, 130, 147
Casilinum, Battle of 126, 134, 136, 147
Cassius Dio 89, 97, 147
Catalaunian Plains, Battle of 131, 147
Cataphracts 119, 124, 126, 128, 137, 148
Cato: *Origines* 76
Catus Decianus 95
Census (Roman) 82–83, 85
Cerialis (Vindolanda) 121
Cestius Gallus 89–90
Chaeronea, Battle of 43, 48–52, 55, 148
Chalcidian Helmet 21–22

Chemical warfare 113
Cherusci 88
Chigi Vase 25
Chnodomarius (king) 127
Cisalpine Gaul 69–70
Claudia Severa 120–121, 148
Claudius (emperor) 95
Claudius II (emperor) 118
Cleisthenes 31
Cleombrotus (King) 42
Cleopatra (VII) 86, 118
Colchester (Camulodunum) 96–98
Column of Trajan 98–99, *106*, 127–128, 148
Combined Arms 47–48, 55, 148
Comitatenses 124
Corinthian Helmet 18, *19*, 21–22
Cornuti 126
Corvus, crow 66, 148

Dacia 82, 98–101, 118, 130
Dacian Wars 98–101, 148
Dara, Battle of 126
Darius III 20, 54–56, 148
Decebalus 99, 148
Demetrius I (of Bactria) *61*
Demetius the Besieger (Macedonian King) *61*, 68
Demosthenes x, 29, 48–49; *On the Crowns* x; *Philippics* 49
Diekplous 66
Dilectus 84
Diodorus Siculus (of Sicily) 17, 40, 50, 62, 84–85
Dionysius I (of Syracuse/Sicily) 40
Diploma (Roman military) 99–101, 106–108, 149
Domitian 98–100
Dromedarii (camel-riders) 121, 125
Drusus 86
Dura-Europos: Siege of 103, 109–112, 117, 120–121, 137

Egadi/*Aegates* Islands, Battle of 65–66, *67*, 149

Egypt/Egyptians 11, 45, 54, 60, 64, 71, 105–106, 118–120, 125, 138–139
Elagabal 119
Elephants 56, 69–71, 79
Elysium 37
Epaminondas 36, 42–43, 48, 50, 149
Erastes 43
Eros 43
Euripides 4, 24, 26, 149; *Electra* 26; *Suppliants* 26
Eutropius 81, 84, 149; *Brevarium* 84

Fabius Maximus, Quintus (Cunctator) 73–75
Face of Battle (John Keegan) 28, 149
Feriale Duranum 121
Flaminius, Gaius 72
Franks 126, 134

Gallienus 117–118
Gaugamela, Battle of 54, 71
Gaul/Gauls 65, 71, 85, 119, 128
Gelon (of Syracuse) 34
George of Pisidia 138
Germanicus 88
Germany 82, 86–87, 89, 120
Gisgo 78–79
Gorgan, Great Wall of 132, 137, 149
Goths 128, 130, 132, 136
Granicus, River/Battle of 54, 56

Hadrian 121
Hamilcar 67
Han (China) 129
Hannibal 37, 59, 68–74, 150
Hanno 66–67
Hanson, Victor Davis 23, 159–160
Harzhorn 86
Hasdrubal 59, 78
Hauran 109, 141
Hector 7, 52
Helots 41, 43, 150
Hephthalites 137

Hera 6
Heraclius 138, 141, 150
Herodotus 15–16, 20, 25, 33, 44–45, 85, 129, 150
Heruls 126, 134
Hillforts 86, 104
Himera, Battle of 34–35, 159
Historia Augusta: *Life of Aurelian* 116
Hittites 10–12, 150
Hoplite 8–9, 16–23, 26–27, 39–41, 48, 60, 150
Homer 18, 23, 56, 135, 150; *Iliad* 3, 5–6, 8–9, 52
Horse archery 3, 126, 131, 133–137
Humayma 119
Huns 126, 129–137
Hyphasis, River 55

Immortals 45
Impedimenta 78
Iphicrates 17, 41, 48
Iuniores 74, 128

Jerusalem 89, 94–95, 110, 139–141
Jewish War (First/Great) 81, 89–95, 151
Jordan 3, 103, 109, 114, *115*, 141
Jordanes 131
Josephus 3, 89–91, 93–95, 151
Judea 81, 94–96, 98, 113
Julian (emperor) 52, 126, 128

Kalkriese 86–89
Keegan, John 27, 149
Kerameikos 31
Khusro II 137–138

Legion 40, 76–77, 83–87, 91, 97, 104, 106, 124, 127, 129, 151; Second (II) 76, 99, 105; Ninth (VIIII) 96; Fourteenth (XIIII) 97; Eighteenth (XVIII) 87; Twentieth (XX) 97–98; Thirtieth (XXX) 99; Primani (late antiquity) 126

194 INDEX

Leuktra, Battle of 42–43, 55, 151
Linear B 9–10, 151
Livy 33, 69, 73, 75–79, 82, 84–85; *Ab Urbe Condita* 33, 69, 75–77, 82–83
London (*Londinium*) 96–98
Lucian 37, 56; *Dialogues of the Dead* 37
Lutatius 66–67
Luttwak, Edward 99–100

Macedon (Macedonians) 15, 46–50, 52–55, 60–61, 63, 107
Magnesia, Battle of 71
Mago 78–79
Mamilla Cave (Jerusalem) 140
Mantinea, Battle of (418 BCE) 27
Mantinea, Battle of (362 BCE) 43, 50
Marathon, Battle of 20, 30, *30*, 33, 44, 151
Marc Antony 52, 86, 118
Marcus Caelius 87, *87*, 88, 144
Masada, Siege of 92–95, 101, 110, 112, 144
Masters of the Air 1, 3
Maurice (emperor) 138
Maurice (pseudo, author) 3, 123, 125, 136, 144, 151; *Strategikon* 3, 123, 125, 136, 144
Mecca 142
Menelaus 6, 8
Messenia 43
Miltiades 20
Minos (King) 37
Moesia 98–99; Superior (Upper) 101, 107
Mona (Anglesey) 95, 97
Mons Graupius, Battle of 104, 151
Mt. Vesuvius 103, 109
Murmillones 127
Mycenae 6–7, 9–11
Myrmidons 6, 9

Nabataea/Nabataeans 109
Narcissus 43

Nerva 99, 107
Nessana 109
Notitia Dignitatum 124–125, 128, 152

Odainath 117–118
Oedipus 41
Onasander 33
Oppida 86
Orestes 26
Orosius 84
Othismos 22, 25–26, 152

The Pacific 1
Pahlavi (papyri) 138–139, 152
Palmyra 98, 112, 116–119, 152
Paris 6–8
Parthians 109, 111, 121, 129, 136–137, 152
Paterfamilias 83, 152
Pausanias 20
Peleus 6
Pelopidas 42–43, 48
Peloponnesian War 15, 17, 24, 41, 152
Peltast 17, 41
Pergamum 60
Pericles 30–31, 153
Periplous 66
Phalanx 16–17, 22–23, 27, 42, 47, 51, 55, 134, 153
Philip II. 46–50, 53, 60, 65, 153
Philo Mechanicus: *On Sieges* 62
Phocas 138
Phyle (tribe) 31
Plato 38, 60; *Symposium* 38
Pliny the Elder 11, 84
Pliny the Younger x, 103
Plutarch 28, 43, 50; *Life of Alexander* 50; *Spartan Women* 28–29
Polyaenus 50
Polybius 17, 62, 66–69, 73, 78, 82–85, 95, 153; *Histories* 68–69, 73, 83–85; *Tactica* 62
Pompeii 54, 109, 153

Porus (King) 55–56, 71
Prasutagus 95–96
Praxiteles (sculptor) 60
Procopius 3, 123, 126, 130, 135, 153
Pseudo-Joshua the Stylite 123
Ptolemies 60, 64, 71, 153
Ptolemy IV Philopator 63, 68
PTSD 153
Punic Wars 59, 154; First 65–66, 85; Second 17, 69, 73, 77, 82, 84–86, 95; Third 79
Pyrrhic victory 65
Pyrrhus (King) 62, 65, 71

Qadesh, Battle of 11
Qadisiyya, Battle of 141, 154

Rams (ship) 62–63, 65–68
Ramses II 11
Raphia, Battle of 64, 71
Roster (Roman–Dura-Europos) 121

Sacred Band 13, 42–43, 49–52, 154
Safaitic 4, 103, 109, 114, *115*, 154
Salamis, Battle of 44, 63
Sarmatians 128–130
Sarmizegethusa 99
Sasanians 110–113, 135, 137, 154
Saxons 128
Scipio (Africanus) 37, 59, 75, 78–79, 154
Scotland 104
Scythians 44, 46, 127, 129, 134, 136, 154
Seleucids 60, 64, 71, 109, 111
Seniores 74
Septimius Severus 100, 121, 154
Shapur I (King, *Shahanshah*) 117, 154
Shapur II (King, *Shahanshah*, the Great) 110, 154
Sicily 13, 34–35, 40, 62, 65–66, 85
Sidebottom, Harry 3–4
Single combat 8, 20, 154

Slaves/slavery 49, 66, 74, 76–77, 89, 91, 93–95
Socrates 39
Sophocles 24, 154
Spain 70, 77–79, 86
Sparta 6, 15, 20, 27–29, 40–43, 50
Spartiates 41, 43, 154
St. Albans (*Verulamium*) 96–97
Standards 83, 111, 127
Strasburg, Battle of 126–129
Strategos 24
Strategy, Grand 99–101
Suetonius Paulus 95–97
Sulpicia Lepidina 121
Syene 45
Syria 3, 11, 60, 64, 71, 89, 103, 106–107, 109, 114, 117, 120, *138*, 141–142
Syriac (language) 123

Tacitus 89, 97, 103–104, 154; *Agricola* 103–104; *Annals* 104; *Germania* (*barditus*) 104; *Histories* 103
Technai 61
Temple Mount (Jerusalem) 91
Terentius, Julius (frescoes of) 111, 121
Testudo 127–128, 155
Teutoburg Forest, Battle of 81, 86–89, 144, 155
Thebes (Greece) 27, 41–43, 48–50
Theodosius II (emperor) 131
Theophanes 138–139
Thermopylae, Battle of 20, 44, 49, 155
Theseus 5, 26
Thetis 6
Thucydides 3, 15–16, 22, 26–28, 30, 60, 62, 85
Thureophoros 64
Thureos 64, *64*
Tiberius (emperor) 86
Trajan 81, 89, 98–100, 106, *106*, 107, 127–128, 148, 155
Trasimene, Lake, Battle of 72, 74

Tributum 74
Trinovantes 96
Trireme 63, 67–68, 155
Trojan War 4–12, 155
Troy 5–7, 11–12, *12*
Tunnel 19 (Dura-Europos) 119
Turma/Turmae 121
Tychai 112
Tyre, Siege of 54, 56
Tyrtaeus 18, 155

Umar ibn al-Khaṭṭāb 141
Umayyad Caliphate 142
Umm el-Jimal 109
Uthman ibn Affan 142

Valens 130
Valentinian III 131
Valerius Antipas 76
Varus, Quinctilius 81, 86–89, 155
Vegetius 123, 127, 144, 155;
 Epitoma Rei Militaris 123, 127

Vexillations/*Vexillationes* 124
Vindolanda 155

Wahballath 117–118
Wales 96–97
Wedge/cunei 47, 55, 124, 127, 134
Western Way of War 4, 22–23, 60, 156
Wilusa 11
World War II 1–2, 29

Xenophon 3, 16, 45, 85, 156;
 Anabasis 45; *On Horsemanship* 51
Xerxes 20, *44*
Xiongnu 129, 156

Yarmuk, Battle of 141, 156

Zabdas 119
Zama, Battle of 59, 156
Zenobia 98, 116–120, 137, 144

For Product Safety Concerns and Information please contact our EU representative GPSR@taylorandfrancis.com
Taylor & Francis Verlag GmbH, Kaufingerstraße 24, 80331 München, Germany

www.ingramcontent.com/pod-product-compliance
Lightning Source LLC
Chambersburg PA
CBHW071818230426
43670CB00013B/2498